PRAISE FOR *CROSSROADS*

"We never know the true meaning of courage until we face it head-on in life: Kaleb's story is truly a story of courage. *Crossroads* is an amazing book that will take you back to your early days of hockey and sports and make you realize how important community and family really are. I know you will love this book and it will remind you how wonderful our country of Canada really is. Enjoy the read. *Crossroads* will change your life for the better."

—WAYNE GRETZKY

"You might assume this book is going to engage you, enrapture you, inspire you, and motivate you because of Kaleb's story about how he's making his way through the Broncos tragedy and its aftermath, but you'd be wrong. It's going to do all of those things, but because of much more than that single incident."

—HAYLEY WICKENHEISER, four-time Olympic gold medallist

"Kaleb has every excuse to be bitter and angry for everything he has been through, but instead he has chosen to be the complete opposite. He has inspired me to live every day to the fullest, and after reading *Crossroads*, I know you will feel the same way."

—KATE BEIRNESS, sportscaster

"This is a book you should read: the story of a young man who has dealt with, and lives with, more than most of us do in our lifetime. Go, Kaleb."

—BOBBY CLARKE, NHL legend

"Moving and inspiring, Kaleb Dahlgren's incredible story of optimism and grit at every crossroad in his life shows us all what's possible on our own journeys."

—MARILYN DENIS

"There are few things more Canadian than a group of hockey-loving teenagers taking a bus to a big game on the Prairies. That's why the Humboldt tragedy hit us all so hard. It felt like the Broncos were all our boys. And so Kaleb's remarkable story moves us and shatters us, and ultimately gives us hope. It's an incredible account of a young man who refuses to be defined by one horrific moment."
— JAMES DUTHIE, TSN host and bestselling author of *Beauties*

"This story truly touched my heart. When this tragic accident happened, Canada—and really the whole world—lost so much. We are all stronger when we come together, and *Crossroads* honours a team and their legacy in such a beautiful way."
— KAITLYN BRISTOWE, TV personality, podcaster, and entrepreneur

"Kaleb Dahlgren has done a great job providing insight into what makes a team strong: as the Humboldt Broncos' Core Covenant states, 'Family first.' A tribute to those lost and a gripping read."
— MITCHELL MARNER, Toronto Maple Leafs

"Sixteen Broncos—their eyes dance and their smiles appear everywhere in *Crossroads*. With anguish and hope breaking through every line, Kaleb's book shows it's not the end of those lives. Deeply affecting and beautiful."
— RON MACLEAN

CROSSROADS

MY STORY
OF TRAGEDY AND RESILIENCE
AS A HUMBOLDT BRONCO

CROSSROADS

KALEB
DAHLGREN

Collins
An imprint of HarperCollins*Publishers*Ltd

Published by Collins, an imprint of HarperCollins Publishers Ltd

First edition

HarperCollins books may be purchased for educational, business,
or sales promotional use through our Special Markets Department.

HarperCollins Publishers Ltd
Bay Adelaide Centre, East Tower
22 Adelaide Street West, 41st Floor
Toronto, Ontario, Canada
M5H 4E3

www.harpercollins.ca

Library and Archives Canada Cataloguing in Publication

Title: Crossroads : my story of tragedy and resilience as a
Humboldt Bronco / Kaleb Dahlgren | Names: Dahlgren, Kaleb, author.
Identifiers: Canadiana (print) 20200412299 | Canadiana (ebook) 20200412302
ISBN 9781443462877 (hardcover) | ISBN 9781443462891 (ebook)
Subjects: LCSH: Dahlgren, Kaleb. | LCSH: Humboldt Broncos (Hockey team)
LCSH: Hockey players—Canada—Biography. | LCSH: Traffic accident victims—
Canada—Biography. | LCSH: Traffic accidents—Saskatchewan.
LCGFT: Autobiographies.
Classification: LCC GV848.5.D295 A3 2021 | DDC 796.962092—dc23

Printed and bound in the United States of America
LSC/H 9 8 7 6 5 4 3 2 1

For the sixteen members of my Broncos family who live on in my heart.

Tyler Bieber
Logan Boulet
Dayna Brons
Mark Cross
Glen Doerksen
Darcy Haugan
Adam Herold
Brody Hinz
Logan Hunter
Jaxon Joseph
Jacob Leicht
Conner Lukan
Logan Schatz
Evan Thomas
Parker Tobin
Stephen Wack

I will always treasure how our paths crossed in this world and will remain forever #HumboldtStrong.

PROLOGUE

—

APRIL 6, 2018.

The day everything changed.

It was just another road trip, like the thousands that sports teams take every year. We weren't thinking about life or death when we tossed our green and gold bags into the cargo hold, walked up the stairs with our necessities, and claimed our seats on the bus.

There was a game to play—two hours away, against a team that had beaten us in triple overtime two nights before. The Nipawin Hawks had a three-games-to-one lead over us heading into Game 5 of the second round in the Saskatchewan Junior Hockey League playoffs. We needed to win this game. It was the only thing on our minds.

The Humboldt Broncos have been a fixture in Saskatchewan hockey for more than five decades. The green and gold sweaters were originally hand-me-downs from the Swift Current Broncos of the Western Hockey League way back in the early 1970s. However, the team quickly formed an identity of its own. Humboldt is an agricultural city of under 6,000 people, about an hour and a half east of Saskatoon, Saskatchewan. The team was run entirely by local volunteers, including the first coach. This tells you a lot about the nature of the Broncos. They are a team built by a community—and they remain a part of that community in every sense of the word.

Our team was the latest generation in that long tradition, and we wore our jerseys with pride every time we pulled them over our heads.

Row 12.

Our spots weren't assigned, but we always gravitated to the same location every time we travelled on the bus—the force of habit that only makes sense when you are part of a team. There are just certain things you know if you've been part of one—rookies load the bus, vets get first dibs on seats.

I was one of nine twenty-year-old vets on the team, all of us in our last year of junior eligibility. I sat where I always did, in the fourth row from the back of the bus. If I wasn't involved in the card games and bad jokes going on around me, I could usually drown out the noise just long enough for a pre-game nap or to listen to music and think about life.

The bus was a safe place. Sort of like a home on the road. It was filled with teammates who were like brothers, and a collective group of personnel that was like a big family. Some of the best memories I have come from being on the bus . . . also, some of the worst.

There were twenty-nine people with us—twenty-nine different stories, and mine was just one of them. Each individual was an important part of the group we had become: from our veterans to our rookies and affiliate players, our play-by-play announcer to our statistician, our bus driver, our athletic therapist, and our coaches. Everyone played a pivotal role in building a team culture unlike any other.

Of course, I think we were pretty extraordinary—that's why I wanted to be a Bronco—but truth be told, we were also pretty ordinary in so many ways. A team just like any other, covering excessive numbers of kilometres, criss-crossing the flat prairies to different cities and towns.

Aisle seat. Driver's side.

We pulled out of the parking lot at the Elgar Petersen Arena in Humboldt close to 2:50 p.m. and drove across the street, turned a corner, and arrived at our coach's house. Darcy Haugan was much more than a bench boss; he was the kind of coach whose influence stays with you for a lifetime. The kind of coach who is more interested in what kind of men his players become than how many points they score or how many games the team wins. His wife, Christina, had cooked a pre-game pasta meal for our team—each pre-packaged into containers for every person on the bus. I remember Darcy running into his house to grab a belt he'd forgotten for his suit, or maybe it was his shoes—there are just so many of those small details that I try hard to remember these days, but simply can't.

There are many things I do remember, though. Like how we took a slightly different route out of town that day. Just over halfway to Nipawin, we turned right towards Tisdale, instead of continuing on, like we usually did. Another small detail that charted our course that day. Not a big deal. It was just a five-minute detour. We hardly even noticed that our path had changed.

From Tisdale, Nipawin was just forty minutes away and we were just a couple of hours from game time. The game was still the only thing that mattered. Most of us were still in our stylish charcoal-grey Broncos track suits, which we always wore on the bus. These were the nicest track suits I have ever worn. Our suits were laid out flat in the overhead compartments above the seats.

We turned out of Tisdale, heading north.

Highway 35.

When we practised that morning, Darcy wanted to make sure we had taken care of every last detail. We had our backs to the wall against Nipawin but were not about to surrender. You'll know the feeling if you've spent any time with a team that is facing elimination. As we continued to make our way north, we were all in various states of pre-game preparation. Some of us sat quietly. Others had their headphones on and were listening to music. A card game involving some of the guys was finishing up just in front of me at the table with inverted seats. We were about thirty minutes out by then. So close.

It was the most important game—and potentially the last—of my junior career. I sat in my seat and turned on one of my go-to playlists to get ready.

This was going to be the best game I would ever play in my life. The best game *we* would ever play in our lives.

A few of the guys were standing in the aisle, putting on their suits. There was banter and laughter. I turned up the volume.

Highway 335.

And everything went black.

CHAPTER 1

—

One of the very first memories I have is of being in a hospital, desperate to get out. There were so many needles. I can still feel the sting, pricking through my skin. The doctors and nurses stuck them all over my arms, prodding me like a human science experiment.

It was the first time I ever used the word *hate*.

"I hate this doctor's house," I cried to my parents when he left the room. "I'm going to throw this chair through the window so he tells me to go home!"

I was just shy of my fifth birthday. My mother and father had never heard that kind of rage come out of me before.

It was hard for them to witness this new circumstance I faced. I'd been extremely healthy through the first few years of my young life, aside from the occasional cold and the chicken pox I caught from the babysitter's granddaughter. I was peeing so much more than usual. I was losing weight. I was sweaty and thirsty all the time.

Mark, my father, got a call from the sitter that afternoon. She said I'd drunk everything my parents had sent and everything she had in the fridge. She also said I had thrown up—the first time I'd ever done that.

"He's just drinking and drinking—and always wanting more," she told him. "There's something going on."

My dad came to pick me up right away. He and my mom are both nurses. They met at nursing school in Regina and started dating after they shared a practicum in Moose Jaw, Saskatchewan—a city of about 30,000, roughly seventy kilometres west of the provincial capital along the Trans-Canada Highway. It's my dad's hometown and old stomping grounds.

They met in 1988, both young but wise beyond their years. My mom, Anita, was apprehensive about Dad at first. He has an outgoing personality—he's "larger than life." Most people find him charming, but she thought he was a little too "grandiose." Nevertheless, they actually had a lot in common. My mom was drawn to nursing because she cared deeply about helping people. My father, gregarious as he might be, is also very endearing and loves to build relationships with people.

Over their psychiatric nursing practicum, they became good friends and he started to grow on her. Within months, they realized how perfect they were for each other. They started dating and got married in 1990, when Dad was twenty-two and Mom was twenty-one.

I didn't show up until some seven years later—on June 10, 1997. We settled into life in Moose Jaw, where they both found work in the health care profession after graduating from nursing. And for the first four years of my life, everything was fine.

Until the day it wasn't: February 22, 2002.

When Dad picked me up from the babysitter's that day, he knew something was wrong. I kept telling him how thirsty I was. Because I had thrown up, and my abdomen was distended, he thought I was constipated and told me to go and sit on the toilet while he called the doctor. When he came back to get me in the bathroom, I was on the counter, lapping water into my mouth with a toothbrush. The doctor checked my urine first and then returned to take a sample of my blood, the first of the many needle pricks. The reading at the doctor's office was on a glucometer machine, and it read *HI* when we went to the hospital. They did a blood test and got the real value. My blood glucose levels were through the roof: 36.8 millimoles per litre—the normal range is 4.4 to 7.2 mmol/L.

The doctor looked at my father.

"Your son has type 1 diabetes. He's going to be insulin-dependent for the rest of his life," he said, coldly and matter-of-factly. "I'll call ahead to the hospital. You need to take him there immediately."

My mom was frantically rushing to the clinic from work by then. Dad didn't want the doctor to tell Mom the news as bluntly as he'd told him, so he took her aside and told her the news before she came into the room. Working in health care, they both knew a fair amount about diabetes, but they had never thought it was something that could affect their own child. There was no history in our family. It completely blindsided them.

Mom went quiet when Dad told her. She was numb from head to toe and couldn't react right away. She was just running the reality of a life with diabetes through her mind.

You see, while the exact cause of type 1 diabetes—also known as juvenile diabetes—is not known, usually what happens is that your body's immune system destroys these little insulin-producing cells in the pancreas. Once many of these cells are destroyed, your body doesn't produce enough insulin, which is what allows sugar to enter your cells. When there is no insulin to allow sugar (or glucose) into your cells, it builds up in your bloodstream, and this is where it can become life-threatening.

There are immediate concerns. If your blood sugar level goes too high, you can fall into a coma and die. If it goes too low, which can happen if you take too much insulin, you can collapse into a seizure and die.

As well, there are the concerns beyond the immediate, and these are what worried my mom and dad the most. If you don't control the disease and don't take care of yourself properly, you might not see the results today, tomorrow, or even next year. But then, fifteen years down the road, you could have high blood pressure and heart disease. Even worse, there's the possibility of having to go on dialysis, losing a limb, or going blind.

I was admitted into the pediatric ward at the hospital for three days to undergo more tests.

While my mom stayed with me the night I was diagnosed, my dad went home and phoned my grandparents to tell them. He is usually a very composed man. Nothing seems to faze him. But as my mother's parents asked him more about what the diagnosis meant, he started to cry uncontrollably. It was the first time he really started to think about what my life was going to look like.

At the hospital, the nurse poked my finger with a needle six times a day. Then there were needles for insulin, four times a day. And every day, they drew blood. The lab tech would wake me up at 6:30 in the morning, just to stick me with a needle again.

Mom and Dad had been painstaking about never using negative words around me. They didn't swear or use words in anger. So they were shocked when, after a couple days of needle after needle, four-and-a-half-year-old me just snapped.

I hated that place with everything my little heart could feel. Therefore, I wanted to break that window. I wanted to go home.

That was the first time my mom and dad couldn't make things better for me.

As nurses in long-term care homes, my parents had some experience taking care of diabetic people, but not their son. When I was able to go home, Mom emptied all of the cupboards of anything that had excess sugar, which was bags and bags of items. There was sugar in practically everything. My parents had to start learning about what was in the food we ate, and all of our meals were planned out by a dietitian. All carbs had to be measured. No sugar. And I had to receive insulin regularly to maintain the right blood sugar levels.

Mom was militant at first. She took an entire month off work just to regain some normalcy at home, while we all got used to our new reality together.

Everything I ate was exactly the same, always. The same food, the same amount, the same time of day. Back then, you couldn't just go to Google to find out what's in specific kinds of food—and even food labels didn't provide the detailed information they show you now. So, my parents were only able to give me food that they were familiar with.

It was a nightmare for all of us.

At home, from the very start, I was given four needles and four finger pricks each day. I didn't understand why the needles had to come home from the hospital with us. I kicked, screamed, and fought. I'd run away when I knew it was time for another needle. I always hid in the basement, beside the bar. It was my secret spot. It was hide-and-go-seek, but I didn't want to be found. They had to chase me down and hold me still while I wailed.

"Why are you doing this?" I screamed. "Why are you hurting me? Why don't you love me?!"

It took quite a while to settle into a new routine.

There wasn't the technology that there is today, with sensors that can immediately sound an alert if something is wrong. So, every night, my parents would take turns getting up and coming into my room, just to check that I was still breathing or that I hadn't had a seizure. And every morning when my father walked by my door, he'd peek in to make sure I was okay. There was an abundance to learn, and we would have to teach others as well.

My babysitter didn't know how to give the needles, or what kind of food I was able to eat. But she was phenomenal. I called her Grandma Leona. She had worked with my father as a nurse's aide, and he begged her to help take care of me when she retired. She started taking care of me when I was seven months old. Grandma Leona was the kind of lady who always asks you how you are doing, and just makes you feel warm with her smile. My parents knew they could trust her. She learned everything about diabetes that she could, and she became an expert. She was a blessing.

However, I was almost old enough to go to school for a full day. What would happen then?

At the time, very few adults had cellphones. But I did. When I was in kindergarten, my parents gave me a big phone with a tall antenna sticking out the top, which I kept in my backpack. The teacher would be able to call my mother at any time of day to tell her what my blood sugar level was. By that time, Mom had it all down to an art. She would pack me a small lunch that didn't raise my blood sugar too much, so I usually wouldn't have to take an insulin needle at lunch. But if it was high, one of my parents would have to leave work to come into school to give me the insulin.

Those were some of the hurdles yet to come.

After the hospital, the most important thing to me was my fifth birthday, which was coming up that June. If the needles were my first bad memory, that party at the hockey rink was my first happy one.

From the very start, we were a hockey family.

When I was born, my parents put the birth notice in the paper announcing me as a future NHL draft pick. (It didn't turn out as they expected.) They thanked everyone involved by giving them a position on the team—Dad was the coach, Mom was the general manager, the doctors were the assistant coaches, the nurses were trainers, and the cheering fan club were my proud grandparents. A couple months later, Dad took a photo of me surrounded by his hockey equipment. His skates, gloves, and helmet were about the same size as I was. For my first Christmas, Santa got me a little net and two blue plastic hockey sticks. And every Christmas throughout my childhood, I received a new hockey stick. (They just got a little more expensive as I got older.)

By the time I was diagnosed with diabetes, I was already a passionate fan. Dad and I used to watch Calgary Flames games on television together. We would pretend that we were actually part of the team, and I even had a Flames sweater with my name embroidered on the back. When the games ended, Dad would tell me where the next game was and we would pretend that we were going on the road trip together. One time, I was at Grandma Leona's and I wouldn't play with the toys. I just sat on the couch, looking serious. She asked me what was wrong and why I wouldn't play. I told her that I didn't have time to play because I had a game in San Jose that night and was on the airplane. The poor lady had no idea what I was talking about.

When I got older and could really understand the game, my favourite players were Joe Sakic and Jarome Iginla, because of the way they carried themselves on and off the ice. But when I was little, it was Jaromir Jagr. I had a little Pittsburgh Penguins jersey. It was probably because Jagr was my mother's favourite player. She wasn't much of a hockey fan growing up, but when she started dating my father, he took her to a game—and she saw Jagr skating around in warm-ups with his flowing locks and decided that he was handsome enough to be her favourite player. I guess he was pretty good at hockey, too.

I was two and a half when my parents got me my first pair of skates. They took me out to the public skating rink, where I balanced on a tiny stool while moving my feet, figuring out how it all worked while my long curly hair flew in the wind. One time, I fell over and my stool slid across the ice, where another kid picked it up. I was furious. Dad tried to calm me down and got me another stool so we could keep skating. But I wanted *that* stool. When we got moving again, I started to pick up speed, with Dad trailing behind. I saw the kid just a few strides ahead of me and went right at him. We collided and both went flying. Dad rushed over to see if we were okay. I looked up at him from the ice. "I bodychecked him," I said.

When I had just turned three, my parents found a figure skating program that would enroll children at a younger age than the local hockey program, so that's where I really got my start. This was our dirty little family secret. We did figure skating shows on the ice with music and lights for our parents. I wore a cowboy outfit with a black vest that was lined with sparkly red sequins. But my ice dancing career was short-lived.

I wanted to play hockey so bad. When I finished the figure skating lessons, I was finally able to join the hockey learn-to-skate program in Moose Jaw. And I had to miss my final skating lesson that year because I was in the hospital. They had planned to set up an actual game with the kids who were part of the program. I was absolutely crushed.

This is where my fifth birthday comes in.

Dad went to work putting together a massive skating party for me, to make up for what I'd missed. If there is one thing you need to know about my father, it's that when he does something, it's never a half measure. He went as big as possible for this. He rented out the ice at the Moose Jaw Civic Centre, where the Warriors, the city's Western Hockey League team, played.

We were regulars at the arena, known locally as the "Crushed Can" for its roof, which sloped in from the edges, making it look like it was caving in. It earned Canada's top architectural prize, the Massey Medal, after it was built in 1959.

For years, the Warriors were a tradition for us. We went to a game at least once a week. My parents never bought season tickets, but we probably went to 80 percent of the games. With the inverted roof, if you sat at the top of one row of seats, you couldn't see the top dozen rows on the other side, but you could hear everything they said. The arena seated around 3,000 fans, and it was almost always full. It was one of those large rinks that feel intimate. You could hear everything that was said on the bench. People would bring in compressed-air tanks hooked up to horns from semi-trucks, and others brought the air horns attached to little canisters of compressed air. The sound filled the rink. Loud music. Light show. Smoke machine. AC/DC's "Thunderstruck" playing full blast. It was wild.

For my fifth birthday, Dad tried his best to make it feel like we were skating out for an NHL game. They brought back everyone from my skating lesson and gave us all special jerseys. All of my friends from learn-to-skate were there. One of my father's friends knew a guy who worked at a guitar shop, which hooked him up with a lighting system. They let him borrow these big poles with lights that attach, and a smoke machine.

Mom was the "manager of chaos," herding a bunch of kids. Dad was the PA announcer. He called us out, one by one, to the beat of music blasting. With all the flashing lights and smoke-filled air, we felt like superstars as we skated onto the ice. They played "O Canada" over the PA system, just like they did at Warriors games. We all lined up on the blue line and sang along to the national anthem. The music blared as we shuffled through the warm-up. Lights flashed all around the rink, like it was a rock concert.

We sat on the same benches the WHL players sat on. They called penalties that sent us to the penalty boxes the WHL players were sent to. Mom was by my side, making sure my blood sugar levels were stable, while Dad called the play-by-play from the sidelines. Sitting in the announcer's box that day, calling my name as I shuffled across the ice, Dad knew that my hockey dream was likely impossible. With diabetes, a future in the game was probably not in the cards for me. It broke my parents' hearts to know that their son's dream could end so young.

But we spent the next decades together—Dad, Mom, and I— proving the impossible wrong.

CHAPTER 2

▬

Mom, Dad, and me. Growing up, it was just the three of us—and, of course, our dog, Koko, a bichon–shih tzu mix we got when I was four. But even though I was an only child, there were always people around. I grew up hanging out with friends every single day, and my parents made sure I didn't think that our small world revolved around me. That was always important to them.

The summer before I started Grade 1, we moved from Moose Jaw to Saskatoon. My parents decided it was time for a change. As I mentioned before, Dad grew up in Moose Jaw, and Mom grew up in Regina. Both wanted a change of scenery, while also remaining close to family. The next best thing was the "Paris of the Prairies." We had spent most of our weekends in Saskatoon for quite a while. There was just a lot more to do there—shopping and restaurants. The job prospects were better, too—and, for me, so was the hockey. That, of course, was really the only part that mattered to me.

Dad took a job in management at a facility for people who needed long-term care. Mom quickly found a full-time nursing job. I was young enough that I didn't really have to leave many friends behind, other than my good childhood friend, Regan Seiferling. Saskatoon was where I'd find the kind of friendships that last.

I'd missed out on the first year of organized hockey in Saskatoon. But in Moose Jaw, I was the only one who could raise the puck. Parents would stand in net, acting as goalies, thinking the puck wouldn't be raised—but I'd shoot it right at their knees or crotch. Eventually, whenever I got the puck, whichever parent was in net would just move out of the way.

When I got to Saskatoon, I was finally able to play Timbits initiation hockey—which was the youngest program for kids in the city. I scored so often that they made an internal team rule that I could only get three goals a game, and then I'd have to pass the puck. I'd skate down to the other end of the ice and wait for the other kids to get there so I could make a pass.

The next season, I was seven years old and could officially play in an organized city league. We were broken up into teams based on where we lived within the city. Each zone had its own roster of kids within a year of each other who would compete against the other zones throughout the city. Our house was located in zone W at the time, which meant that I belonged to a team called the Bobcats.

The league was divided into three tiers—the first tier being the highest, the third being the least competitive. Each level was made up of two age groups, and there were two teams per tier. After my first tryouts for the Bobcats minor hockey zone, I was selected to play on one of the top-tier teams, the Bobcat Thrashers. I was the only player born in 1997 on my stacked novice team of '96es.

One of the benefits of playing organized hockey was that players were allowed to fill a roster spot on the next age group up if they were playing well enough at their own level. At every level throughout minor hockey, I was able to play on my actual team as well as being an affiliated player for an older age group ('95s and '96s). I'd go to all of their practices and games, on top of my own practices and games with my team. Whenever I could get extra ice time, I took it. We had a lake a few blocks from my home. Volunteers would create a hockey rink during the winter, using a quad that was rigged up with a rotating brush to clean the ice and a pump to flood the surface. It also had a fire barrel, and my friend David Sheppard, who lived next to the lake, had lights that lit up the ice for us. I spent countless hours on that lake.

During Christmas and Easter holidays, I'd go to skills camps or would play shinny on an outdoor rink during the days away from school. All through the summer break, I did the same.

Thankfully, pretty much everything in Saskatoon is about twenty minutes from everywhere else. We played at numerous rinks across the city, but most often we ended up at a four-pad arena called Canlan Ice Sports Jemini, on the south side of the city. We spent up to four nights a week at arenas like the Jemini, if not more if we could get ice.

The ice was like our home away from home. And when we weren't at the rink, I was finding ways to keep playing.

Our house in Saskatoon didn't have a finished basement. Concrete floors and walls are a dream for a kid who loves sports. The minute I'd get home from school, I would head downstairs and strap on my Rollerblades. I'd spend hours down there, zipping around, shooting pucks at the net set up on the far wall. I cranked up the AC/DC hits and sometimes even turned on a disco ball and strobe light for extra-special effects (I am my father's son, after all). I loved every minute of it. I would be down there for hours, with a brief intermission for supper, before heading back to the basement for more practice and fun before bed.

Often, a couple of my neighbourhood friends would join me. One of them was Collin Shirley. He went on to play for the Kamloops Blazers of the Western Hockey League for several years and captained them before joining the men's varsity hockey team at the University of Saskatchewan. Another buddy—and still my best friend—was Wyatt Tyndall, who ended up becoming a member of the Canadian national gymnastics team and earned a scholarship to compete for Penn State University.

Needless to say, we were a pretty active group. We'd rotate through the goalie position, while the other two battled one-on-one. We would have shootouts and play Pig or Horse to see who could hit the targets we set up. These games were so intense that one time I chipped my front tooth after a stick hit me in the Chiclets. It was a permanent tooth, and I needed a root canal to repair it. There are very few things in life that can compare to the endless fun we had day after day down in that unfinished basement.

So, I wasn't exaggerating about us being a hockey family. I played the game every day.

But both of my parents worked full time and my mom did shift work, which meant an incredible amount of sacrifice on their part to get me where I needed to be. Dad actually coached or helped out with many of my teams. That also meant that he could be close by in case I suffered a diabetic emergency. Despite my passion for hockey, the reality of my disease hadn't changed. But we learned to manage it. In just a few years, I learned how to do all my own finger pokes and read my blood sugar levels. I could check in with my parents and let them know what they were. I knew what to eat and what not to eat. I could recognize how I was feeling—whether I was high or low. The teachers at my school had become familiar with my situation, and my parents met with every new teacher I had to make sure they were updated on what to do in case of an emergency. I had that brick of a cellphone, to be used in case something happened.

We made up binders of information about the amount of carbs in different kinds of foods, collected over the years. As we learned more, we didn't have to limit what I ate as much as we did initially. As a family, we were a walking encyclopedia of nutritional facts. And most importantly, I'd grown used to the needles. They no longer scared me the way they once did. I no longer cried when it was time to take one. They were an uncomfortable and inescapable reality of my life, something I had to live with. But I wasn't going to let diabetes defeat me.

As hockey parents go, mine were actually pretty quiet. Dad would usually just stand by himself in the arena. Since he was often the manager of the team, he kind of settled into that role and didn't say much as he watched—because he didn't want to come off as biased or upset any of the other parents. Mom was also pretty muted; she wasn't your typical "hockey mom." She was always focused on watching me play and learned the game because I loved it. She took pride in my development as a player. She knew my skating style and how I shot the puck. She didn't spend a lot of time chatting with the other moms during games because she wanted to focus on what was happening on the ice. She didn't want to be distracted.

Both of my parents, though, were also very good about making sure that I stayed grounded. Even though I was excelling in my small corner of the game, they knew that there were a lot of talented players out there—and the worst thing I could do was get ahead of myself and start to get cocky. My mother and father are both very modest people, and above all they made sure that I stayed modest, too. They very rarely pumped my tires, as they'd say. Even when I played well, they pointed out areas where they thought I could improve, without making me feel bad about it. Whenever Dad had a pointer for me, he'd focus on several positives before tossing in an area that I could work on. My mom would always say, "I'm going to be real with you," and would give me her opinion on how I played, even if I didn't like what she had to say. I appreciated that. I always knew she would tell me what she really thought.

My parents also always tried to compliment other kids on my team to their parents after every game, pointing out particular moments where they excelled or mentioning an area where they had made a noticeable improvement.

Dad was always careful to navigate what he calls the "cow pies" of competitive hockey. There are all kinds of things you can step in if you're not careful, he would say. My parents taught me that you never wanted to do something that would shine a negative light on yourself or on your family. So, it was important to stay out of petty arguments and avoid talking about another player or family behind their back. The world of minor hockey can be very devious and ruthless at times, and that kind of stuff is far too common in hockey rinks across the country. Hockey parents and players are stomping in cow patties all over the place.

In Saskatoon, when you reach the peewee level, the top tier is made up of six teams. And instead of trying out only against the kids in your zone, you were competing for a spot with the best players from all across the city. It didn't matter if you were in a zone that had tons of good players or one that didn't. It was a draft-style process, and you'd be chosen strictly on your ability.

When I was eleven years old, I was really excited to make one of the six teams in my first year of peewee. Not only because it felt unique to represent the entire city instead of just your little slice, but also because it created a new opportunity to make friends. I think this was when I first realized the importance of being part of a team.

I think it was a great way of developing people, because you're able to create relationships across the city, while also playing with and against elite players.

At that time, Saskatoon had loads of talent. Guys who were part of the city-wide teams went pretty far in the game. Some of my teammates and opponents were Rourke Chartier, Garrett Pilon, and Lane Pederson, who are all now playing in the American Hockey League.

That year was the first time I started to feel like I might actually have a shot at a future in the game. A year and a bit earlier, I had been selected as a member of Team Saskatchewan, a collection of the province's best players in my age group. It was a team formed for spring hockey, just off-season from our regular loop of play. We travelled to Edmonton to play in the very well-known Brick Invitational hockey tournament, which attracts teams from all over the world. It takes place at the rink inside the West Edmonton Mall—people walking through the mall stop by and watch as you play. Countless players who have eventually gone on to the NHL have played in the tournament over the years. One of our opponents that year was Matt Barzal, who played for the Vancouver Vipers team that won the championship, and another was Mitchell Marner, who played for the Toronto Bulldogs.

It was a once-in-a-lifetime experience. They hyped up the tournament so much, and every game was packed to the point where there was no space to watch. We'd have to put eye black on our cheeks to block the glare of the sunlight shining down on us. But the best part was travelling with our team. I met one of my close friends, Connor Ingram, during that trip to Edmonton. Connor was our goalie—and a very good one. He now plays in the Nashville Predators' system.

Over the next few years, I always played spring hockey. We'd travel with the team to places like Minneapolis and Calgary. We would play against the best from places like Vancouver, Winnipeg, and Fargo, North Dakota. All of the teams were the same age and the same calibre. It gave us a chance to really see how we stacked up against the best of the best.

Again, Dad always volunteered to be the manager of the team. It allowed him to come out on the road with me, knowing that he'd be there beside me if anything ever went wrong. He was a really fun manager, at least from the players' perspective. He'd let us watch movies like *American Pie* on the bus, even though he knew he'd hear about it from the other parents. He always felt the daggers from the other parents who came along for the bus trips as the cursing and questionable content filled the bus with laughter.

But Dad was always like that. He didn't try to sugar-coat reality. We'd blast Eminem while driving when I was young, and we'd rap along—even though I didn't know what most of the words meant. He was always careful to point out the words that I was never to use in public. Dad went the extra mile with the summer teams, too. He brought along the stereo, lights, and smoke machine on all of our trips, so the locker room would flash like a nightclub with music blaring while we got dressed. The other teams must have thought we were nuts.

Those are the memories I still cherish. They are the kind of ridiculous moments you share as a team—silly, inconsequential memories that help make up the fabric of the lifelong friendships and bonds you form over those days and nights on the road and in hotels.

I'm an only child, but I found brothers on the road. Because, in the end, family is about the journey and who you take it with.

Two other teammates on those spring hockey teams would end up playing an even bigger part in my life not too far down the road: Logan Schatz and Bryce Fiske.

In just a few years, we would all suit up together again, as members of the Humboldt Broncos.

CHAPTER 3

—

Why am I still here? And why aren't they?

The first time I asked myself those questions, I was twelve years old. I couldn't move. I was drenched in sweat and my heart beat so quickly that I could feel it pounding in my head. As I tried to catch my breath, I opened my eyes and looked up at the blue sky.

My body had never felt so tired. It was pure and absolute exhaustion from my head down to my toes.

It was my very first workout with Chad Martin (a.k.a. Pablo), a well-known strength coach in Saskatoon who agreed to take me on as a client, even though I was so young. I had decided that hockey was going to be a big part of my future, and I was determined to work as hard as I possibly could to make that dream a reality. Chad was going to help me get there.

He was one of the co-founders of the Next Level Training Centre in Saskatoon, which he started with his friend Kelly Riou, another strength coach. With the goal of helping people use fitness to accomplish their goals—whether they were an average person looking to lose weight and live a healthy life, or an elite athlete looking to increase their endurance and improve performance. They wanted to create a gym that was "next level," focused entirely on healthy results. It was not for those who were interested; it was for those who were committed. Chad and Kelly had experience training players who went on to play in the NHL, like Luke and Brayden Schenn, as well as Chandler Stephenson. They had also helped some clients who weren't high-performance athletes lose hundreds of pounds.

When I left after my first session with Chad, I wasn't sure what to think. We went to the tennis courts outside of Mawson Fitness, where Chad and Kelly were based at the time. We did banded walks, ladder drills, sprints, tire flips, tire slams with a weighted bar, "cock push-ups," and the killer: sled pushes. Welcome to day one, Kaleb.

Chad was a very friendly—and very fit—guy in his mid-thirties. He had tattoos, a genuine smile, and a great sense of humour, and he was absolutely jacked. He pushed me to work as hard as I could. I knew that achieving my dreams would take every ounce of effort I had. But I didn't know that I had *this* much effort in me.

After my heart slowed down and I caught my breath while staring up at the sky, Chad said, "See you Wednesday, brah." The workout was over. I got picked up and fell right to sleep once I arrived at home. When I woke up the next day, I could barely move. Every limb felt like it weighed 200 pounds. It took a Herculean effort just to pull myself out of the bed. I took the longest walk to the bathroom of my life—and when I finally got there, I couldn't sit down on the toilet. I turned on the shower and stood there under the hot water, trying to will my body back to life. I squeezed some shampoo into my hands but couldn't reach the top of my head with either arm.

I was walking like a stiff board the next time I saw Chad.

"This is insane," I said. "I feel like absolute garbage."

He smiled. He was so charismatic, he could make feeling like garbage seem like an accomplishment.

"This is what working out is, my man," he replied.

Chad explained that I was experiencing a buildup of lactic acid. It would eventually go away, he said—and with time and work, it wouldn't hurt as much.

"It's your muscle building strength," Chad said. "Keep it up and learn to love the burn. If you keep on creating the burning sensation throughout your body, you're going to get better."

Of course, the second workout was even worse, and there were going to be three every week. But Chad was such a magnetic guy, I couldn't wait to get to the next one.

That was how I learned the importance of pushing beyond what you might believe your limits are. Chad lived that mindset every day, and he passed it on to me. One of the fundamental parts of being physically tough is learning how to be mentally tough. You have to know how to fight through the pain, because it's worth it. Pain can stop us in our tracks if we let it. But it can also propel us forward if we know how to use it.

That meant that instead of going just partway down on a push-up, you did what Chad called a "cock push-up"—which meant your entire body had to touch the ground with every rep, from your nose down to your crotch. We did a lot of cock push-ups. With Chad, nothing was done by half measures. He pushed everyone to their limits, knowing how to get the best out of every individual. He would go above and beyond to make you feel proud of your accomplishments, big or small. To him, it was not just a hi and a bye; he cultivated a relationship beyond the gym. He wanted to know you down to your core.

I had come to Mawson Fitness because of a hockey tournament my Saskatchewan AAA team had played in Minneapolis earlier that year, in May 2009. Instead of chartering a bus, everyone on the team was responsible for getting out to the tournament themselves. Therefore, we took the fourteen-hour drive to Minnesota as a family. On our way back, I asked if we could take a small detour to the University of North Dakota.

When we arrived at Ralph Engelstad Arena in Grand Forks, where the UND Fighting Hawks play, I was astounded. We took a tour of the rink, which has been called the Taj Mahal of hockey.

It cost $104 million to build—with a granite floor in the lobby, escalators taking spectators to each level, and seats made of cherry wood with leather upholstery. During our tour, I must have asked so many questions, which slowed the whole thing down for everyone else. The tour guide asked me to hang on to my questions until the very end, with a promise that he would do something special for us if I did. At the end of the regular tour, when everyone else left, the guide told us he'd take us on the "real tour" now. He took us to all sorts of places in the arena that most people never got to see. He took us down to ice level, showed us the hallway to the dressing room—though we weren't allowed to go in—the workout facility, and the organ room. We spent another hour walking through the place. The Ralph was mesmerizing.

That day, I decided I wanted to play university hockey. It's what is commonly referred to in hockey as the "school route." It meant that when I was old enough, I would look to play Tier II junior hockey (also known as provincial Junior A) rather than major junior hockey in the WHL. It's a path many competitive hockey players in Western Canada have taken so that they could keep their options open in the NCAA. That meant playing in a league like the Saskatchewan Junior Hockey League or the Alberta Junior Hockey League, both of which have a storied history in smaller hockey communities.

It was a path towards a future that was tied to more than the game itself. It was a chance to make sure that all of my hard work on the ice would translate to opportunities off of it. I didn't want hockey alone to define who I was; I wanted to use it to help propel myself forward in life. I wanted it to help build character and life skills that I would be able to transfer to school and to work.

The previous summer, I had been scouted at a AAA spring hockey tournament in Edmonton and approached to be a part of a hand-picked team called the Team Canada Polar Bears, which was playing in the Czech Hockey Challenge Cup.

The invitation came completely out of the blue, and I had no clue what to expect. After receiving the details and talking to my parents about this opportunity, we jumped on it. I ended up having the trip of a lifetime and was named captain of the team. After the tournament in Prague, we travelled on a bus, touring around Europe. This experience opened my eyes to new possibilities of playing professional hockey abroad, something I knew nothing about. I loved the trip so much that I would return as the team's captain the following summer. The historic culture, beautiful atmosphere, and new experiences left an impression on me.

The entire ride home from Grand Forks, I couldn't get the idea out of my head. I'd made up my mind: I was going to play university hockey, receive an education doing it—and then go overseas to play professionally.

Right away, my parents told me that if I wanted to play hockey at the college level, I was going to have to get my grades up, get stronger, and work harder than ever—because nothing comes easy.

"You get what you work for," Dad said.

I wasn't a poor student at the time, but I hadn't really taken school super seriously, either. I was a good hockey player, too—but I could be better. Looking back, that was the first time I realized that being good at the things that came easily to me wasn't going to be enough for me to achieve my goals. I had to work harder than I thought I could. It was going to take sacrifice.

On the ride home, I told my parents that I wanted to start training seriously. I was going to change my diet. I vowed to work even harder in class. I was determined to make it happen. Anything less than the honour roll wasn't going to be good enough.

This was a turning point for me.

When we got back to Saskatoon, I found Mawson Health & Fitness through family friends, and Mom drove me over to check it out. That's when I met Chad for the first time. That summer, he quickly became one of the most important mentors of my life.

Both of my parents were very busy with work, which required them to work eight-to-twelve-hour shifts. They arranged their schedules so that I wasn't alone often, which meant that one would be heading to work just as the other was getting home. It also meant that it was sometimes difficult for them to drive me to strength training. The gym was five kilometres from our house along a busy street, which was fine for a twelve-year-old to bike every day in the summer, but nearly impossible during a "Sasky" winter. Chad knew how hard my parents worked and that it was going to be difficult for me to get into the gym with the regularity required to see a real benefit. Therefore, he offered to pick me up and drive me, even though our home was out of the way for him.

It was a small gesture, but it showed his dedication as a coach. It wasn't just about the business for him. He cared about the people he worked with. He went out of his way, literally, to make sure we had everything we needed to succeed. Even though I was still quite young, those drives with Chad taught me about being generous and kind. He taught me that those traits are just as important as the hard work that you put in. It's not just about the success you want to have, but the type of person you want to be.

Chad was thoughtful, but he was also tough. He knew what it took to excel. He knew that even at a young age, it was essential for an athlete like me to understand the importance of hard work and dedication. He taught me that pain is part of the process— and that I have the strength to push myself further and endure more than I thought I was able. Chad taught me the importance of perseverance.

Each time I ran a sprint, I learned that I could run several more. Every time it felt like my body wanted to give up as it hit the ground during a push-up, my mind learned that I could make myself rise again. I felt my body getting stronger. I knew that I was improving, day by day. Every time I went to the gym, I came home exhausted and sore. But I knew that the temporary pain was worth it.

As someone with diabetes, it was imperative that I eat well and stay focused on my nutrition. Chad helped me understand that I needed fuel to run the machine I was building. I needed to think about what I was putting into my body, especially because of my condition. He taught me that I was able to overcome that, too.

Chad taught me to believe in my goals and provided me with a plan to get there.

For a long time, I didn't know that Chad wasn't well. He was in remission after a battle with brain cancer when he founded Next Level Training with Kelly, who had suffered a head injury that ended his hockey career. They had brain trauma in common, and that's how they met, becoming friends and eventually business partners.

Chad never brought up the battle that he had already endured during our drives to the gym together. When he was encouraging me to fight through the pain—to do one more push-up, or run that extra kilometre—he never told me how much he'd already fought through in his own life.

To me, Chad was not just a coach; he was much more. He was a family man, a man who'd worked hard to begin a successful gym and a career as a trainer. He was an example of what it meant to combine hard work and character. And he was just getting started.

The entire time, though, Chad knew he was dying.

The cancer had returned. It was there when he was telling me about the importance of believing that I could overcome any obstacle. He knew that there are some obstacles you just can't overcome. But that doesn't mean you should give up.

I first really started to think about death in March of 2010, when one of my teammates on my AAA spring league hockey team was killed in a car accident. Brock Pulock was part of our hockey family. I played with him for only one season. He was quiet at first, but once you got to know him, he opened up into a caring and thoughtful person. He was a solid hockey player as well, and a good defenceman. His older brothers Derrick and Ryan both played—and today, Ryan is a defenceman with the New York Islanders. On March 29, 2010, they were in the car coming home from one of Derrick's hockey games with the Grandview Comets senior hockey team. Rylee Zimmer, one of my teammates on that spring team, was also in the vehicle. The SUV they were driving flipped off the road. Rylee suffered severe injuries but survived. Tragically, Brock died from injuries sustained in the crash. He was just thirteen years old. It was terrible.

My parents knew it was going to be difficult for me to understand what had happened. I was still so young. They sat me down to tell me what had happened to Brock. They told me that death is something that is going to happen to all of us. We don't know when it's going to happen, or how—but it's going to happen at some point. It was going to happen to them. It was going to happen to me. There is nothing we can do about it. So, we have to learn how to live with the fact of it. That's why we need to love the people who are around us today. We just don't know if they will be here tomorrow.

We mourn when the people we love die, and that's okay—it hurts, and it should. At the same time, though, we should celebrate the lives that they lived. We should smile at the memories they gave us and never forget the joy they brought.

Death is a painful and scary reality, but it also reminds us that we need to appreciate what we have in life. We can't take this gift for granted. There is no point in worrying about when or why it's going to happen. We can't control that.

"Let's just live as big as we can," my father said. "The only thing we can control is how we live our lives now and how we celebrate people when they pass away. We need to move in their light and not in their darkness."

I understood the inevitability of loss and the value of life—and learned to have gratitude for the gift of having known people, as opposed to the anger of having lost them.

One thing my parents would always remind me of whenever I was upset about something not going well was that life is too short to be upset when things don't go the way we planned. They'd tell me to slow down. The worst thing that can happen in life is someone dying young. That's the hardest thing to understand and the most painful to endure. But even when the worst happens, we need to celebrate the lives that they lived.

I learned that lesson when I was thirteen years old. I had no idea how quickly it would become essential.

Why am I still here? And why aren't they? I didn't have the answer then, and I still don't. I don't think I ever will.

The first time Chad told me he was sick was just after he took me home from the gym sometime during the last year that I trained with him. It was a shock. I sat there speechless. It was something I did not know how to react to. He told me how his cancer was spreading and that he would be unable to train me much longer. It meant I'd begin training with Kelly instead. Chad literally changed my life, and I couldn't repay him in any way. I felt helpless.

Not long after, wristbands were created in support of Chad. They were black, one-inch-thick rubber bands that stated "Pablo's Ultimate Fight *#Believe*." I bought one and never took it off.

He never asked for sympathy. He never seemed angry. Even though I was working mostly with Kelly, Chad continued to mentor and shape me into the person I am today, until he just couldn't anymore. I said one last goodbye to him with a visit at St. Paul's Hospital. I took him an inspirational magazine and tried to brighten his spirits. I walked into the hospital room and my heart sank. He looked frail and in poor health. I kept asking myself, *Why him?* He was the toughest person I'd ever met, even as his cancer progressed the following spring.

Pablo's ultimate fight ended on March 12, 2011, at St. Paul's Hospital in Saskatoon. He was thirty-seven years old. Instead of a funeral, there was a celebration of his life. This was the first time I had ever attended such an event. Even though they were sad, people were legitimately celebrating Chad. The beautiful stories told about all of the fun times he shared with his loved ones, rather than the fact that he was no longer here—which we couldn't change—made a lasting impression on me. Chad changed my perspective on death, just like his presence changed my life.

I think about him all the time, as I do so many other people whose lives have touched me in ways I'll never forget.

At night, I look up at the stars and think about his light. It still shines.

CHAPTER 4

—

I t *could have been me.*

The one-tonne truck careened through the intersection at highway speed. There wasn't any time to react. It collided on the passenger's side, crumpling the frame like it was made of paper.

That was where I was supposed to be sitting that day. The entire seat was twisted in crushed metal. Had I been there, I have no doubt that I'd have been killed.

Instead, the phone rang as Mom and I pulled into our driveway. It was my father. He was supposed to pick me up from the gym, but I finished early and took a ride with Mom instead. Dad had to run some errands, which I would have helped him with.

He was turning left on an advanced green arrow, but the driver of the truck coming the other way didn't notice that the light had changed. Dad saw the truck at the last second, right before it T-boned our Chevy Malibu Maxx. It was hauling a trailer of cement products. The force of the crash threw our car into a metal stanchion, and the Malibu crumpled like an accordion. The passenger's side was gone and Dad was stuck on the driver's side. He shook his head and tried to figure out where he was. He felt like his guts had been slammed out one side of him and back across the other, before falling back in place inside of him.

People came running out of their cars nearby to see if he was okay, but the door was pinned against a metal pole. No one could get it open. Dad sat there, stuck in his seat, telling himself he was okay and that everything was fine, even though he couldn't be sure. Adrenalin was pumping through his system.

The fire department arrived on the scene first. They checked to see if Dad could move his legs. He could. They checked his arms. Still working. There were no sharp pains, other than the feeling that he'd been turned inside out and back again. Finally, they managed to pull him out of the mangled Chevy. When the paramedics arrived, they told Dad they had to take him to the hospital to get checked out, but he refused to go. His priority was getting his phone and calling us.

When Mom answered, we didn't think it was that serious. After all, he'd managed to call us—how bad could it be? But when we drove up to the scene of the accident, we were shocked. Our car was destroyed. We went as white as the snow that was falling that night. It looked like a scene out of a demolition derby. It was astounding that Dad had survived at all. It was hard to process just how lucky he'd been. Then I remembered where I would have been sitting had our schedules run according to plan that day. One small detour and lives change forever.

It could have been me.

It was December 11, 2012. I was fifteen years old and I was playing for the Saskatoon Sabercats city-wide Midget AA team at the time. We were not the best team, but not the worst. Earlier that fall, I had been one of the last cuts from the Beardy's Blackhawks Midget AAA team and became affiliated with the Saskatoon Blazers Midget AAA team. I had a chip on my shoulder, determined to prove I should have been playing in Midget AAA that year, and was having a great season individually, improving every game.

I had been fully managing my diabetes for the past two years and had begun to adapt to the way puberty was affecting my blood sugar. It was an extremely challenging time as my levels fluctuated between high and low, even though I was receiving the same insulin dose as usual. When I was high, I'd have an enhanced sense of smell and, oddly enough, would smell insulin. I'd have a tingling sensation all over my body and would be slightly irritable, extremely thirsty, and need to urinate frequently. When my blood sugar was low, my legs and hands would shake, I was unable to concentrate, and I became weak and sweaty. It was a period of trial and error, but nothing I couldn't handle. My parents were supportive, adding their two cents' worth, but I continually warned them that I had aspirations to move away the following year for Midget AAA hockey and would not be able to rely on their guidance as I tackled these situations. Even though I loved it at home, I had my mind set on challenging myself to grow as an individual, and I believed that moving away into a billet house would achieve that.

Dad felt fine when he came home after the accident. He's a thick guy. He only had a few bruises on his shoulder, but later that night he started to stiffen up. The next day, he had a hard time walking, but he pushed through and went to work. He hoped that it was just a little whiplash and that his muscles were just tense from the collision.

But through the Christmas holidays and into the new year, Dad just didn't feel quite right. Little did I know that this was just the beginning.

That January, we went to a hockey tournament in Regina. On the way back, my father started to feel sick, like he had the flu. He was drenched with sweat, felt exhausted, and had a difficult time staying awake at the wheel. His entire body was sore—almost like how he felt right after he was in the crash. Dad went right to bed as soon as we got home, hoping it was just a bug that he could sleep off. But when he woke up the next morning, he still felt terrible. Once again, he was soaked with sweat. He couldn't get out of bed. In fact, he could hardly move at all.

This went on for several days until he realized that his illness was something worse than a typical flu and he agreed to visit a doctor.

That wasn't much help, though. Dad was diagnosed with a bacterial virus and sent home with some antibiotics.

They didn't work. He just kept getting worse and worse. He'd wake up in the middle of the night and struggle to pull himself out of bed. The sweat from his body would drip right down his legs. His hair was drenched, too. His sweating was so out of control that they would have to change the sheets—and eventually they put down a liner beneath him, so his perspiration wouldn't soak through to the mattress.

It was very scary because we had no idea what was wrong—and even less of a clue about how to fix it. When he returned to the doctor, Dad was given a different antibiotic to try. But that didn't work, either.

Soon, the symptoms shifted from the sweats to severe chills, where my father felt like he was freezing and would shake uncontrollably, almost like he was having a seizure. We'd put blankets in the dryer to warm them up and cover him. My mother even went out and bought special heated blankets, to make sure Dad had something warm to wrap himself in through the night. He'd have as many as four blankets covering him until he stopped shivering. Many times, I would cuddle up beside him or lie right on top of him, for hours, just trying to warm him up with my body heat. The minute after the chills went away, Dad would be drenched in sweat again. During all of this, he was so lethargic. This was not my father at all.

He returned to the doctor a third time and had blood work done. That night, the phone rang. It was the doctor. Dad's blood work was all over the place, he said—and it was dangerous.

"You need to go to emergency," he said. "Your C-reactive protein test is critically high and you could have a heart attack or a stroke."

We rushed my father to the hospital, where he underwent a thorough evaluation, but the doctors were still unable to figure out what was wrong with him. One concern was that he might have cancer. They ran every test for cancer under the sun: a bone biopsy, a spinal tap, a colonoscopy, a gastroscopy, an MRI, a CT scan. With each test, they found nothing.

For a while, the doctors thought they had ruled out everything except HIV or tuberculosis. He had numerous HIV tests, and he went on a medication regimen for tuberculosis, in which a nurse would come to the house and watch him take the medication, because it makes people so nauseous that many will try to avoid it. Dad vomited the medication up, over and over again. He couldn't keep it down. We had a hematologist looking into possible blood diseases that might have gone undetected. We thought about hosting a fundraiser to raise money so that dad could go to the Mayo Clinic in Rochester, Minnesota.

Through all of this, he stopped eating. Mom and I would bring him food and help him eat it, but he couldn't stomach it. He just didn't have an appetite. Dad was a big guy normally—close to 300 pounds—but in just a few months his weight dropped to 160. He was literally half the size and was almost unrecognizable. A lot of that loss was muscle mass, which meant that Dad had a hard time holding himself up. He would actually fall down when he started to walk. He couldn't do anything but lie around all day, being helped from the bedroom down to the couch.

It was horrible to see him this way. Every morning, I would poke my head through his bedroom door to double-check that he was still breathing. This experience weighed heavily on me; it felt like I was carrying his life on my shoulders. My father was always so full of life. He was the guy who taught me to always live big, because tomorrow wasn't a guarantee. He and my mother had worked so hard to give me the opportunities that I had and to live a privileged life.

Now, he needed me. My mother had to work constantly, because Dad was on disability leave from his job. She spent every spare moment she had taking care of him. I did the same. After school, I would come right home to check on him. If I went to the gym, I'd rush back, too. I avoided going out with friends for a long time, because I knew my father needed me. It was a sense of duty, but also a sense of guilt. Any time I spent away from my father felt like I was abandoning him. I know that he didn't feel that way. He wanted me to live my life, but we needed to stay together—to stay strong, the three of us—while we tried to figure out and defeat whatever it was that seemed to be killing him.

That March, while we were still trying to understand what was happening to Dad, I played in the SaskFirst tournament in Regina, which was a showcase of the top players from across the province, organized into eight teams for an all-star tournament. This was the tournament I had been cut from a year before as a bantam-aged player, which ultimately ruined my chances of being drafted into the Western Hockey League. Many players' careers are promoted and are able to blossom over the weekend, as plenty of scouts are in attendance. I was one of the few fifteen-year-olds selected from our city's representative midget team. I had earned a spot a month earlier as one of the top players from my zone and was hoping my dad would be able to be part of it. He did everything he could, with Mom's help, but he was so sick that he only made it out to a handful of my games. The few times he was able to attend, he was covered in a blanket because his chills were so bad, or he was drenched in sweat, dripping, while everyone else tried not to look at him. A couple of times, Mom had to leave the rink early with Dad because he was severely nauseous or couldn't stay awake.

It was a huge honour and probably one of the bigger moments in my hockey career up to that point. Several scouts watched me play and wanted to speak with me and my parents about joining their teams. Dad was able to be part of a few of the conversations, but he was so incredibly sick that he wouldn't be able to really remember any of them.

Of all the pain, sickness, and uncertainty he was going through, I know that having to miss me on the ice tore his heart up the most. Looking up and not seeing him in the stands did the same to me.

Dad was my best friend, and I didn't know how much longer he had. I'd lie beside him to keep him warm all day and night if I had to. He was literally wasting away before our eyes—and there was nothing we could do.

After the tournament in Regina, I committed to the Battlefords Stars AAA team for the 2013–14 season—a little more than an hour away from home. The team recruited me during the SaskFirst tournament, and the head coach, Martin Smith, even took the time to come and visit me in my home afterwards. The program was undergoing a culture change with the goal of creating something special, and the coaching staff was going after highly touted free agents with great character to load up for the Saskatchewan Midget AAA Hockey League championship. I was lucky to have several other teams ask me to join them that spring, but North Battleford was the closest to home and I wanted to be a part of the atmosphere that they were trying to create.

I turned sixteen that June. If I was going to chase my dream of playing hockey at the highest level possible and use it to get an education, this was going to be a major step in that direction.

But this would be the first time I'd live away from my parents, and it was happening when it seemed like they both needed me the most. I spoke to them about the decision, and they both agreed the move was what was best for me, even if it would take me away from them—even if we weren't really sure what was happening with Dad.

I told him that I wasn't sure if I could leave, but Dad told me I had to pursue my passion.

"You know what? Just chase it. Go for it," he said. "I don't want to hold you back. I never want to hold you back. You've got to go try it out."

That fall, we packed up the car and headed northwest to my new home. The Stars connected one of my best friends, Michael Korol, and me with a billet family. We had just found out about our billet home a week prior. I had no idea what to expect.

When we arrived at our billet, we were shocked at how nice of a spot we received. When you're first recruited to a team, you do not always get the most ideal places. Michael and I absolutely hit the jackpot when we scored Anne Cole and Ryan Haughian as our billets.

Billets are truly the difference makers for your experience away from the rink. If there are problems in your billet home, your only escape is the arena. And if there is no escape in the arena, then you will not be in a good spot mentally.

Upon arrival, I knew it was a good fit instantly as Anne made us feel like we were right at home. With three kids of her own, all of whom were moved out, she had a welcoming charm and a motherly presence about her. I felt like I had known her for years after just ten minutes of chatting with her. She was so loving and caring.

To be honest, she had her worries about me. I was a type 1 diabetic, I was an only child, I had a father who was severely ill, and I was living away from home for the first time. I also drove a used red Hummer H3 with a licence plate that read BARDOWN—my dad's idea. On the surface, I definitely did not seem like an ideal person for them to have moving into their home.

The first week was strictly about adjusting to the new life. It was absolutely hectic. First, I unpacked all of my belongings to make it feel like home. Then I met all of my new "brothers" for the season. Training camp started, which included fitness testing, gruelling workouts and practices every day, and scrimmages twice a day on the weekend. This was physically draining because we all wanted to display the hard work we had put in that summer and earn our spot in the lineup. I had a lot to prove, being one of their first commitments. I wanted to be a leader on the Stars, even though it was my first year with the team. I wanted to go the extra mile to demonstrate that I hold myself to a high standard and to display my values.

Being away from home for the first time meant I had to pay more attention to my diabetes than ever before. By now, the disease was actually very stable and under control. I had minimal issues with it, other than experiencing the occasional low or high. With the additional physical activity, I had to have a snack before practice and another one between practice and our team workout to eliminate the possibility of going low. The goal was to stay in the range of 8 to 10 mmol/L when doing physical activity. During games, I was continuously going high because of the adrenalin, so I started to give myself a couple units of insulin during the game to bring my blood sugar down to a healthy level. Things were running quite smoothly.

But that doesn't mean things were easy. I was still trying to juggle the relationships I had back home, cope with my father's illness, and create new friendships with the people I would be with every day. Grade 11 was starting up and I was the new kid on the block at John Paul II Collegiate. I was trying to get settled into my new courses and find my way around the school.

This sounds chaotic—and it was. But I believe I was ready to move away, even at the age of sixteen. I ended up settling into a groove extremely quickly. I already knew several players who were returning to the team that season, and I hit it off with the other incoming recruits. We meshed as a team seamlessly; because many of us had moved away from home to become Stars, the only family we had were our billets and each other.

When the season started, the hardest part was the feeling that, for the first time, my family wasn't bonded around my sport. It was weird. It was just so normal to have both of my parents around. My entire life, it was the three of us. Then, all of a sudden, my father was deathly ill and my mother was trying to work, take care of him, and visit me as much as possible.

My mother later described those months of uncertainty when Dad was sick as filled with complete emptiness. I agree with her. Nothing felt complete. Ever since I was a kid and we were pretending to fly to hockey games in our basement, my father was always central to my experience in hockey. He loved watching me play the game more than anything. It brought him so much joy. Now he wasn't able to enjoy that. Amid the uncertainty of his health, that seemed like the cruellest blow of all. It was frustrating. It was heartbreaking.

Mom and I had a glimpse of what life could be like without Dad, and neither of us was quite ready for it.

Despite the pain, we had to push on. I had to try—because Dad would never want me to stop chasing my dream. He wouldn't want me to get stuck in the darkness that I felt. I had to fight to live big in the light, for him.

CHAPTER 5

—

9:33 a.m.

Good morning, how's Dad doing? I couldn't sleep
and thought about him all night! 🖤

10:00 a.m.

Good morning hon 😊, good luck tonight in your game.
I will be thinking of you as I will not be able to make
your game. Dad isn't doing well . . . 🖤🖤🖤 😢

11:08 a.m.

What is wrong!?!?

12:49 p.m.

Mom!?!?

12:57 p.m.

He's not looking good.

1:19 p.m.

What do you mean, is he okay??!? I need to get my head
in the game, talk to you later! I love you guys lots 🖤

1:52 p.m.

You need to come home NOW!!!! Dad is not going to make it . . .

Y ou never forget the gut-wrenching moment when you first find out that someone you love might be gone forever.

For me, it was supposed to be a routine morning ahead of a regular-season game with the Battlefords Midget AAA Stars in the 2013–14 season. I woke up thinking that it was just another game day.

It wasn't.

O f course, the year itself had been far from ordinary. I'd tried my best to settle into life in North Battleford. But as Dad's health continued to spiral, he started to weigh heavier on my mind. Every morning, I would ask Mom how he was doing and get an update, then do my best to continue to live my life to the fullest in his honour. Attitude and perspective are everything. I could have chosen to focus on the negative fact that my dad was ill and we didn't know what was wrong with him; or I could focus on the positive by taking life one day at a time and knowing that my dad was still fighting. I used his battle as an internal motivation to push myself on the days when it was tough. Everything I did, I gave it my all. That was who I was and the standard I set for myself; I wasn't going to change.

More than anything, I knew how badly my parents wanted me to succeed and how much they had sacrificed in their lives for me to follow my passion. I was privileged to have earned this opportunity, and I desired to make the most of it, for them and myself.

Very few knew what rough shape my dad actually was in. I did not even know the full extent. I knew he was dealing with something serious, but I didn't actually grasp how severe it was until I realized that he wasn't going to be able to attend any of my games. I knew that even with all of the complications and uncertainty he was going through with his illness, the hardest part for my father was not being able to witness this next chapter in my life.

46

Even though I was only an hour away from my parents in North Battleford, it felt like ten. Dad had always been very involved with every team I played for. Watching me play was one of his biggest joys, and it was being taken away without any real understanding as to why.

He'd text me before and after each game and would follow along with updates online. I'd fill him in on the details of what happened every time the game ended. Dad made the best effort he could, but it broke his heart to not be able to be there. I knew he also worried about me and Mom all the time. Not being able to take care of us was the most frustrating thing he'd ever dealt with.

It was difficult to play without him in the stands, because he and Mom had literally been there for every single game I had played up until he fell ill. The rink felt hollow without him. Mom was missing her partner in crime. As hard as it was for me that Dad couldn't be there, I knew that it was even harder for him. We spent so much time together as a family on the road, driving to my hockey games across North America. Now I was living away from home and Mom was making the journey alone.

Whenever I had a game, she'd drive out to North Battleford or catch a ride with another family and be there in the stands to cheer me on. If we had an away game, Mom still made the trip—even to places like Swift Current, which is three hours away. She would bring me care packages of fresh fruits, veggies, dried mangos, yogurt, meat, cheese, and crackers. Sometimes, she'd have packages made up for my linemates, too, which would make the rest of my teammates envious.

My mother was working overtime in her career, as a wife, and as a mother. After working full time, never missing a day, she spent every waking minute by my father's side or coming to watch me play. It was a full twenty-four-hour clock for her.

I asked her how she managed to do it all.

"You just do," she said.

My billet mom, Anne Cole, was so supportive and loving. She did everything she could to comfort me—coming to all my games and spending hours chatting with me at the house. But not even Anne truly knew what I was experiencing internally.

Nobody did.

Late-night thoughts are sometimes a silent killer. The odd night, I would worry about the things that were out of my control and question my values. The constant possibility of my dad not being around tomorrow and me "selfishly" pursuing my passion while he was slowly dying tortured my sixteen-year-old brain.

Am I even doing the right thing? I wondered. *Doesn't he need me at home?*

Even though Dad wanted me to follow my dreams, these thoughts still emerged. How could they not cross your mind at least once?

Through the fall of 2013, Dad's health had continued to worsen. He had been in and out of the hospital several times since he'd become sick. He was always sent home after the tests, because they weren't sure what was wrong with him and didn't have any beds to spare. Mom would prepare food and leave it in a cooler beside the couch when she left for work each morning, so that Dad wouldn't try to get up and make something for himself—he was so weak and he kept falling. She would come home after her shift hoping that he was okay and still alive.

Late that October, two months after I left home, Dad suffered a gallbladder attack. He went to the hospital for laparoscopic day surgery. We were told that it would only take about an hour to complete. Dad went in on Halloween, which is one of his favourite days of the year. He always goes big, dressing up as something frightening and joining the rest of our neighbours in scaring the living daylight out of the kids—and even some of the parents.

Despite not being well, he figured he would at least be able to hand out candy to the little kids who stopped by in their cute costumes.

When he woke up in the hospital bed after surgery, there were tubes coming out of him everywhere. He literally felt worse than he'd ever felt before. Dad looked over and saw my mother sitting beside him, looking distraught and worn out. Right away, he assumed that the worst had finally caught up with him. We'd been told several times by doctors that there was a good possibility that dad had cancer, even though they couldn't detect it. They must have finally found it, he thought.

When Mom saw that my father was awake, she held his hand.

"This isn't how we planned for it to go," she said.

No shit, he thought.

When the surgeons opened my dad up, they found all kinds of scar tissue built up around his gallbladder and liver. It was so extreme that it was hard for the surgeon to distinguish exactly where his gallbladder was. They took out as much as they could know for sure was actually his gallbladder and left the rest. The symptoms were consistent with a rare autoimmune disorder known as hepatic sarcoidosis. Doctors remain unsure why people develop the disease. Often, it's in people's lungs and can be resolved. Very rarely, it affects the liver. This is what had caused the inflammation around Dad's internal organs and led to such odd readings in his blood work, where one day everything looks normal, then spikes, returns to normal, and spikes again. When the liver is affected by a disease like this, it tries to protect itself by storing protein, which prevents it from getting to other parts of the body. This effectively shrank all of his muscles, leading to his lack of strength, severe weight loss, and difficulty walking. It also led to severe cirrhosis of the liver, which is essentially scar tissue in the liver.

After the surgery, he also developed a peritoneal and urinary tract infection. It caused him to have excess fluid around the area, which expanded so large that the internal sutures popped. A long needle had to be stuck into his abdomen to drain about a litre and a half of fluid daily.

Dad didn't get home in time to hand out his Halloween candy that day. The infections nearly killed him.

The doctors looked at my father with the pity you would have towards someone who was going to die too soon. But even though he could see it in the doctors' eyes, my father didn't believe he was going to die. He just knew that it wasn't his time, regardless of how bad things got.

I'd check in with my parents whenever I could, usually with a quick phone call or text message—just like the one I sent that morning, thinking that it was just another day.

On November 10, I was getting ready for the second game of our weekend series in Tisdale. I'd had a hard time falling asleep the night before the game. I was constantly thinking and worrying about Dad. His condition and symptoms were progressively worsening. Now it looked like he was reaching the end.

You need to come home NOW!!!! Mom texted. *Dad is not going to make it . . .*

When I saw her last message, I was at least two hours away from home and we had a game to play in eight minutes. There was no way for me to get home without taking the team bus. I felt sick with worry that we were going to lose him and that I wasn't going to be there when he died. I wanted to go home. I thought of Dad lying in that hospital bed, trying to stay alive—knowing how badly he wanted to see me out on the ice. I thought about what Dad and Mom had taught me about death and living—about making the most of what we have and being grateful for everything in life. I knew that my father would be disappointed if I'd given it anything less than my all in Tisdale.

That afternoon, I tied up my skates, pulled my jersey over my head, and stepped out on the ice with Dad's initials written on the knob of my stick. I played the game for him. I played like he was in the stands for the last time. He didn't leave my mind the entire game. I felt like I had to do it for him.

I scored the opening goal and had two assists in a 5–2 win. It was the best game I'd played all season. It felt like it was one of my best games ever.

I called my Mom as soon as I got off the ice. Dad was still alive. We boarded the bus after the game and got back to North Battleford late that night. I drove my roommate home to our billets', rushed inside, and threw a few things in a bag before I was out the door, on my way to the hospital in Saskatoon. That whole night, I was expecting a phone call saying he was gone.

He looked weak. I didn't think he was going to make it. He was in the worst shape I had ever seen him. Face whiter than his bedsheets. Tubes coming out of every opening. His belly looked like he was nine months pregnant. His face and temples were sunken in due to malnutrition. He was awake and smiled when he saw me. I stood beside his bed and grabbed his hand, still wearing my full suit. I had a huge lump in my throat. I could barely talk. What do you say to somebody when it could be your *last* words to them?

"It's Kaleb, I am here for you. I love you very much," I told him. "You can't leave us just yet. You have to keep fighting, Dad."

He was still really surprised and confused, wondering how I'd got there if I was playing a game today. He showed me his incisions, his bruises, and every single staple—thirty-one of them. He tried to be positive and upbeat, because he did not want me to be worried. However, I was worried sick. I couldn't picture life without my best friend.

But it wasn't the end.

I think that being reunited as a family in that hospital room was another turning point in my life. Dad's condition started to improve after he saw me. I think that deep inside, he realized he still needed to be here, and that he *wanted* to be here—generating more motivation to get better. I think he knew it wasn't time yet.

Shortly after that stay in the hospital, Dad would start to take a medication called prednisone that helped reduce the inflammation, allowed him to gain weight, and gave him a little bit more energy, so he wasn't as fatigued. Still, he didn't leave the hospital for forty days—not until just before Christmas.

During that time, my mother visited him every day, sometimes twice if she could. I don't know how she managed to hold it together through those difficult dark and cold months, holding us together—but she did. She is the strongest woman I know.

Even after Dad was out of the hospital, his health continued to worsen. We had a working diagnosis and a better idea of what was wrong, but very little information about how to actually make him better.

For a home game in North Battleford several months later, Dad took the trip with Mom. He could still barely walk up the stairs to their seats. It took him about ten minutes. He was still frail and gaunt. Anne, my billet mother, didn't recognize him at first. She said he looked like a completely different person. And he did. I skated around the ice during warm-ups and saw him there. I couldn't believe it. I had the biggest smile on my face. I was ecstatic and proud of how hard he fought to be back. The arena didn't feel hollow anymore. I had an extra step in my game and a chip on my shoulder to show Dad how much I had improved that year. I still had *M.D.* written on the knob of my stick in his honour. Every game I played was for him. Dad was on his way back, and nothing was going to stop our family from continuing this journey together.

When I returned home at the end of the season, he was heading towards a recovery. The prednisone had helped, but you can't take it forever because it has severe side effects. My dad suffered from cataracts, insulin-dependent type 2 diabetes, and puffiness, especially in the face. Eventually, he is going to need a liver transplant. I wanted to give him part of mine, but I can't because I'm diabetic.

Recovery was slow for Dad. He had to start working on his strength because he had lost all his muscle mass and had trouble walking. He would tire easily and still slept excessively. The side effects from all the medications he was taking only complicated things further. They made him easily fatigued and it was hard to control his blood sugar. This meant lots of blood glucose checks, insulin adjustments, and food intake changes. He needed to gain weight back, but not fat. This meant his diet was high in protein, moderate in fat, and low in salt to control fluid retention. I could also tell that Dad was having trouble remembering words, and sometimes his memory wasn't the greatest. I am not sure if that was because of the illness, the trauma to his body, or side effects from the medications he was on. Recovery wasn't easy—he had to have eye surgery to remove the cataracts—but he persevered. He wasn't the same Dad as before, but I was just happy I still had him.

In all, Dad spent two years in and out of the hospital, fighting for his life.

Today, he's still not fully recovered, but he's able to function. Over the course of two years, he was able to return to work. He was able to get back on the road and come to the rink to watch me play. He was able to smile and laugh. Dad was able to be himself, which means he was able to live *big* again.

CHAPTER 6

I don't remember a day in my life when I was living without diabetes. There are many young people who understand what that means. It means you live in a constant state of monitoring yourself, 24/7, knowing that your life is in danger if you slip too far one way or the other. It means that the pursuits you dream about are often that much more difficult to do, because you have to corral a disease at the same time you're seeking to defeat your own doubts and push yourself to the limits required to find success in any area of life.

Growing up, you are often looked at differently than others. Even though the illness is not visible, the things you have to do to maintain your health are evident. What other eight-year-old child has to leave midway through class to give themselves a needle in the school bathroom? Imagine being a young male, carrying around your diabetic supplies and being called derogatory names because you're carrying what looks like a purse. Or even an athlete, having to sit out a couple shifts during tryouts while devouring snacks on the bench because of a low blood glucose level. The constant reminders of being "different" weigh on your shoulders.

It can be a very lonely and discouraging experience.

Yes, it could be much worse, and I am grateful to have this disease over countless others, but there are definitely negative features about being a diabetic.

However, I embraced the disease and chose to focus on the positives at a young age. I learned to be independent and responsible. I was fortunate to have really good friends who accepted me for who I was, regardless of the illness I lived with. When I was younger, we would always guess what my glucose reading would be, and it was a great way to educate my friends about diabetes. They would even try poking their own fingers to put themselves in my shoes, learning that your finger burns for a solid minute after each poke—and if you didn't draw enough blood, you would have to do it again.

When I was sixteen years old, playing my first year of Midget AAA with North Battleford, I decided I wanted to find a way to support and encourage other teenagers and children who were living the same reality as me. This realization hit me after I met Josh Lilly at John Paul II Collegiate. He was newly diagnosed with type 1 diabetes and was in the same grade as me. I ended up becoming good buddies with him by helping him navigate the diabetic way of life and answering any questions or concerns he had about the disease.

I had a very good understanding of how my body reacted to different situations, but I was never perfect. Nobody is. The one time when my diabetes took over was during a bag skate. We had all played pathetically and lost to a team we never should have allowed to beat us the previous weekend. It was one of those games where you did not even want to hear what the coaches had to say. We showed up to the rink on Monday to find that there were no pucks laid out for us to take on the ice, the way there normally was. I remember looking around for pucks and even asking the rink attendant, but I could not find any. Once it dawned on me what was happening, my stomach went numb. We all knew what was coming. A no-puck practice.

As a hockey player, I can tell you these practices absolutely suck. You truly don't know what it feels like until you have experienced one yourself. To make matters worse, I was running high that afternoon, so I gave myself some insulin to bring my blood sugar levels down to a range that was a good fit for a typical practice. And this one wasn't going to be typical.

We ended up skating for the full sixty-minute time slot, with two-minute breaks for water every eighteen minutes. The idea was that since we only played up to our standard level for about six minutes in that previous game, we would pay for the fifty-four minutes when we did not play.

Everything was going as well as it could until I hit a wall. I was near the front of the pack throughout the whole skate, but then I dropped to the rear. *Noticeably* last—by five to ten seconds. You knew it was bad when guys started to worry and ask if I was okay. I knew I wasn't, but I didn't want to let my teammates down. I wanted to show I was a leader and was not going to take the easy way out.

After the next rep, I knew my blood sugar was extremely low and I was going to collapse into a full seizure on the ice if I did not get some carbohydrates into me. My assistant coach, Jody Reiter, skated up to me and asked if everything was all right. He said I looked terrible and needed to stop. I listened to him and told him my blood sugar was severely low. Thankfully, he was carrying the Scooby-Doo fruit snacks in his pocket that I'd given him as a precaution at the start of the year. I quickly jammed them down my throat as I skated to the bench. Then I got to the bench and collapsed. I couldn't move, and I lay down, looking up to the bright white lights on the arena ceiling, faintly saying, "Scooby." Thankfully, someone—and I'm sad to say I do not remember who—was able to get more snacks into my system. Within twenty minutes, I felt back to my normal self.

After that near-seizure experience, I promised myself I would never mess around with low blood sugar, regardless of the situation I was in.

Growing up, I found that there wasn't much awareness or advocacy for type 1 diabetes—especially in athletics. When I was younger, I didn't really have an influential person to look up to. In hockey, Bobby Clarke was the best-known current player to have diabetes, but his career was already done by the time I was growing up. (Today, Max Domi is the best-known hockey player who lives with diabetes. He's only two years older than me.) So, I wanted to create a way for young people with diabetes to be able to connect with someone they could look up to.

When I told my parents about the idea, they were both on board. I've always been taught that it is important to give back. However, they also taught me to manage my time and the goals that I set for myself. This seemed like a very big feat to pull off while still trying to acquire honour-roll grades in school, play hockey at a high enough level to earn a spot on a collegiate team, and give back with various events in the North Battleford community. My parents told me to wait until I had finished high school to focus on such a time-consuming project. I agreed, but the thought remained at the forefront of my mind. I knew it was going to be a massive segment of my future plans.

After my first year of Midget AAA in Battleford, I was in constant talks with the team in the Saskatchewan Junior Hockey League that held my Junior A rights: the Notre Dame Hounds, based in Wilcox, a tiny village about three hours south of Saskatoon. The team is affiliated with a private Catholic boarding school that was founded in 1920. Over the decades, the Hounds developed a rich hockey tradition. Players like Rod Brind'Amour, Curtis Joseph, Wendel Clark, and Vincent Lecavalier all played for Notre Dame. It was an extremely reputable program in a great community setting; therefore, I had tremendous interest in joining the team. I went to their training camp in late August of 2014 and was offered a spot as an underage player. This would mean I would need to transfer from North Battleford to Notre Dame for my final year of high school. It was a big move, but initially it was one that I felt ready to make. I went through the whole process to initiate the transfer and prepared myself to move even farther from my parents, even though Dad was still quite sick.

During one of our exhibition games with the Hounds, the coach pulled me aside and told me he wanted me to focus on playing less of a skilled brand of hockey. Instead of thinking ahead and passing the puck on an offensive zone entry, he wanted me to just dump it in when I crossed the red line. I realized that the style of hockey the coach wanted the team to play that year wasn't going to help me develop as a player. Even though I would be playing at a higher level, in Junior A, my abilities and skills would likely diminish. Instead of making the jump up to the SJHL that season, I decided to return to North Battleford and play out my final year of Midget AAA as a seventeen-year-old, where I could continue to develop. This was an important lesson for me—and one that I have carried ever since. Sometimes the best choice isn't the one that seems the most prestigious. Sometimes you advance by having a sense of where you are at a certain time and place. It's hard to turn down what appears to be a promotion, but if you have goals, you need to factor in the best route to achieving them. It's not always a step forward. Sometimes a step back will actually better prepare you for the steps you take ahead. Patience is difficult, but it's incredibly valuable in the bigger picture.

I packed my bags and returned to North Battleford to play one more season of minor hockey, with a vision for greater things—both within the game and outside of it.

Returning to such a good environment eased the hardships back home. I loved going to school, the rink, and the gym, spending time with my billet family, and hanging out with teammates. I created a new family. It was my second home.

That season, my father started to come to more games with my mother. He was starting to gain some weight and get some muscle back, but he was still weak and would get tired quickly. He would take lots of naps and was dealing with side effects from his medications, which were both physical and mental. He said he felt like he was "in a fog"; he would have trouble remembering words and would pause in mid-sentence because he couldn't remember one, or he would forget things. He had been to Edmonton for a three-day liver transplant assessment and they found he didn't need one immediately but would need one in the future. He asked the specialists if this illness was something I could get, and they said it is very rare and they didn't know enough about it to say whether it is hereditary or not. Since it is so rare, they couldn't give us a prognosis, but I knew my dad would remain positive and continue moving forward. He was still very sick, but we at least had a better idea of what the problem was.

At first, Dad tried to reclaim his role as the one in the driver's seat. He loved driving. That was always his job on our long trips as a family. He still didn't have the strength, though, and Mom had to take the wheel. Dad would sleep in the passenger's seat while she drove. It was another sign of just how sick he was. When they arrived at the rink, mom would have to help him in. She'd lead him up the stairs. They weren't able to sit where my mom usually sat because it was too far away and he just didn't have the strength. Sometimes Dad had to fight to stay awake through all three periods.

Even though he was still struggling, it was great to see him back in the stands. It started to feel like we were back together again.

That final year in North Battleford was incredibly important to me. It was my final year in high school and the last chance I had to take care of one of the key pieces in my plan to play collegiate hockey: excelling in the classroom. The Battlefords Stars organization was very committed to academics. They didn't just bring in players who were good at hockey; they wanted players who also worked hard in school. That was one of the things I loved about the program. On our AAA team, I'd say about 75 percent of us really tried hard in school, which is rare for a hockey team—normally there are only maybe three or four. It was really nice to have teammates who were of the same mindset as mine. We pushed each other to study, the same way that we'd push each other to understand the systems we were using on the ice. It was all one and the same. I'd never experienced anything like that before and I was grateful to have that kind of support. John Paul II Collegiate was a great place to spend my final year of high school. I had become accustomed to the school, the teachers had an idea of the kind of person I was, I made lots of new friends, and we were provided with the support we needed to succeed. We also had our annual floor hockey tournament showdowns at lunch that I couldn't miss.

Those two years of being a Star were the best two years of my hockey career up to that point. It was the greatest group of guys I have ever been a part of. Of course, you are never best friends with everyone on a team, but we were an extremely close-knit group that respected each other in both of my years there. It was similar to what I would experience a few years later.

We were a solid team as well—good enough to make it all the way to the league finals in both years that I was there.

Unfortunately, we weren't quite good enough to win the championship in either season, losing out both years in the finals. When the 2014–15 season ended with that disappointment in late March, I decided that it was best for me to head home and finish off the school year in Saskatoon, where I could be closer to my family and graduate with my childhood buddies. It was super hard to leave my teammates and good friends that I had created during my time in North Battleford. I even contemplated staying there until I graduated in June. I loved my time there.

I wasn't quite certain where I was heading next, but I knew it was likely going to take me even farther from my family and friends. It was going to be nice to spend some time with my parents, while Dad continued his fight. Dad was able to make it to all my playoff games in North Battleford that season and was even able to make it all the way up to my mom's regular spot. He was getting stronger every day but still had a long way to go to get back to his old self. Dad would always tell me how much he enjoyed watching me play hockey. After my first playoff game he told me that he'd really missed watching me and was happy he was still able to. Honestly, that was very nice to hear. It's the little things you appreciate after your life gets flipped.

As we were unloading all of my stuff from the car, moving it back into my childhood home, my phone rang. It was the head coach from Notre Dame, Clint Mylymok. The Hounds were about to start round two of the SJHL playoffs and still had interest in me being part of the roster as an underage player. I felt as though I'd developed into an even better player through my second season of Midget AAA, and I realized it would be a great experience to join a Junior A team for the playoffs now that minor hockey was finished.

"Load it back up," I told my parents as they unpacked the car. "I have to go."

I set out for the long drive to Wilcox that night.

CHAPTER 7

L uctor et *Emergo*.

Struggle and emerge.

That was the Notre Dame way. The saying was a founding principle of the school in 1920—and it had governed the generations of students and athletes that attended ever since. It was painted across a wall of the Hounds' dressing room, and it's something that stuck with me right away.

As a family, we'd struggled so much over the past couple of years. I knew we were about to emerge.

After arriving in Wilcox, I joined the Hounds for a playoff run that took the team right to the Canalta Cup finals. I was able to suit up and play a few games. It was the second championship series I'd been involved in within just a couple of weeks—and it was also the second league final I'd been on the losing side of. But there were plenty of lessons to learn, despite falling short.

One of those lessons came off the ice.

As is often the case with hockey, high school can get complicated with all of the moving around you have to do. I'd transferred to Holy Cross High School in Saskatoon from John Paul II Collegiate in North Battleford, but left for Wilcox before I could even step foot in the classroom. The school in Saskatoon was not highly interested in accommodating my unique situation. I asked them to send me the work to do remotely, but I was told they wouldn't do that and I would have to catch up on what I missed when I returned. I didn't know how long I was going to be in Wilcox, so this put me in a difficult position. I couldn't afford to lose an entire year of school. I had to find a way to complete the courses I was enrolled in, while being absent for an indefinite period of time.

I had several friends in my classes who helped me out by sending me their notes. These gave me a decent foundation, and I advanced on some of the concepts by watching videos on YouTube while doing my best to study. I was taking an online course at the time, so I was significantly ahead in that course and ended up finishing it at the start of May, even though it was supposed to end July 1. When I returned to Saskatoon after about a month in Wilcox, I had to sprint to catch up on all the assignments I had missed, while keeping up with the new ones. It was an exhausting time, but I knew how much these marks mattered if I wanted to earn a scholarship.

The teachers at Holy Cross were understanding of my situation for the most part. And I worked my butt off to catch up and keep my grades high enough. The effort paid off. I managed to keep all of my marks above 85—all, that is, except one. I went from a 94 in physics in North Battleford to a final grade of 67 in Saskatoon. The physics teacher was just not interested in helping me. He basically said that anything I'd missed was my own fault and that he wasn't going to provide me with any information on the previous units. I essentially had to teach myself. It was the worst mark I'd ever receive. I kind of think of it now as motivation to overcome obstacles, even when people who are in a position to help you are actively working against you. Looking back at it now, he was preparing me for the real world. There are always going to be people who don't want to see you succeed, for whatever reason. The important thing is to believe in yourself, despite them.

I wasn't going to let one disappointment throw me off course. Despite that 67, I still made the honour roll.

After deliberating all spring, looking at different options for my first full season of junior hockey, I decided that returning to Wilcox was the best move for me. I still had concerns that the lack of emphasis on skill in the team's system was going to be a challenge for me, but the roster was made up of great guys and I had a lot of respect for the coaching staff. They'd been to the SJHL finals the year before and were now in a rebuilding phase. I could be a key piece in their puzzle. And the team boasted such a rich history. It was an honour to wear the Hounds jersey and continue that legacy.

My parents were supportive of the decision to take my passion to Notre Dame. They knew I was ready. I was still able to remain somewhat close to home in case my dad's illness flared up. After everything we'd endured over the past two years, we knew that a little distance was nothing.

Dad also had missed games to make up for. Luckily for him, Notre Dame had only a handful of games that weren't on the weekend. My parents would drive three hours to Wilcox and three hours back in their Equinox just to watch us play. Those drives brought my father so much joy. The Hounds played teams as far away as La Ronge, four hours north of Saskatoon; Flin Flon, six hours away on the Manitoban border; and Estevan, four and a half hours southeast of Saskatoon, near the American border. In our division, we also played against teams like Battleford, Kindersley, and Humboldt, each of which was an hour or two from Saskatoon. The first sign that really showed me my father was back was when my parents showed up to my first home game against Humboldt at Notre Dame in the fall of 2015.

Notre Dame was a special team. When I first got listed with

them at the age of fifteen, Kevin White, the head coach at the time, took my family on a tour of the town. It's a tiny village in the middle of nowhere, just down the road from where *Corner Gas*, the television show, was set.

"All you do here is practise, work out, and play games," he told us.

"Perfect," I said. "That's all I want."

All of the players lived on the Notre Dame campus in a dorm that was right across the street from the arena. It takes approximately forty steps from our dorm to reach the main doors of Duncan McNeill Arena. The junior dorm was separated from the high school dorms, and we had a few offices underneath us as well as on our floor. These were occupied by Athol Murray College staff during school hours. We were also very close to the cafeteria where we would go for all of our meals—another 100 steps away in a different direction.

I think tradition was one of the major things that I learned to appreciate during my time at Notre Dame. They take their history very seriously. They respect it. Each player carries the responsibility of adding to that tradition. The school's Midget AAA team was one of the best in the province. They were developing talent for years to come. That's how you build a winning culture, I believe: by taking pride in the past, present, and future of the team that you are part of. It was particularly effective because even players the school didn't develop felt like they were included in that tradition. You could feel that pride as soon as you put on the jersey and did the pre-game prayer chant, which ended with "for Hounds and Hounds everywhere."

Every player was given the responsibility of taking on a role away from the ice that helped benefit the collective group. In my years at Notre Dame, I worked as a scorekeeper for bantam and midget games, as a supervisor at the Meier Performance Centre and a cleaner on our days off, and helped with their renowned summer camps. It felt awesome to be involved in a community like that. You felt like you were part of the Notre Dame Hounds legacy.

I actually enjoyed living in a dorm. I think you either love it or hate it—nothing in the middle. I lived in a room with two sets of bunk beds and three other teammates staying with me. We had a pretty good set-up, with a mini-fridge, microwave, toaster, TV, and gaming console, but it was definitely a tight squeeze. Rookies always were assigned four to a room by the vets, and they always got the smallest rooms in the dorm.

Being able to live with your teammates is a unique experience. Growing up as an only child, I didn't get to share a space with other kids, even though I had friends around all the time.

It was something competitive hockey in Saskatchewan allows for, because teams are so far apart. Many players have to leave home at a young age, and they have to take total responsibility for themselves while they're still teenagers. You can't just rely on your parents. But it also gives you a chance to connect and bond with teammates in a unique way. I was grateful for the opportunity. I was still a couple years away from understanding just how strong the bonds formed by living with teammates can be.

In my second year, I was named assistant captain, which was a responsibility that I took very seriously. It was an honour to have the *A* stitched onto my Hounds jersey.

We were an average team on the ice, which was frustrating. In both of my seasons with Notre Dame, we finished just outside of a top-six playoff spot and had to play in the survivor series.

But the program was also a key part of my development as a player. Although I was a finesse forward and didn't appreciate the dump-and-chase brand of hockey we played, the reality was that I still had a tremendous amount to learn about the game. I grew into a critical shutdown player for our team, playing against the most elite players in the SJHL every single shift. I became more detailed in my game play and came to be defensively reliable in all key situations. Even though I preferred to play a different way, I learned the value of listening to new perspectives, accepting instruction, and taking great pride in my role on the team. It was one of those lessons that doesn't always seem obvious but ends up being one of the most important in the long run.

Still, I knew that Notre Dame wasn't the right place for me to finish my junior career. I was nineteen years old and was still set on playing hockey at the collegiate level. I had attracted some interest from other junior teams in the United States, from as far away as Boston and Alaska. An NCAA Division III school in Vermont recruited me heavily. But I was set on either making it to a Division I school or going the Canadian route, playing U Sports—each of which is the highest level of hockey you can play in either country at the college or university level.

There was much more than hockey on my mind, though. Early in my first season with the Hounds, I joined up with the Juvenile Diabetes Research Foundation, becoming a provincial ambassador. My teammate Conor MacLean and I were the only type 1 diabetics in the whole league, and he was the one who introduced me to JDRF. My connection with Conor was different because we both understood the additional challenges that we endured daily to get where we were, and to where we were aspiring to go. We had an elevated level of love and respect for each other.

My role with JDRF allowed me to connect with younger kids with diabetes and mentor them the way I'd always wished someone had done for me. Working with the organization was one of the most enriching experiences of my life. It reminded me of the idea I'd first had a couple of years earlier to create a program that would inspire and support the kind of kids I was connecting with through JDRF. I wanted to use my platform in hockey to reach them.

I decided that junior hockey was the best way to do that. Most teams had arenas that were packed with young fans. It was the perfect place to create the kind of connections I was looking to make.

The only problem was that Notre Dame was one of the only places that didn't have that kind of connection with fans.

With only about 400 people in the entire community, the arena was never packed, except for the home opener and playoffs, when we had the locally famous Red & White nights where all the students would pack the lower bowl. In fact, we probably averaged about fifty fans per game, most of whom were parents, families, and girlfriends who drove in to watch—the rest were students. There were not many fans or children watching us play, dreaming about playing themselves one day.

I knew that if I wanted to create this program, Wilcox was not a large enough place to launch it. I needed someplace bigger.

Before I went into my final meeting with the coaches at the end of my second season, I made up my mind to ask for a trade. I was going into my final season in junior hockey, and I wanted to use it to make the greatest difference I could in other people's lives.

As I was walking to the rink, our captain was just leaving. He had just finished his meeting with the coaches.

"Congrats on being our new captain, buddy," he said. "Have a good meeting."

It threw me a little off balance. It was a massive honour that the coaches wanted me to lead our team in the upcoming season. It would be a tough accolade to pass up.

My coach asked me for my thoughts on the season. I'd remained positive all year, even though we struggled at points. It was a great place to play and to mature, and he was a great coach to play for.

He asked what I planned to do the following season.

There was no way to go around it. I told him I wanted to be traded.

He looked quite bewildered. As far as he was concerned, this was coming completely out of the blue. That was fair, because I'd never indicated that I wanted out before.

"Are you sure about this decision? We want you to lead our team next season," he said. "Take a couple of days to think about it."

I told him about the program I wanted to start and that it had nothing to do with the team. It was something larger than hockey or myself. He understood. A couple of days later, he texted me, just to be sure. But I had made up my mind. He went to work trying to find a team to trade me to in a bigger market.

I went back to Saskatoon that summer, not knowing where I would wind up next. But I was excited about a fresh start. I turned twenty that June. My father was more like his old self; he was back to work and his medications were more stable. He was even going for walks regularly. He was doing more around the yard and house and was once again larger than life, having emerged from the edge of death. We'd spend the summer together, as a family, looking forward to whatever the future would bring.

A couple of months went by after I asked to be moved. Then my cellphone rang one day in the middle of July.

It was Darcy Haugan, the head coach of Humboldt's Junior A team.

"Welcome to the Broncos," he said.

That call changed my life forever.

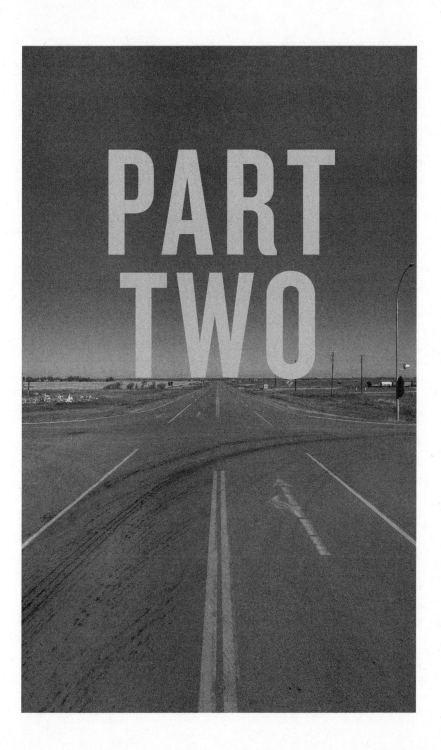

PART
TWO

CHAPTER 8

—

When you drive to Humboldt from Saskatoon, you head east, following the slopes of several hills, as fields of wheat and canola surround you. Once you pass the hills, the rest of the trip is flat and open Saskatchewan prairie. When you reach the city, you're greeted by a big sign that says *Humboldt*, with *Go Broncos Go* beneath it on a digital screen.

You know instantly that this is a hockey town.

One of the first buildings you see on the right-hand side is the Elgar Petersen Arena, attached to the Humboldt Uniplex. The rink, now over thirty years old, carries the long tradition of hockey in Humboldt. When you walk into the lobby, you see banners from the team's two national titles and ten provincial championships—the most of any team in the SJHL. There are photos of the teams that built the Broncos tradition along the wall of the main concourse. Green and blue seats fill the rink. There is a big Broncos logo in the middle of the glossy ice.

For any hockey-loving kid growing up in Saskatoon, the Humboldt Broncos were the Junior A team you wanted to play for. It was the place to go. So, from the start, the boy in me was excited to be part of this team. Through those first few weeks with the team, I got a sense of what made the organization extremely special. Right away, I felt like I was part of a family.

I was billeted with Wes and Carla Clement, who own a restaurant called Johnny's Bistro, located a couple blocks from the arena, near downtown. It's named after Carla's father, who had passed away.

Carla has a vivid, infectious smile and is the kind of person who lights up a place. I called her the Energizer Bunny. She's always moving and on the go. Aside from running her own restaurant and a house full of kids, dogs, and hockey players, Carla always had several side hustles—like creating and selling apparel for several minor hockey teams, a line of clothing related to the restaurant, and a catering service. Carla would get up at 7:30 in the morning and not sit down until 11:30 at night, every single day. This kind of work ethic and selflessness struck me.

Wes, her husband, is the more laid-back of the two. He is a CN train conductor, but he also spends most of his spare time on the ice, coaching his kids in minor hockey. When Wes is not at work, he likes to kick back and relax, watching sports. Carla is the dominant figure in the household, but Wes is the support that keeps things moving.

The Clements have three children—Jaya, Rowan, and Madden—all younger than eleven when I billeted with them. They also had two dogs, a bichon–shih tzu named Dexter and a Lhaso Apso named Panda, as well as a hamster that didn't last too long (long story short: Panda caught the hamster when it escaped). The family are huge supporters of the Broncos. Carla's parents had billeted Broncos players throughout Carla's childhood, so really, she was continuing a family tradition.

They regularly billet several players at a time. When I showed up, they already had two other guys living in the basement. One of them was Stephen Wack.

When I first met Carla in the summer, before my move to Humboldt, she told me she knew that Stephen and I would connect right off the bat. After I met her a second time, she told me that he and I would become best friends. I didn't know Stephen at all before I arrived in Humboldt, aside from playing against him. He'd grown up just outside of Edmonton and played in the Alberta Junior Hockey League before coming to Humboldt the season before I arrived. He was not a fun player to play against, as he would let you know in some way every time you were on the ice with him, whether it was a slash to the back of your leg, a cross-check to your back, or a quick poke of the puck with his long reach.

Before training camp started, we had a team meeting for all of the returning players and the guys who had been traded to Humboldt in the off-season. I was one of the first players in the locker room.

When I arrived, I introduced myself to the coaching staff— Darcy Haugan, Mark Cross, and Chris Beaudry—then to all of the players who were there and the others as they arrived.

"Hi, my name is Kaleb," I said about a dozen times. "It's nice to meet you."

Unfortunately for me, I had developed pneumonia in early August and was bedridden for two weeks before I arrived in Humboldt. Instead of taking some time off, I stubbornly pushed ahead and joined the team for our preseason fitness testing, wanting to make a strong impression on my new team. In the small world of Saskatchewan hockey, I knew only a handful of players on the Broncos before I joined the team. I knew Logan Schatz from playing with him in spring AAA hockey and Team Saskatchewan ball hockey. We were actually roommates and "lineys" at the ball hockey nationals in Vancouver—it was a blast. I knew Xavier LaBelle through playing three-on-three adult safe hockey together in the summer, on the Dekes of Hazzard—a team full of all my good buddies. I played with Xavier's brother Isaac in city-wide bantam. I also played with Cole Young, a returning player, in city-wide bantam.

Brayden Camrud was another one I knew going into camp. We skated together that previous summer with the CounterMove Hockey Elite Skills Camp. Layne Matechuk and I worked out together that previous summer, but he did not arrive in Humboldt until after our training camp. I had heard of a few others, like Evan Thomas, Antonio Di Paolo, and Tristen Elder, from around the hockey world but had never actually met them.

I had lost about thirteen pounds and was still on antibiotics and using an inhaler, but I felt like I was just starting to be on the mend when I arrived. I told the coaching staff I was on meds and was still a bit under the weather. They told me to participate only in whatever exercises I felt comfortable with, but I hated the idea of starting out as a Bronco like that. There were several players on the team that I didn't know, and I didn't want them to think less of me because I was so out of shape—and I wasn't inclined to go around telling everyone I was sick. And after I had put in the work all off-season, I didn't want anyone to think I was taking the easy way out by opting out of some of the fitness testing.

As a twenty-year-old, I also intended to be a leader and set an example. To me, that meant taking part, no matter what. So, I told the coaches I had no intention of skipping any of the tests. That was probably a poor choice. I struggled through most of the tests well enough—until the final one.

It was the thirty-metre shuttle run. We had to sprint back and forth between two pylons six times in under a minute. I had done the same test in July and was perfectly fine, completing it in fifty-five seconds. This time was different. On my third trip between the pylons, I hit a wall. I could feel my legs lose strength, I couldn't breathe, and I couldn't see straight.

This is not *good*, I thought.

On the sixth lap, my legs literally gave out. I collapsed on the floor before I even hit the finish line. It was a full face plant. It took me about ten seconds to crawl to the end point and put my hand on the line. Then I rolled over on the floor, trying to catch my breath, as the other group started running.

All the guys looked at me like they were wondering what the hell was wrong with me. That was the Broncos' first impression of me: a face plant and a crawl across the finish line. Awesome. There had been several trades through the summer, because Humboldt was going for a championship that year. The team had a lot of new faces and everyone was trying to figure each other out. Aside from the coaches, the only other person who knew that I'd been suffering from pneumonia was Logan Schatz, our captain.

Despite that questionable introduction, I think I recovered pretty quickly and connected with my new teammates from the start. I took a few days off before training camp officially started and managed to get my legs back. When I started skating, I went excessively hard on the ice, trying to make up for my poor show-ing in fitness testing and trying to prove that the team had made a good trade when they brought me in. Anyone who knows me will tell you I have only one gear, and that is maximum effort always. I was just trying to show my teammates I belonged.

I was a teddy bear off the ice, and I took a few of the guys who were on the bubble under my wing. Striving for a roster spot is a tough position to be in, so I tried to offer as much advice as I could and encourage them to stay confident while playing their game. I tried to make them feel as comfortable as I could. We were all going through similar battles, or else we had been through the same kind of pressure at some point along the way. Even though I was new to the team, I tried to act the way I would if I were still playing for Notre Dame. As a leader, I think it's important to set a tone and establish the culture of a team early on. Making new players feel comfortable is essential to any team. The faster you are able to gel as a unit, the faster you will find success.

For me, the relationships were built as soon as I was traded to Humboldt. Logan Hunter reached out to me and wanted to connect about the Broncos. I actually didn't know who he was, but he tossed me a follow on Instagram. In his bio, it said "Humboldt Broncos," along with the brown horse and green saddle emoji. I asked Schatzy about him, and he told me Hunts had signed with us in the summer. Hunts and I ended up exchanging numbers before camp. We texted to get to know each other a bit better, and he told me how nervous he was about fitness testing, but how excited he was to get the season started.

I've always felt that it is important to lead by example. I was positive and encouraging at the rink and away from it. During practices, I was always in the first row, taking a knee in front of the board while the coach explained the next drill. Picking up pucks, putting away the nets. Thanking the coaches after practice for the skate. Being the last one off the ice. I was never the best player on my teams throughout my hockey career, but I always tried to be the most respectful. It was just something that had stuck with me since I was young. It's one of the lessons I learned playing hockey that I intend to carry with me through the rest of my life. Always be respectful, always listen, always be grateful, and always be eager to learn.

At the end of training camp, we were split into two teams to play for the intra-squad championship. It's a Broncos tradition, with the Elgar Petersen Cup awarded to the winners. My squad was the green team, which was made up of a lot of the younger players who were on the bubble. The other team was the gold team, which had most of the veteran players. Schatzy and I tried to rally our team together right away. We called ourselves the Green Machine and dubbed the other squad Old Gold. We even came with a pre-game chant around the net before the opening faceoff. Everyone took the game seriously. We were a competitive bunch, which was a good sign. Our group formed a bond over that short time. Of course we beat the Old Gold guys and hoisted the Elgar Petersen Cup. When I spoke to some of the guys afterwards, they told me that it was one of the best camp experiences they'd ever had, because they had never before felt like they were part of a team before the season even began.

The day before our season opener, we held a community night at the Humboldt Uniplex.

The best way to describe Humboldt is that it is a small, very tightly knit community. It was the kind of place where everybody knows everybody, and the Broncos were central to that community. Whenever I was there as an opponent, I knew there would always be a great crowd inside the arena. I was excited to have them on my side for once.

More than a hundred fans, billets, and friends showed up to the event, picking up their season tickets and interacting with the players and coaching staff. Outside, there was a pad where you could take shots on a Broncos player, play catch with a football, or try to hit flashing targets with a ball. Inside the lobby, we hosted a huge cook-off and ran a raffle. I was in charge of the team's Snapchat account for the event, so I went around, meeting the fans and taking videos of all the action. At one point, Jacob Leicht had four kids latched onto each of his limbs. He was a magnet, and the kids loved him.

This was when I first understood what the team meant to the community.

Afterwards, we went to the locker room and took a seat in our stalls, painted green with yellow trim, to unveil our jerseys for the season. Darcy stood near the Broncos logo on a black carpet in the middle of the locker room and addressed us as a group. He paused for a second and looked at each of us around the room.

"It's a great day to be a Bronco, gentlemen."

He said that he was happy and proud with how we interacted with the community this evening.

It was time to reveal our new uniforms, introduce the team, and get a picture on the stairs of the concourse in front of the Humboldt community members that had joined us that evening.

Before arriving in Humboldt, I asked several good friends who had previously played for the Broncos what they thought of Darcy as a coach. Every one of them went on about how much they respected and valued him. Now, even though I'd only spent a couple of weeks with him as my coach, I knew that all the rave reviews were true.

When it came to hockey, Darcy was a players' coach. He was the kind of coach who let you be creative and do your own thing on the ice. He was there to guide you and correct your play when you needed it, but he let each individual play to their strengths—and he utilized those strengths to lead a stronger team on the ice. That appealed to me right away. I was always comfortable operating with coaching like that.

One thing that astounded me was that after a loss, Darcy would never come into the dressing room and address us as a team. He would always wait till the next day, after emotions had settled down and thoughts could be analyzed. Normally after a loss, a coach will come into the dressing room to verbally rip the team apart, call out some players who played poorly, maybe kick a garbage can, and then storm off. This was the first and only time I had a coach who would not address a team after a loss, big or small.

As good as he was on the bench, Darcy was even better outside of the game. He was one of the nicest men I've ever met. He genuinely cared about his players as young men. He knew that there is much more to life than hockey, but that we could all learn from the opportunity to be part of a team and members of a community like Humboldt. For Darcy, what we did on the ice was less important than what we represented off of it.

When Darcy took over as the Broncos' head coach for the 2015–16 season, he came up with what he called the Broncos' "Core Covenant." He had it painted in green on the wall between our locker room and the coaches' room:

Family first
To treat my teammates and co-workers with respect
To be thankful for the opportunity to wear the Bronco jersey
To play each game and practise with passion and determination
To conduct ourselves with honesty and integrity
To treat all volunteers, billets, sponsors, and fans with respect
and gratitude
To understand that we are building foundations for future
generations with our words and actions
To always have hope and believe that everything is possible
To always give more than you take
To strive for greatness in all areas of life

I loved that this was the focus of our team, but at the time, I still didn't know just how important it was to our identity as Broncos.

Darcy announced that Logan Schatz would once again be the team's captain. Schatzy and I used to have sleepovers all the time in the summer. When I was still unsure about where I would end up, Schatzy kept asking me if I would come to Humboldt. "This is the year," he told me, meaning this was the year the Broncos were going for it and he wanted me to be a part of it. He often helped Darcy recruit players, because he knew many players in Saskatchewan and their personalities. I truly think he was the reason why Darcy brought me into the organization. I was really excited that we'd been able to reunite for our last year of junior. It felt like we had come full circle.

One of the unique things about the Broncos was that the players had a hand in deciding who the assistant captains would be. We had all put in our votes for who we wanted to wear the *A*s.

Darcy picked a white, green, and yellow jersey out of the box in front of him.

"One of our assistant captains this year is Kaleb Dahlgren," he said, holding up a jersey with my last name on it. "We're very pleased to have you here. Your leadership has shown throughout training camp."

I was absolutely pumped. Internally, I was jumping up and down, but I had to hold it in and say thank you. It was definitely a huge honour, because going in I knew that being captain wasn't an option and I hoped to earn the honour of wearing an *A*. During our initial call, I had told Darcy that I intended to be a leader on the team. Through training camp, I'd done my best to show him that I was one. But this wasn't Darcy's choice alone. To have been chosen as a leader by my peers after just a couple weeks of training camp—which started with me crawling across a finish line, no less—meant the world to me.

The guys clapped as Darcy tossed me my number 16 jersey. He pulled another one out of the box.

"Our next assistant captain is Logan Boulet," he said. "He's been with us for one and a half seasons and he's been nothing but great for us since the second he walked in. And we believe that he'll lead and push our team through his work ethic."

Boulet sat next to me in the middle of the locker room, where all the twenty-year-olds sat. I looked over at him, shook his hand, and congratulated him while the boys called for him. He collected his jersey with a wide smile across his face.

Darcy continued, holding up a jersey with the number 7.

"Our final assistant captain is Stephen Wack," he said. "We're honoured to have watched you grow into a leadership role over the last year. We believe that you will help carry us to the championship with your presence."

Wacker, as everyone called him, was a six-foot-six, 220-pound defenceman from St. Albert, Alberta, just outside of Edmonton. It was his second year with the Broncos.

I looked over at him directly across the room and gave him a head nod. He knew that I thought he was a great leader and deserving of the honour. We had discussed it at length the day before.

We'd only lived together for a couple of weeks at that time, but I already knew that Carla was right about him. We were already inseparable.

After we all received our jerseys, we walked out into the lobby of the Uniplex to take a team photo of the 2017–18 Humboldt Broncos on the concourse stairs.

The first game of the season was the very next day, September 16—against the Notre Dame Hounds. They were still a very good team and were poised to make a run at the championship.

From Saskatoon, Saskatchewan, wearing number 16 . . . Kaleb Dahlgren!" the announcer roared. The smoke machine cast an emerald haze as I skated out onto the ice, into the spotlight in the green and gold colours of the Broncos. Fans cheered and cowbells rang. My body shook with nerves as I saluted the crowd with my stick and skated to the blue line. During the national anthem, it felt like I was on the wrong side of the ice. The previous two years, I had worn red and white, ready to ruin the Broncos' home opener by shutting down their top players, like Schatzy. This time, playing on the first line with Schatzy, I was now considered to be an enemy of the Hounds.

It was even more bizarre lining up against my old team for the opening draw of the season. Seeing one of my best buds from the past two years, Chance Longjohn—wearing the well-deserved *C* for the Hounds—and lots of my other good buddies from Notre Dame jokingly chirping my Broncos colours was very unusual. However, I was focused and eager to impress the crowd at Elgar Petersen.

Once the game started, all of the thoughts and distractions went away. I was in game mode. We ended up on the power play five minutes into the first period. I hopped over the boards on the first unit. After a faceoff scrum, we popped the puck out and started to work it around Notre Dame's zone. Elder took a one-timer shot on the half-wall, and the rebound redirected to Schatzy. He settled it down, and all eyes were on him. I found a little gap and popped out to the slot for a quick one-timer. Schatzy threw the puck to me and I slammed it home in the open white mesh. The rink erupted. My body flooded with excitement. I'd just scored the first goal of the Broncos' 2017–18 season—against my former team. Before I could think, I was quickly bombarded by the power-play unit for a group hug, then we skated for a fly-by as the horn and music blared. I ended up playing one of my best games, scoring a goal and being defensively reliable in a 3–2 overtime win.

The next day, we boarded our bus and took the three-hour trip south to Wilcox. The Notre Dame crowd hadn't forgotten me—but they weren't about to welcome me back, either.

As soon as I stepped on the ice for the opening faceoff, the chants started to fill the rink. As usual, the students were packed in the lower bowl for the Hounds' season opener. The ringleader, who is usually a Grade 12 student, had a megaphone and pointed his arm at me the way a ref would point at the net to signal a goal. The rest of the student body followed suit, pointing their arms at me chanting, "Trait-or . . . trait-or . . . trait-or . . ."

I loved it. I thought it was hilarious. I thrive on that and always play better when the fans are on me. My parents and my girlfriend, Erykah, had made the trip, and I found them in the crowd and smiled. They just smiled back, laughing and shaking their heads.

We were trailing by a goal with half a minute left in the third period and our goalie pulled. Darcy called a time out on a whistle in the Hounds end. When I skated back to the faceoff circle in the offensive zone, the jeers got even louder as students were still standing over the glass pointing their arms and chanting:

"Trait-or . . . trait-or . . . trait-or . . ."

The puck went back into the corner off the draw. There was a huge scrum for the puck, and Conner Lukan came out with it. He sent it back to Wacker with five seconds left. Wacker tried to throw it on net, but it got blocked. Luckily, the puck bounced to Schatzy. As Wacker was shooting, I rushed towards the net from the point, just behind one of their wingers who was standing in between the hash marks. Schatzy heard me screaming for it and zipped me a backdoor pass from the corner. I snapped it bar down to tie the game with 0.9 seconds left. Our bench went wild while I indulged in a little celly of sweeping the ice. As we skated back to our bench for the fly-by, Schatzy, who was behind me, put his finger to his mouth, shushing the crowd of students and Hounds players.

Off to overtime we went.

The action was heated in the extra period, with chances on either side. I was able to spring Lukes on a breakaway, and Notre Dame's goalie robbed him. Next shift, they came down on a two-on-one, but Jacob Wassermann turned them away. Still undecided as the buzzer rang.

Shootout time.

I knew I really wanted to shoot. I loved the pressure and the thought of winning it all for the team.

We went second. Chaz Smedsrud, one of my buddies, was the Hounds' first shooter. He is a silky-smooth guy who could finish. But Wass stood his ground and stopped him.

Brayden Camrud was our first shooter. Camo tried a quick move but was denied.

Wass shut the door on the Hounds' next shooter, and then Darcy tapped Schatzy to seal the deal. He went with his go-to move but he got robbed.

Next up was Notre Dame's captain, Longjohn—we called him LJ. He was another crafty player who had good mitts. He tried to go backhand and was stopped by Wass's long reach.

Darcy looked at me next and said, "Go end it."

I jumped over the bench, jittering with excitement. I had the opportunity to close out the game. I skated to the centre-ice circle hearing the support from our bench. I heard cheers of "Go, Dahly, you got this!" and "Come on, Dahly, put it home!" This was my shot to close out the game. To make a statement around the SJHL.

I picked up the puck with speed and swooped to the right side of the ice. I was aiming to shoot high glove, since the last two shooters on our team had shot blocker side. As I got past the blue line, I started to attack the net diagonally, coming in hot. Someone in the stands yelled, "Choke!" I faked a shot, then shifted to my left side and brought the puck over with me to my backhand.

The goalie didn't flinch.

I quickly adjusted, making four fast stickhandles so he would drop to his knees.

Still the goalie didn't move.

I was now in close, so I slammed on the brakes, hoping their goalie might shift over in his crease and give me space on the glove side. He played his position well. I reached my stick as far as I could to the right on his glove side and tried to go top shelf.

The puck hit the top of his glove and went up in the air, seemingly in slow motion. I turned my body to watch the puck come back down as it was in the air. It felt like ten seconds. As it came down, their goalie was lying on his belly since he'd had to sprawl out to make the save.

He tried to bat the puck away with his foot. He missed—and ended up kicking the puck across the goal line.

The red light turned on behind the net.

The ref pointed his hand to signify a goal.

I threw both my hands in the air instantly and started to skate over to centre ice to greet Wass. The guys jumped over the boards and piled onto the ice to celebrate. We took the weekend sweep in a 4–3 shootout victory.

We were all excited in the dressing room, whooping it up after a thrilling nail-biter of a win—and two in a row against a tough team to start our season, a great start to the campaign. I ended up receiving the hard hat that is handed out to the player of the game, and I wore it proudly the rest of my time in the dressing room. We turned on one of our favourite team songs—"4 AM" by 2 Chainz, featuring Travis Scott—and started singing along.

We showered and dressed quickly, then loaded our gear back onto the bus for the long journey home. I was able to visit with my parents, Erykah, my maternal grandparents Stella and Rudy, my uncle Rick, my aunt Shelley, my cousin Dominique, and a bunch of my former teammates and friends from the Hounds community.

When I walked onto the bus after visiting, lots of the guys started to cheer me, chanting "Dahl-yyy," and gave me fist pumps for my performance on my old stomping grounds. I leaned back in my seat as the boys continued to holler and laugh around me. We were the Humboldt Broncos and proud of it.

I turned on my overhead seat lights, got some snacks out from the care package Granny made for me, turned to the right, and started to chat with my other stall mate, Derek Patter. As we pulled out of the Duncan McNeill Arena parking lot, the veterans at the back of the bus yelled, "Two honks," signalling our bus driver to honk twice for the two points we captured—*honk, honnnkkk*—and we drove off into the night.

CHAPTER 9

—

What makes a team?

In my opinion, it means a group working together towards a common goal, while aligned on the same vision for how to get there. It means that a group trusts and relies on one another to do their jobs. It means sacrificing the "me" aspect in favour of the "we." It means respecting the people beside you and loving who they are. A team is like a family in that way. You stand beside each other through good times and bad times—the highs and lows, knowing that you'll never stand alone.

That's what I found in Humboldt.

The first tenet of the creed on the wall outside our coaches' room was no mistake: *Family first.*

It was Darcy's reminder to us that, no matter what happened, the relationships in our lives were more important than anything else. That meant our relationships with our families, but also with the family that we created as a group.

What makes a team? When it comes down to it, a team is a family.

They are the people you spend your days with. The people you struggle with and celebrate with. The people you challenge, and who challenge you. The people you rely on.

The family I ended up finishing the season in Humboldt with was made up of nine twenty-year-olds playing their final season of junior hockey, five guys in the middle of their journey, ten rookies playing their first, and a handful of "affiliate players" getting their feet wet. We were led by a forty-two-year-old coach who had two sons and a wife of almost seventeen years who worked in the Broncos office. From our two assistant coaches, Mark Cross and Chris Beaudry, to our athletic therapist, Dayna Brons, our volunteer trainer, Clinton Thiel, our statistician, Brody Hinz, our play-by-play announcer, Tyler Bieber, and our bus driver, Glen Doerksen, each of us played an essential role in that family. We were a group of individuals who had various aspirations to play hockey professionally, or become lawyers, broadcasters, doctors, electricians, teachers, accountants, chiropractors, musicians, coaches, physiotherapists, and tomorrow's leaders. The organization had many other individuals who played an important role in the background, like the billets, the fans, the Broncos' board of directors. There was the front office, the hockey operations personnel, the scouts, the strength coaches, the volunteers, the rink and Uniplex staff—everyone played a role.

We were the Broncos—and we were a family.

From the start, our leadership core wanted to make sure that was exactly how the other players on the team viewed it. The four of us—Schatzy, Wacker, Bouls, and me—became close very quickly.

I already expected to get along well with Schatzy, whom I'd known since we were kids. He was in his fourth full season with the Broncos and his third as captain. Wacker and Bouls were complete strangers when I arrived.

Logan Boulet was in his third season with the Broncos. He was twenty years old and grew up in Lethbridge, Alberta. We all called him Bouls, since there were three Logans on our team. He planned to go to the University of Lethbridge and play for its varsity hockey team after his final season as a Bronco. He wanted to become a teacher, a profession that ran in his family. I sat between Bouls and Derek Patter in the dressing room. Both were awesome

stall mates and good buddies. Bouls and I had quite a bit in common. We both liked giving back to the community, working out,
and listening to '80s hit songs. We had the same values, were both
injured for the same portion of the season, and loved spending
time with the guys.

Bouls would come over to the Clements' house to hang out
with Wacker and me all the time, usually coming over to catch a
movie with us and have a good chat about life. Sometimes, all of
us would just relax in the hot tub while listening to music.

Through that first month together, Wacker and I had continued to find more and more in common. His room was just
down the hall from mine in the basement. But even away from the
Clements, we were already inseparable. We were both independent and shared an even-keeled approach to life. He also loved
school and was interested in learning new things—I was the same.
We both took pride in our off-ice recovery. He liked to have deep
conversations about life perspectives, and I did too. Neither of
us partied very much during the season; we just weren't into it.
We liked the same music and enjoyed finding the newest banger
songs. We both thought going into the hot tub to kick back and
relax was a good time. Wacker didn't really like to leave the house
often and was a huge homebody. In fact, that's one area where we
differed. I loved to get out and get involved in community events
and initiatives.

Still, we were like-minded and complemented each other very
well. Wacker planned to go to business school in Toronto or to
Simon Fraser University in Vancouver when he was done playing. We liked to eat healthily and work out. We'd go to the gym
together all the time. We also both knew there was much more to
life than hockey, which is not always the case for guys who spend
so much time at the rink.

Even though Wacker loved the game as much as anyone, he was
intellectual and talented in so many other areas. I really admired

that about him. He had a creative side to him and was a videographer who made these fantastic short films about small things, like travelling or just hanging out at the lake with friends. My first appearance in a video Stephen created was a "thriller" video of us scaring kids who came to the Clements' door for Halloween trick-or-treating. I hid in our garage, which was connected to the walkway to the front door, and once the kids rang the doorbell, I would quietly open the door and stand behind them with a shovel, mask, red plaid coat, toque, and hood up. We caught lots of screams and some hilarious moments.

I also helped with the last video Stephen ever created, filming the intro, which featured Stephen sitting at his computer and leaving the dining table at our billets'. He knew how to capture the beauty in the things that other people took for granted.

Wacker and I also shared a love for music. We always shared different hip hop, dance, and rap songs that we liked. Stephen and I had a group chat with Tyler Smith called Banger Bros, where we would post the newest hit banger songs that we liked. Stephen and I took charge of creating our pre-game mixtape and ended up creating three different mixes that season, with Fisker and Smitty providing their input. I took on the responsibility of being the team DJ. Anyone who has done this knows it is one of the most important jobs in the locker room—but can also attract some fierce criticism. I'd take a lot of heat if the "aux wasn't fire." So, I took great pride in my role and always accepted requests to please the guys. On game days, we always had to play the song "Animals" by Nickelback on our way out of the dressing room—it was Patter's go-to. But our team song that year was really "You Came to Party" by Meter Mobb. Everyone knew the lyrics, and it would be a shame if you didn't sing along to the song whenever it was on. We made a mix of the song and the team skated out onto the ice for warm-ups to it.

Wacker's sense of humour was another quality I loved about

him. Once you really got to know him, he was actually a really funny dude. We would send different pictures or jokes to each other all the time. When we weren't playing or didn't have something going on in the community, Wacker, Fisker, and I spent a lot of time just hanging out with the Clements. The kids were at a fun age and it was neat that we were able to connect with them. I helped out with Rowan's and Madden's practices, whenever I could. I didn't have much experience with dance, but I'd drive Jaya back and forth to her classes and got to go to her dance recital, too. I wanted to be heavily involved with the family and be a part of their lives.

Looking back, it was all of the moments that seemed small at the time that really showed me what I learned during my time in Humboldt. I was lucky to have parents who always did what they could to be by my side, cheering me on. Now, as a twenty-year-old, it felt great to be able to do that for others.

As leaders on the team, the four of us wanted to make the team as tight as possible. We wanted all of our teammates to feel comfortable and welcome. Every time we had an event, we made sure that everyone on the team knew about it and that the invitation was always open. One of the best ways to have success on the ice is to have a genuine bond with your teammates off of it. We planned accordingly.

As a team, once or twice a month, we would go to a church—which was down the street from the Clements'—to do a team-building exercise. It was mandatory for everyone on the roster, other than the high school kids who had class—Morgan Gobeil, Layne Matechuk, and Jacob Wassermann. Pastor Sean Brandow would run the event for us and explain life values while we had a delicious feast. Meetings would cover various topics, including love, commitment, and integrity. I always enjoyed these talks and found great value in them. Not only would we have a good time with each other and build a team culture, we were able to take something away to better ourselves after every meeting. We would also do activities, such as skeet shooting, bowling, and board games.

There was a Ping-Pong table inside the church, and it commanded most of our attention. The games got *real*. We had some epic battles before and after our team-building sessions. We took them seriously. People broke out into full sweats and got legitimately mad when they lost. I brought out my old skills from my time in North Battleford. Jaxon Joseph was always a favourite to take control on the table. It was a little moment that was always fun.

We had an NHL regular-season fantasy pool with twelve guys in it. We acted like we were all NHL GMs—sitting around the Clements' basement with our laptops and phones out, researching the players we were after. I remember us completing the draft and going over our team rosters for finalization. I sat there thinking, *My team looks solid*, but then Evan Thomas piped up with his and I couldn't get over how stacked his team was. You legitimately could have thought he cheated if you hadn't been there. I was in last place for a solid three months—and boy, did I get chirped. My running joke with Morgan Gobeil was sending him a trade offer every week. At first, I was on everybody to make trades and stirring the pot, but my tactics quickly got noticed and people would intentionally reject my offers, even if they were fair, just because I was the one sending them. Even so, my roster ended up making a huge turnaround and I finished second to Tommy that season, but never got to celebrate.

On Monday nights, the entire team would come over to Wes and Carla's basement for one of the most essential bonding traditions a junior hockey team can have: *Bachelor* night. Every week, the guys gathered to watch America's favourite reality dating show. After the first episode of the season, we conducted a draft in which each of us picked one contestant who we thought would be the one to get engaged. The oldest guys on the team picked first

94

and the youngest guys picked last. We'd put money in the pot, and whoever picked correctly would collect at the end of the season.

It was a bring-your-own-wine event every week. Monday nights were the best. We'd usually have a practice in the morning, but never played any games, so we didn't miss a show. It was one of many off-ice bonding sessions our squad had that year. We'd consistently have sixteen to eighteen guys over to watch. We genuinely liked to hang out together, so it wasn't difficult to get everyone on board. The roster was full of guys who just enjoyed being around each other.

Along with *Bachelor* Mondays, we had *Riverdale* Thursdays, which took place at the billet house where Derek Patter and Graysen Cameron lived. The popular drama series based on the Archie comic book characters was a hit at the time, and a good group of us were just as nerdy about Archie and Jughead as we were about *The Bachelor*. Usually, we'd have about ten or twelve Broncos in attendance. Of course, whenever the show was done, we'd turn on Thursday night hockey to catch the end of whatever NHL game was on until our team-imposed curfew sent us all home.

Our coaching staff was big on making sure that we were responsible away from the ice. We all abided by the team curfew and the other rules governing how we conducted ourselves as members of the Broncos. At the same time, we were encouraged to have some fun. Like most junior hockey teams, we had a rookie party to welcome the guys to the league at Blake Berschiminsky's farm just outside of the city. It was my first-ever experience with a well-known Humboldt Broncos tradition: the rookie party scavenger hunt. Every rookie was divided between two rookie teams, and their team had a list of items to complete for points. I left my mark on the scavenger hunt by adding a requirement for video proof of two good deeds being done, worth ten points each.

During the season, we were allowed to have about one team

party a month, usually at the home of a player born in Humboldt, like the Leichts' or the Gobeils'. Whenever Darcy gave us the green light, we quickly mobilized the troops. He never really encouraged it, but if we'd played well and he knew we needed a break, he'd say something like, "Green light tonight, fellas," and left it at that. He knew that getting together was part of team building, and he wanted to make sure we were always growing as a group. It helped reinforce our bond.

That season, we had nine twenty-year-olds on the roster, even though we could only dress eight for each game. Three of us "twenties" were in the same house—Wacker, Fisker, and me. Bryce Fiske got traded to Humboldt on October 23 from his hometown squad, the La Ronge Ice Wolves, where he'd been captain, and he moved into the Clements' house shortly after. I was excited to welcome him into our home and knew he would be a great addition after having played with him previously in spring hockey. He quickly fit right in with everyone in the house and gelled with the team. We had a household group chat that displayed the panda emoji as the title, named after the Clements' dog Panda.

My roomie, Fisker, and I were jokingly called Dad and Mom. These names couldn't have been more accurate in reflecting our personalities. Fisker was a prototypical dad who liked to have a good time and a casual beer while sitting on the couch. He was a "super vet," meaning he had four years of experience in the league, so many of the guys would look up to him. I was a prototypical mom who cared almost too much and always wanted to make sure everyone was healthy and safe. After every party, I would help clean up the room and take care of individuals who went a little too hard.

We picked up Jaxon Joseph in a trade that sent twenty-year-old Tristen Elder the other way. As the trade deadline neared, with a lot of the twenty-year-olds battling various injuries, we acquired a high-end skill player in Flin Flon assistant captain Nick

Shumlanski, giving us a needed offensive boost. That meant our team was pretty evenly split between veterans and younger players.

We had a team full of leaders and a good group of guys in the locker room, and Darcy made sure the culture of our team was positive. At the same time, though, we did enforce a few age-old (but mild) measures to mark the rookies' standard rite of passage into junior hockey.

We maintained order through a standard "finable offence" system, with violations adjudicated by the twenty-year-olds and administered by Schatzy, who was in charge of "court." Both rookies and vets were susceptible to fines, and all the proceeds went towards a year-end party.

There were penalties for keeping a messy stall in the locker room or stepping on the Broncos logo on the floor in the middle of the room. We also implemented "juice boy," which is a game we played after practice. It was a Humboldt tradition.

Each player would get two pucks to shoot: one from the ringette line, and then they would get a chance to try to deke the goalie. When you scored, you were out. But if you didn't score on either attempt, you had to keep going. The last person to score would have to go to the store across the street to buy juice for the entire team right after he got off the ice—wearing full gear, his Broncos jersey, and a red helmet with the words "Juice Boy" written on it in pink tape. Our goalies—Parker Tobin, Jacob Wassermann, and Sam-Jaxon Visscher—were always spared the duty; in the end, they were the ones who decided who the juice boy would be. Whichever one of them was slated for the backup role in the upcoming game would take to the crease. And they'd deliberately whiff on shots from some players and try super hard against others. If you'd ticked one of them off by shooting high during practice, you were screwed at juice boy time. For the most part, the goalies and vets had a truce, so the juice boy was usually a rookie.

After the juice boy had picked all of the pucks up off the ice, they'd have to go and get juice right away—or, if it was late, have the juice in the dressing room before practice the next morning.

Sometimes, the juice boy would retaliate by buying the worst no-name juice possible. That was a finable offence, too.

Every rookie on the team had the responsibility of bringing movies for each road game, one for the ride there and one for the way back. If the movies were bad, they'd be fined two dollars, which would go towards our year-end banquet. Our group of nine twenty-year-olds would make the call on the quality of the films, and Schatzy would administer the fines. The rookies *rarely* had good movies. On the way to one game, we watched *Frozen*. The other choice we were given was *Aladdin*.

"What are we doing?" I asked the guys as we listened to Elsa sing "Let It Go."

Our road games were usually two hours away, so we'd take a coach bus there and back on the same day. Sometimes, on weekends, we'd have games in places like La Ronge, which was four hours away, or Flin Flon, which was a five-and-a-half-hour ride. We'd play three games over a weekend on trips like that. The rookies were under extra pressure to make sure they brought some quality flicks for those trips. I tried to be helpful and bring my stack of movies I had collected through the years, which included major classics like *Slap Shot*, *Step Brothers*, *Wedding Crashers*, *Miracle*, *Talladega Nights*, *The Town*, the *Fast and the Furious* franchise, and *American Pie* from our spring hockey days. This got the rookies off the hook numerous times.

Just after our last game before Christmas, we had the annual family holiday party, where we all got together with our families in a hall to have a meal. It was great meeting my teammates' families and loved ones at this event. For me, the highlight was the Christmas carol the rookies sang for the audience. They knew about a week before the event that they would have to come up with a song to sing. I guess it was part of the Broncos tradition.

As soon as they lined up, single file, across the front of the room, I knew it was going to be good.

Tommy belted out "Deck the Halls," and all the rookies behind him peeped their heads out to the side to sing the *fa-la-la-la-la* part. Tommy wore a green Christmas sweater with white lettering that said "Jingle My Balls." They truly did an amazing job and brought laughter to the entire room. Afterwards, we congratulated them on the amazing performance, and then we all posed for a team picture in our Christmas sweaters. It is a memory I've thought about every Christmas since.

Things were going very well for me when the season started, and I quickly became one of the top scorers on the team. I was fortunate enough to earn a spot on the first line with Schatzy and Lukes, filling in on the right wing. We had some chemistry as a line, but we got split up not too long into the season to generate some scoring depth. I remained in the top six and excelled in that role throughout this period.

But starting with pneumonia, it ended up being the worst season I'd ever had when it came to illness and injuries—there was probably only a month or two when I wasn't playing injured. Before the injuries hit, it was probably the best I'd played in my career, both offensively and defensively. After twenty-two games, I had nineteen points, more than in my previous two seasons with Notre Dame, when I was in a shutdown role. I was proving that I could be productive if given the opportunity, just as I'd been in AAA.

I played through a separated AC joint in my shoulder, which made it impossible to lift my right arm above my head and severely impacted my ability to score or make plays. I didn't get in lots of fights, but if I had to, I would have been in trouble because I couldn't throw a punch. A couple of the guys on the team knew about the injury, but I tried my best to keep it to myself, because I didn't want to have to sit out. It was my last year of junior hockey, and I wanted to play regardless. Six games after that injury, in November, I fell awkwardly after being taken down on a breakaway and twisted my wrist. There was no faking this one. It completely destroyed the cartilage and I couldn't grip the stick properly with my top hand, which made stickhandling nearly impossible.

I wasn't able to participate in the SJHL showcase, an all-star tournament that offers a major opportunity to show scouts what you are able to do. Missing that really hurt my chances as a prospect for NCAA Division I, and even U Sports in Canada. It's easy to look good against a rookie who weighs 150 pounds, but it's different when you're up against the top players in the league.

I missed a total of ten games, wrapped around the Christmas break, and I despised watching from the stands. I just wanted to play.

My wrist wasn't healing or improving as the new year rolled around, so the doctors were debating whether to perform surgery. Meanwhile, I was not committed to any university at the time, and I knew that if my season was cut short, it would limit or do away with any opportunity. Therefore, I tried to get back as soon as I could. The only way I could play was by applying numbing cream for the pain and having my arm taped from my knuckles to mid-forearm, like a boxer. I returned to the lineup and battled the pain from January 12 onward. The third game after I got back on the ice, I was on a penalty kill and chased a puck down at the boards by the blue line. As I raced and tried to chip the puck out of our end, I tripped on the other player's skate and fell hard awkwardly. I scorpioned—my legs hit the back of my head as I went headfirst into the boards. I was a mangled mess on the ice. When I tried to get up and skate to the bench right after, I was seriously winded and could hardly catch my breath. Still, I ended up making it to the bench without interruption and playing the rest of the game.

The next day, I was swollen, bruised, and knew that something was wrong. My side and back were killing me. I decided to wait and see how I fared over the next few days. Thinking it was just a muscle strain, I would get many massages and put a super-potent muscle cream on my back for games, which created a burning sensation. I wouldn't find out for another few months that I'd actually broken a couple of ribs and a vertebra on that play.

All of the injuries I had that season meant I got to know our athletic therapist well. It was Dayna Brons's second season with the Broncos. She was twenty-four years old, just a bit older than us, and grew up just outside of Humboldt, in Lake Lenore. She loved sports and had come to Broncos games as a kid. She graduated from the University of Regina's kinesiology program in 2016, and then took the job with Humboldt as the team's athletic therapist.

Dayna took on much more responsibility with the team, though. She was an absolute workhorse. On top of treating all of our injuries and taping us before and after games, Dayna took care of all our gear and jerseys. She organized all of the equipment, sticks, and items that we needed for the season and for every game. Basically, she kept our entire ship running. Without her, we would have been a mess.

I always tried to avoid the athletic trainer's office, but with the season I had, it was impossible. I ended up spending quite a bit of time just chatting with Dayna while grimacing through whatever injury she was helping me through. She was often quiet, but was very interesting and talkative once you got to know her. She also had a quick wit about her. On a hockey team, that's important— the ability to banter is key. Whenever one of our guys needed to be taken down a peg, she was always there with a hilarious joke. We respected and loved Dayna. She was part of the family.

One night, the team volunteered as servers for a fundraiser at the Boston Pizza in town. It was a bit of a disaster because none of us were good at remembering orders, let alone balancing food on trays.

Dayna came in with some of her family members to laugh at how bad of a job we were doing. The guys on the team had a recurring joke that it was always Dayna's birthday. I'm not really sure where it started or why, but I know Matthieu Gomercic had something to do with it. It was one of the inside jokes a team finds funny, I guess. We just always wished her a happy birthday. Our Boston Pizza shift gave us a chance to take the gag to the next level.

We picked out some big sparkler candles in the kitchen at Boston Pizza, lit them, and placed them in an enormous dessert. As soon as Dayna saw the group of us walking towards her table, she knew what we were up to. We belted out "Happy Birthday" as loud as we could, and the whole restaurant joined in. Dayna just shook her head and smiled—the wide smile she always had—and then blew out the candles on her daily birthday.

CHAPTER 10

▬

Shortly after I arrived in Humboldt, I was driving home from one of our exhibition games when I saw a man in a Broncos jersey by the side of the road, fiddling with his bike.

I recognized him from the rink. He was one of a few guys who were "superfans" at our games, who would wait by the gate to give us fist bumps as we went on the ice.

I pulled over and asked him if everything was okay. He told me his bike was broken, that the chain had come off the sprocket and was a twisted mess. It was going to be tough to fix—so I offered to give him a ride home. We picked up the bike and put it in the back of the Hummshow. On the way to his place, he told me his name was Dallas. He was probably in his late forties or early fifties. He lived in a home for people with special needs. He explained that, during the season, he and his friends usually took a shuttle organized by the home to and from the arena to watch our games, but the bus was sometimes late arriving at the rink and often had to leave before the games were over because of the residents' early bedtimes.

"Well, I don't mind giving you guys a ride," I told him. "If you guys want me to pick you up and give you a lift back from the arena, I'll take you. That way, you won't miss the opening faceoff and will be able to stick around if we go into overtime."

"Really?" Dallas said. "I'd love that."

"As long as you're willing to be at the arena two and a half hours before game time and to wait another half hour to an hour after the game for me."

He seemed to really like that idea. We pulled up to the house and grabbed his bike out of the back. I told Dallas I'd pick him up at five minutes to five the next evening on the way to our home opener.

"And I can bring my friends?" he asked.

"As long as we have enough seats, the more the merrier," I said.

That was how our "taxi crew" began.

Riding to and from the games with Dallas and his friends became one of my most memorable experiences while playing in Humboldt. On the day of each home game, Dallas would call to confirm that Bernard, Shane, and Morris were coming and that they'd be ready when I showed up. If I didn't hear from him by 4:30 the odd time, I'd give him a shout and leave a message on his phone. Dallas always called back in time to grab a ride. And there were always four men from the home waiting when I arrived. They were the best. I had a pretty big subwoofer in the Hummer, so we'd blast the music as loud as possible. We'd crank some Drake, Kanye West, or Avicii, getting pumped up for the game.

After our games, the guys would wait in the tunnel the team used to get on the ice, where they would give us fist bumps. If we'd had a big win or if I'd had a good game, we'd all go to Tim Hortons afterwards to celebrate. I'd pick up five donuts and five coffees for us to have in the Hummer. The taxi crew ended up being like just another group of friends to me. To be honest, I don't even know what disabilities they had. We never talked about that. We just talked hockey, listened to good music, and had a celebratory donut or two. We hung out like buddies do.

I picked up the taxi crew before every home game that season. They didn't miss one. Picking them up and driving them home became part of my game-day routine.

When my parents came out for the home opener, I forgot to tell them that I was driving the guys home, so they ended up waiting at a restaurant for me for an extra hour. They were a little annoyed until I told them what I was doing. They had both worked with people who had special needs and had taught me the value of taking time to get to know them. It wasn't just about the support that you can give them, but also about what they can teach you. The energy with which they lived their lives inspired me.

It was definitely a humbling experience. I think they showed me a different perspective on life. I'd been involved with people who had different disabilities throughout my life, but my relationship with the taxi crew reignited my desire to work with and learn from people who have experienced different things in their lives than I have.

I also learned that the guys were more than hockey fans. They were players, too. They took part in a Special Olympics floor hockey program on Monday evenings. Therefore, once a week, instead of bringing them out to watch *me* play, I ended up going to the gym to play with them. I was kind of like a player/coach, instructing the guys while running up and down the floor with them. These Mondays are a Broncos tradition, and my teammates Logan Boulet and Tyler Smith would come out and join us from seven to eight every Monday night (and then we would head back to the Clements' in time for the team *Bachelor* night). The floor hockey games were just part of the extracurriculars that enriched my life while I was in Humboldt.

More than anything, I enjoyed the connections we were encouraged to build with the city of Humboldt. We were constantly involved in events to engage with our fans and the community at large. That was a big thing for Darcy. Hockey was a privilege that came with responsibility, and we were expected to take that responsibility seriously.

That concept had been instilled in me by my parents, but

Darcy certainly reinforced it in Humboldt. Outside of practice and working out, my goal for that year was to get involved in the community as much as I could.

Every Sunday afternoon, I helped run recreational hockey for two hours, which was a program that Mark Cross, our assistant coach, was in charge of. It was set up to introduce children to the basics of hockey and generate a love for the game. This was a great initiative created by the city, which the Broncos took over the same year I arrived. After my first time on the ice with the kids, I was hooked. It was so much fun to run through drills with them. There were some who already knew how to play and were just looking for extra ice. Others were just learning how to skate. It was super hard to give everyone the attention they needed, but I enjoyed the challenge.

After a few weekly sessions, I realized that Mark was running the program on behalf of the Broncos without having any days off. He would work with the team through the week, Monday to Saturday, and then run this program on Sunday, while still having to watch video to prep for our upcoming games and do office work. He would also try to find time to meet with his family and girlfriend of ten years, Molly. On top of all of that, Mark played senior hockey for his hometown team, the Strasbourg Maroons.

I felt bad that he had no time for himself, just to recover. In late October, I started telling him I could handle the drills alone and that he should take a break. He asked if I'd be interested in taking over the program for him.

"Of course," I said. "Let's do it."

From then on, Mark coordinated which Broncos would come out each week, while I took care of all of the on-ice programming and instruction. In December and January, I had to miss two sessions because I was injured. When I returned, Mark laughed and said the kids had missed me—and that they seemed to like me more than him. I loved it so much. Being out there with the kids is one of my favourite memories from Humboldt. I don't know why—I just really enjoyed seeing other people learn to love the game as much as I did.

Mark was about twenty-seven years old at the time. He'd played hockey with the York University Lions, where he was an assistant captain for three years and was named the team's MVP in his final year. He grew up in Strasbourg, a tiny town just north of Regina. After he graduated from university in 2016, he returned to Saskatchewan. He coached for a season in Lumsden before joining the Broncos as an assistant coach the same year I joined the team.

He was a wonderful coach and an even better role model. He was super genuine and caring, and just wanted the best for each of us. Mark never boasted. He never used his position of power to intimidate us. He just tried to help us. After practices, Mark would always stay on the ice late with whoever wanted to work on a specific aspect of their game. I spent a lot of time out there with him, whether to practise taking faceoffs or zipping backhand passes across the ice. He was patient with us, working through the details that we might have missed during practice, making sure that we left the ice better than when we went on.

Mark was also incredibly generous. He had a special program on his computer that had clips from all our shifts, so we could go back and figure out how to improve. Mark and Chris Beaudry, our other assistant coach, sat with me for hours on end, just working on my game, helping me improve. Chris, whom everyone called Critter, even gave me access to his account at the Coaches Site, so that I could learn from some of the best coaches in the world. They were both so dedicated to their players.

Early in the season, Critter also let me borrow his laptop so I could use the video software to make a highlight video. This video was sent out to the universities I was hoping to get interested in me for the following season.

One of the schools I reached out to was Mark's alma mater, York University. He told me great things about the program and encouraged me to consider it. Knowing my style of play and personality, he thought York would be the best fit for me. A few of my friends already played for the Lions and loved it, too. Russ Herrington, the coach at York, responded to my email right away and contacted Mark for an assessment of my play. He gave me a very nice review. After that introduction, I started emailing with Coach Herrington regularly. Near the end of February, Russ told me to register for my area of study for the 2018 fall semester and that we would talk formally about scholarships after the playoffs. The Lions quickly became front-runners, and I was ecstatic to be verbally secured, but nothing was set in stone yet. I decided to keep this quiet since it was not official. I only told my family and the coaches, as I did not want to cause any conflict going into the playoffs.

I knew Mark Cross would put me in a good situation with the Lions, and I trusted his opinion very much. He truly wanted the best for everyone. The Lions had been Ontario University Athletics champions in 2017 and were a well-respected hockey program in U Sports. Mark knew that Coach Herrington was a good person and a players' coach, which is another aspect I wanted. And York had a great reputation as a premier post-secondary institution. They had every program I was looking to study—business commerce, education, and kinesiology. I knew I did not want to stay in the Prairies for my university days; I wanted to expand my horizons, so living in Toronto definitely appealed to me.

As my future beyond Humboldt started to take shape, I focused on another reason why I'd wanted to join the Broncos in the first place: launching Dahlgren's Diabeauties.

I had discussed my idea for the program with Darcy during our first phone call when he welcomed me to the team. He was on board right away. I told him that I was excited to play for a team that had many fans and was very connected to the community. When I brought diabetic children out to the games, I wanted them to feel celebrated for their difference. I wanted them to hear the crowd cheering for them—to hear the *community* cheering for them. I wanted these kids to feel special, in a good way.

As soon as I knew I was heading to Humboldt, I went to work putting the blueprint of the program together. With the help of Jocelyn Doetzel, the Broncos' public relations and game-day coordinator at the time, we created a web page and developed a social media presence to promote the program. Her dad, who owned Doetzel Loader Services, donated the start-up fees to get the program up and running. Erykah's dad, Chris, designed the Diabeauties logo and sent two variations of it. The Broncos promoted the program on the team website. A newspaper story by Kevin Mitchell appeared in the *Saskatoon StarPhoenix* and the *National Post*. And JDRF sent out a news release about the program as well. They have a local chapter in Humboldt, so they reached out to several people directly to let them know what I was planning.

The response was actually quite surprising. We had five inquiries in the first week or so.

In the end, we had five kids who came out to different games as part of the Diabeauties program. For each home game, we arranged to honour a different child with diabetes from the community. The Broncos agreed to pitch in complimentary tickets for each kid's immediate family members. Carla also helped us out by offering to give the families twenty-five dollars off their pre-game meal at Johnny's Bistro. The child was given a custom-made green and gold Diabeauties jersey to wear for the night and rep the Broncos colours. We even had a ceremonial faceoff, where the Diabeauty would drop the puck with me and the captain of the other team at centre ice before the game. During the draw and photo ops, our announcer introduced the Diabeauty and their family to the crowd before the national anthem. Usually, ceremonial faceoffs were the captain's role, but Schatzy was kind enough to let me take the draw. He was nice about it.

"This is your program, buddy," he told me. "You take the draw."

After the game, I would meet up with the child and their family to get to know them on a deeper level. I was able to establish some meaningful connections that way, which was always the most rewarding part. I'd give them some Broncos swag and Diabeauties gear, and then talk to them about growing up with type 1 diabetes and how I managed to pursue athletics despite dealing with the complications that come with it. I did not want these evenings to be one-and-done experiences, so I created a Facebook group chat where they could mingle with other Diabeauties.

At a later date, I would visit each Diabeauty's school—sometimes two hours away—and give a presentation for all of the students and faculty about type 1 diabetes. Occasionally, these experiences led to other areas where I could get involved. After I did a presentation for my first Diabeauties class in Humboldt in mid-September, the teacher asked if I would like to be a volunteer in their classroom for the season. I thought it would be a great opportunity to be involved in a classroom setting and give back to the community. I started to volunteer at St. Dominic elementary school every Wednesday morning, from nine until noon. We did not have a practice until 2 p.m. that day because of ice maintenance in the morning. So, instead of sleeping in, I would spend my time in the Grade 5 classroom, covering multiplication tables, helping with essays or labs, and doing little things that needed to be done around the classroom. I would drive Jaya, Rowan, and Madden on Wednesdays, as they also attended St. Dominic. I was actually volunteering in Jaya's class, so she had to deal with me every Wednesday morning. This was during a time where I was still undecided about what occupation I wanted to pursue, and teaching was on that list, so this was right up my alley.

Dahlgren's Diabeauties also attracted interest from across Canada, which I was hoping for.

I wanted to make sure I was able to develop a personal connection with the children, even if they were far away. I would arrange a special care package to send them, and so that we could make more than a superficial connection, we set up recurring check-ins with each Diabeauty via FaceTime, Skype, a phone call, or text message. I wanted to be able to mentor these kids to become the best individuals they can be, to be there for their good and bad days, and to create the next wave of leaders in the diabetic world. I also wanted to be involved in their lives and address any questions they might have as they got older, like how to face dangerous temptations such as drinking alcohol, and how eating healthy and being physically active can help control diabetes—to be a positive influence to help them with difficult decisions or situations that come with the disease, like relationships, athletics, and being independent. Most importantly, I wanted to be the person I *needed* when I was growing up with type 1 diabetes. I'm still talking to all of them today.

More than anything I was able to do on the ice, getting the Diabeauties program off the ground was by far the most important personal accomplishment of my time in Humboldt.

In the second half of the season, our team was still going strong. We finalized our roster on January 10 and had all the pieces in place to make a push in the postseason. Every team in our division—North Battleford, Kindersley, and Notre Dame—was solid and could win on any given night. Most divisions had a team or two that were near the bottom, but not ours. This helped prepare us for the playoffs because we had to consistently play at the top of our game every night. We would face each of these three teams eight times in the regular season, and each of them was at least a two-hour drive.

We started to really come together and bond as a team even more in the second half. We had a player auction shootout, where the fans "bought" a member of the team for a shootout after the game. The coaches participated, and even Dayna laced up her blades to get in on the action. The skater would have two shootout attempts and had to score on one. If they didn't score, the skater would be out and the bidder who got them in the auction would lose their money. However, if they were in the top three, the individual who selected them would win money—the higher the placing, the bigger the prize. It was a little bit of fun that the high-roller gamblers of Humboldt could enjoy.

I remember how fun it was for us, too. We all went into the dressing room after a game, put on whatever we thought would be acceptable or funny for a fan shootout, and had some fun with it. Guys wore their hats backwards or let their locks flow in the air; some had sunglasses or a funky hat. Wacker pulled a bright pink cowboy hat out of his bag that he surprised everyone with. We all thought it was hilarious. I don't even know how it stayed on his head for the whole shootout, but he managed to finish top three, so it must have worked some magic. I ended up wearing a black cape that I made out of a garbage bag and blue Sherwood sunglasses that I won in a prize pack from Sherwood Hockey. My moves were garbage, just like my cape, and I ended up being stopped on both attempts. Xavier finished second and Hunts won it all, which wasn't a surprise—he always scored in shootouts.

That winter, we had many other events within the community. We would do hot lunches with Johnny's Bistro for students at the local elementary schools; hold fan appreciation nights, where we would skate on the ice with our fans after a game; help out with team practice for the peewee girls in nearby Bruno; tie skates and go on the ice with the elementary schools' skate-a-thon; and call past Broncos donors to see if they would buy tickets for the 50/50 lotto.

I think one of the funnier events a few of us took part in was a financial literacy course. We attended two learning seminars at Conexus Credit Union in Humboldt, detailing how money compounded if you invested your savings and how to put aside money monthly for future savings. Once we passed the course, we would go to a middle-year classroom to give a presentation about financial literacy. What was funny was the irony of us junior hockey players teaching children about this topic. We had no real jobs, were living off money from our summer jobs, and did not have to worry about groceries, utilities, rent, or any other payments because we lived with billets. So, there I was with Logan Hunter and Parker Tobin, teaching children how to save their money.

Looking back at it now, all of these kind gestures within the community were what made our team grow closer together.

In early March, with the playoffs just around the corner, there was a major snowfall in Humboldt. A hundred centimetres of snow fell in one night, and all of the roads were shut down. We had a practice that morning, but Darcy sent a message at 8:06 a.m. on March 5 to our captains' group chat:

Good morning Guys . . . just a slight change of plans here today, practice will be pushed back or postponed . . . I want to make sure all your billets' snow gets removed . . . and we might have some good deeds to do around the community today to help people . . . please fwd on to the group . . . thanks.

We notified the rest of the guys through the team group chat and told them to be dressed in winter gear. When we showed up, Darcy told us our skate was cancelled.

"We're going to go shovel," he said.

Darcy could tell by our faces that we were a bit confused.

Who spends a day shovelling snow when the playoffs are coming up? We wanted to get ready to play.

"The community has been there for us, and we need to be there for them," Darcy said.

The local radio station, Bolt FM, announced that if anyone needed their driveways shovelled, we would go out and do it for them. We received more than twenty calls—and even more from people whose cars were stuck in the snow and who needed us to help pull them out.

We spent four hours shovelling snow off of driveways and pushing cars out of ditches, on a day when the temperature was almost minus-thirty. Absolutely *freezing*.

It was one of my favourite days playing for the Broncos. In all the seasons I'd spent playing junior, this was probably one of the best team-building experiences I had. It was more than bonding with teammates, though. It was bonding with a community. It was seeing the faces of families overwhelmed by regular life, watching us clear one giant chore out of their busy day. It was seeing elderly people who shouldn't be out lifting heavy snow, waving at us from the warmth of their homes. It was tossing heaps of snow at little kids who bounded through drifts around us.

Later, we all went to Johnny's Bistro and shovelled out the entire lot. That was more work than all the driveways combined, but we had quads that could do the heavy lifting. Carla repaid all of us with a meal on the house.

At its best, this is what hockey meant to a community. That's what Darcy taught us. He was really focused on the importance of service.

The impact that we could have off the ice was more important than what we could accomplish on it. If any of us felt that getting ready for the playoffs was more important than helping dig our community out of a snowstorm, then we missed the point.

CHAPTER 11

—

Take care of the seconds and the minutes take care of themselves. Darcy always told us that. He wanted us to focus on what we were able to control in the moment, and to let that define our future. There was little value in worrying about what came next, when everything to come is driven by the decisions you make now.

It's as true on the ice as it is in life.

We lived in the moments before everything went black.

Life in junior hockey is full of routine. Consistency is key. Every morning in Humboldt, I'd wake up and head to the Clements' kitchen to make some oatmeal, have some hard-boiled eggs, or blend up a smoothie to share with Wacker and Fisker. Then we would climb into either Stephen's or my vehicle and head to Elgar Petersen Arena for practice.

We would enter through the side entrance, go down the stairs, turn left and walk past the benches, continue along the tunnel by Dayna's office, kick off our shoes on the mat outside the team's locker room, and then get dressed in our stalls, painted green and lined with gold. I'd plug my phone into the auxiliary cord beside Bouls's stall and occasionally turn on our dressing room TV to watch the sports highlights from the night before. I'd check to see if my stick needed to be retaped, put on my compression undergear, and roll out my muscles with a foam roller before putting my gear on. Get pre-iced on the first few drills we were going to do. We'd pump out our playlist and watch the highlights on mute while we got ready for another day.

On the ice, we would come out early to mess around with pucks and get in a good stretch along the wall near centre ice, and then take off for the first set of drills. I would normally stay out after practice for quite a while to work on little details of my game that get overlooked in practice. Reagan Poncelet and I would work on our deflections, one-timers, backhand passes, rim passes, and other specifics that you might need only once or twice a game but still needed to be able to execute.

After practice, I would quickly get undressed, get a workout in, and then head two blocks down the road to Johnny's Bistro for lunch. There were only a handful of us on practice days, but on game days we would have nearly a dozen side by side, taking advantage of the 50 percent discount Carla offered and fuelling up for the game ahead. Eggs Benedict, the meat lover's ome-lette, and the meat lover's skillet were definitely the favourites of the majority of the group. Every game day, I would have a meat lover's omelette with a substitute of oatmeal on the side instead of hash browns.

It was just the routine. Every day almost identical to the one before. It's how hockey players function. We used that routine to keep us focused so that we were ready when it counted. In other words, we took care of the seconds.

That season, the seconds led us to a second-place finish in our division with thirty-three wins. It wasn't where we had hoped to be when the season started, but we felt good about our chances in the playoffs.

The team voted to dye our hair bleached blond for the post-season, one of the long-standing playoff traditions that the Broncos and many other junior teams do (probably because most of the younger players can barely grow a playoff beard). Everybody knows you have to get your hair dyed in the playoffs. It's just the way it is.

Most of the guys got together after cleaning out the local pharmacy of boxes of blond hair dye to get their new looks. The guys who came from Humboldt put some green in their hair as well.

I didn't join the team hair-dyeing party because I already didn't have much hair to begin with and I wasn't about to trust my linemates with the finer points of applying Clairol Ultra-Light Cool Summer Blonde. The guys understood my concern.

"You *are* balding, Kaleb," they said. "It's okay."

Instead, I booked an appointment at a local salon to get the job done by a professional. I didn't want to risk it. When I called and explained what I wanted, the hairdresser said, "You're a Bronco, aren't you?"

It was the first time I had ever dyed my hair. Not going to lie, it was actually pretty stylish. I posted a photo on my Snapchat story noting my similarity to Slim Shady.

Our fresh look carried us as we faced our heated rivals, the Melfort Mustangs, in the first round of the playoffs. The Mustangs were a good team that had finished with six more wins than us on the season and were the favourites to win it all, as they had the first-place Nipawin Hawks' number all season. They were only an hour away from us and were our closest opponents in the SJHL.

We did not like them. They did not like us. Plain and simple.

The battle to get into the game-day lineup come playoff time was fierce. We had nine twenty-year-olds who were all healthy enough to play, and only eight could be dressed on any night. This meant that if you were irrelevant in the last game, you were sure to watch the next one from the stands. For us twenties, these would be the last playoffs of our junior career, and all of us wanted to play. This internal dogfight probably made our whole team even hungrier.

We all understood that we needed to push each other, but still be happy if others got an opportunity and you were in the stands. But it's a very weird dynamic to be in. I fought and clawed every day to earn my spot in the lineup. I managed to appear in every game in the regular season after coming back from my injury, except for one on February 9. That was the first time in my hockey career that I had ever been a healthy scratch, and it was in my twenty-year-old season.

Being scratched is normally a concern for rookies. As a veteran, it's never on your mind. But now it became a reality. And for a home game like this, there was the feeling of sitting out in front of your own fans and having people ask you why you're on the sidelines.

What's wrong? Are you injured? Did you break team curfew? Come late to a meeting?

I did not want those questions or feelings of embarrassment, shame, and worthlessness to ever happen again. Anyone who has ever been scratched knows what it's like.

I knew I was a valuable piece of the team and a leader, but I obviously had to be more than that. When the playoffs came, I did everything in my power to focus on the things I could control and let my play do the talking.

For Game 1 against Melfort, I was pencilled into the lineup. I ended up having an incredible game and left it all out there. I had two primary assists—one coming off a neutral-zone breakout pass from Adam Herold that I skated into the zone on a two-on-one with Jacob Leicht before dishing it to him for a backdoor goal. Herry was a sixteen-year-old defence stud we'd called up from the Midget AAA Regina Pat Canadians. I tried to take him under my wing when he first arrived, since I knew exactly what it was like to be in his shoes after going through it a few years earlier. He fit in quickly with our group, and surprisingly had his hair already bleached before he came, because his AAA team had the same playoff tradition. He was quickly slotted into the left side on the first pairing with Bryce Fiske and was a regular in the lineup.

The other assist was on a power play when Ryan Straschnitzki threw a puck on net and I deflected it on goal, with the rebound being kicked out to Nick Shumlanski, who put it home. Broncos win, 7–2.

The roster for Game 2 was posted the next day. I went to look at it and was in shock—I was scratched. My mindset kicked into gear: *I cannot settle for this. I can control my own destiny.* I had faced adversity my whole career, being cut from various teams. As I saw it, this was just another bump in the road on my hockey journey. I resolved that when I got another opportunity, I would make the most of it.

We ended up losing that game, 6–3.

I was back in the lineup with a vengeance in Game 3, picking up a goal and an assist in a 4–1 win. From there on out, I played every game against Melfort. We managed to cruise through that series, winning four games to one, finally starting to play as well as we knew we could. We claimed the first-ever Bourgault Cup, a trophy sponsored by a company that was headquartered between Melfort and Humboldt. We took a team picture with the cup after having it handed to us in the dressing room. Bleached blond hair only.

Winning the series meant we faced an even bigger test: playing the Nipawin Hawks in the league semifinals. The Hawks had finished the season with forty-three wins and the best record in the league. They were a *very good* team. In fact, they were ranked in the top five in Canada heading into the playoffs.

Even though we were the underdogs, we felt confident heading into the series. It wasn't like us to be worried about how good the other guys were. The Hawks did not want to play against us because they were scared of how easily we had rolled over Melfort. We were self-assured and had lots of experience. Darcy had assembled a team with a plan to win another championship for Humboldt, and we believed we could do it.

We battled into double overtime in the first game of the series, at Centennial Arena in Nipawin. We had a lead heading into the third period but blew it. Unfortunately, we lost, 3–2, despite forty-four saves from Parker Tobin. We dropped the second game, 5–3, in Nipawin, but still didn't lose hope as the score had been tied in the second period.

There was still time to turn the series around. We managed a 2–1 win in Game 3 at home, with goals from Conner Lukan and Logan Boulet—and twenty-nine saves from Jacob Wassermann.

On Wednesday, April 4, we went into the fourth game with a chance to even the series. We were ready and determined. We knew success was attainable, we had implemented a few small, detailed changes into our system, and we just had to win the 50/50 battles and remain disciplined. We were excited to be in a position to tie the series and knew that the Elgar Petersen Arena was going to be rocking again, the way it had been the night before. We came out hard and got a quick goal from our captain, Schatzy. The Hawks really didn't want to let us back into it and quickly retaliated. We trailed 3–1 in the second period, and I saw some heads on our bench sink. It wasn't the first time we had experienced these feelings this season. Still, I knew the game was far from over and there was still lots of time left. Persistence is key. And Darcy wouldn't let us quit. He was too good of a coach to let us beat ourselves.

I was on the ice, mixing it up in front of the net and providing a screen for a power-play goal from Bouls that brought us within one. Then the Hawks picked up another penalty and I deflected a shot by Hunts off my shin pad and past their netminder, tying the game up. We didn't stop there. The Hawks were getting frustrated and took another penalty. With the man advantage again, Shums put us in the lead. Then, with twenty seconds to go before the second intermission, we picked up another from Lukes to take a two-goal lead. The EPA was rockin'.

The crowd could hardly believe it—and to be honest, neither could we. We went from the lowest despair to supreme confidence in half a period. It's crazy what momentum can do. At that point, it was already one of the most epic games I'd been a part of.

When we came out for the third, the EPA crowd were on the edge of their seats. Despite the rowdy cheers against them, the Hawks had some fight left, too. They managed to battle back and score two in the third to tie it up. We had fought extremely hard to come back to take that lead, so it felt demoralizing—but after what we had already overcome, there was no way we were going to give up.

The first overtime period was thrilling, with several good chances for both sides. On one play, I got the puck in front of the net and shot as the goalie was down and out, scrambling across the net. I should have gone five-hole, but I went high and the goalie just managed to catch the puck in his glove. He made an incredible save. We were that close to winning, several times. We had breakaways, they had breakaways. We had wide-open two-man breaks, they had the same. The game just kept on going. We outshot Nipawin, 16–10, in the period.

We sat in the locker room while the ice was cleared during the intermission, eating granola bars and fruit and drinking as much water as we could. We taped our sticks and got mentally prepared for the next period.

We went back onto the ice and played another twenty minutes of gritty hockey, outshooting the Hawks, 12–7. Wass even faced a penalty shot. Still, no one scored. We sat in the locker room completely gassed. This time, we had chocolate bars, slices of pizza, and sandwiches brought in from the rink cafeteria. Anything that could give us energy. Guys were doing whatever it took to remain focused on the objective and recover quickly. This was *playoff* hockey.

The third overtime was just as frantic as the first two. None of the fans had left their seats. The EPA was still bumpin'. Every rush seemed like an opportunity to end it, but the goalies played phenomenally. It was a thrilling game—and it seemed like it would go on forever.

Maybe when I was eighteen, I wouldn't have noticed how exhausting the game was, but as a twenty-year-old, I could feel it. My legs were starting to cramp up. I know I wasn't the only one. We were all in good condition, but when you play an extra full game on top of a game, you're obviously going to be a bit tired, especially one as intense as this, where any mistake could cost you the win.

Patter and I did our special handshake for the sixth time that night as we made our way onto the ice. Minutes into triple overtime, the Hawks got away with what should have been a boarding call. Then, a couple of plays later, Shums was called for boarding on almost the exact same play. We were livid. About thirty seconds into the power play, the Hawks scored on a one-timer in the slot.

We slumped over while the Hawks celebrated in front of our fans. Guys were furious as we headed into the locker room. We sat there, completely exhausted, feeling deflated. It felt like that game had been for the series. We now trailed three games to one and had to head back to Nipawin to keep our playoff hopes going.

As usual, Darcy didn't come into the locker room after the loss. He said he always wanted to get some space between his emotional reaction and his logical one. He never wanted to say something that he might regret. A couple of the twenty-year-olds piped up in our dressing room. I chimed in, too.

"This is just one game of a seven-game series," I said. "We have to hit the reset button and focus on our next game, and win it."

For the nine twenty-year-olds on the roster, this was the last chance at a championship. We knew that our next game could be our last. We weren't going to let that happen.

After showering, I walked out into the hallway and saw the taxi crew standing in the tunnel, waiting for me. I smiled at them and they smiled back—reminding me that, win or lose, there will always be things in life that are much more important.

The next day at noon, we had a mandatory check-in at the rink, and there was optional ice for anyone who hadn't played in Game 4 at 1 p.m. Pretty much everyone who played skipped the extra ice and got some rest. We needed to recover for Game 5, back in Nipawin on Friday.

The break was necessary, because there was still a lot of hockey left to play in the series. Game 6 would bring us back to Humboldt on Sunday. Game 7 would be the following Tuesday, in Nipawin. And we fully expected to get there.

That afternoon, I did a yoga session and took an ice bath in our dressing room's tub. I was always a baby about getting into a tub of freezing ice water, but it helped alleviate some of the pain the playoffs had already inflicted. I could still feel every hit from the previous night. My legs were rubber. My back was still giving me pain. My body was covered in bruises.

I still was taping my wrist like a boxer. There had been instances earlier in the year where I wanted to step in and drop the gloves to stand up for my teammates, but I would face a three-game suspension for illegal taping of the hands in a fight if that happened. Lots of the guys went on the bikes to get their legs moving and lined up in Dayna's office to receive treatment. That Thursday night at 7:30, we had a video meeting to go over a detailed analysis of how we were going to approach the Hawks in twenty-four hours. Darcy reminded us that we weren't out of it. We'd had a lead starting the third period in three out of the four games in the series so far. If we were good enough to take the lead, we were good enough to hold it. We just needed to focus on winning this game, and then worry about the next one. Mark and Chris went into the specifics, showing us the mistakes in the last game and explaining in detail the changes we needed to make on the power play and penalty kill.

On Friday morning Wacker, Fisker, and I went to the rink for a pre-game skate and then met a handful of the guys at Johnny's Bistro for a late breakfast. Even though we had our backs against the wall in a do-or-die match that night, we had to treat it like just another game day. We had to take care of those seconds.

After breakfast, we drove back to the house and had a quick snooze. I woke up in time to have a hot shower—another pre-game ritual—and change into my Broncos track suit, which we always wore on long bus rides before changing into our suits. I slipped on my loafer-style dress shoes—an odd look with sweats, but it's an old trick to make sure you don't have to deal with two pairs of shoes on the road. Then I said goodbye to Erykah, who had just arrived from Regina to watch the game in Nipawin that night.

On the way to the rink, Fisker and I stopped in at Johnny's Bistro again to pick up all of our pre-game meals, as we were running early. Wacker met us at the rink. For road trips, Wacker, Fisker, and I would always put in an order at Johnny's—pasta, wraps, and so on—that we would pick up on the way to the rink and eat on the bus. Because of my diabetes, I've always been very strict about sticking to my eating schedule. Usually, our games started at 7:30 p.m., so I'd start eating whatever I'd picked up at the bistro that day right at 4 p.m., and then put on my suit. (Pro tip: you have to keep your suit clean, so you always eat in your track suit.)

I'd texted with my parents several times that day. Our conversation that day was mostly about the future. I was pretty sure that I was going to head to York University in the fall, but wanted to consider all the logistics and financial factors. Dad, Mom, and I went back and forth, making sure that everything was looking good. They planned to arrive in Nipawin in the late afternoon, in time to grab a meal before puck drop, like they always did. With an extra hour to log coming from Saskatoon, they were already on the road by the time I arrived at Elgar Petersen Arena for our team meeting at quarter after two.

A couple guys showed up late to the 2:15 meeting, and it got pushed back fifteen minutes. Once Lukes and Brayden Camrud arrived, we had a quick team highlight-video session, displaying all the positives that had got us to this point. Darcy and Mark also reiterated what we had discussed the night before, so everyone was refreshed on their roles. Before we wrapped up, Darcy echoed his message from the night before.

"I don't want anyone leaving this dressing room thinking that we are out of this," he said. "If you do, then don't come."

I looked around the Broncos locker room. All eyes were on Darcy. I didn't see any doubt on the faces of my teammates. They looked determined and ready.

It was time.

Before we left the locker room, I took a picture of the lineup that Darcy had written on the board. It was just a habit I had, so I was able to remember who was playing with who, and what lines we'd be matched up against. I was playing a shutdown role that game and wanted to prepare mentally for what I'd have to do up against the Hawks' top scorers.

We all grabbed our gear sitting in the bags in front of our stalls and carried it out to the bus, along with our suit bags. The rookies loaded up the bags, along with the skate sharpener, medical table, and extra gear, jerseys, and sticks.

As we climbed up the stairs to the coach, we were greeted by our driver, Glen Doerksen—who was nearly sixty, had been married for almost three decades, and was a master carpenter. He'd been hired by Charlie's Charters in Tisdale to be our driver. Glen was a regular and we'd had him before. I always liked to strike a conversation up with our bus drivers.

"Hi Glen, how are you today?" I asked.

"Doing good, thanks. Hoping that you guys pull out the win."

"That's good to hear," I responded. "And don't worry, we will."

The twenties took the seats at the very back of the bus—Matthieu Gomercic, Jaxon Joseph, Logan Schatz, Logan Boulet, Bryce Fiske, Stephen Wack, Conner Lukan, Nick Shumlanski, and me. Next came the nineteen-year-olds—Derek Patter, Brayden Camrud, and Tyler Smith. Then the eighteen-year-olds—Parker Tobin, Xavier LaBelle, Graysen Cameron, Jacob Leicht, Evan Thomas, Logan Hunter, Morgan Gobeil, and Ryan Straschnitzki. Finally, the youngest—Jacob Wassermann, Layne Matechuk, and Adam Herold—sat near the front, where the coaches and team staff sat. It was a pretty informal system, just kind of like an unwritten rule. Veterans also had two seats to themselves.

Dayna sat near the front of the bus. So did Brody Hinz, our eighteen-year-old volunteer statistician, who was a two-sport Special Olympics athlete, in bowling and floor hockey, and a massive sports fan. He sat close to Tyler Bieber, who was in his first year as the play-by-play announcer for games, which were aired on Bolt FM. Tyler grew up in Humboldt and was in the midst of a burgeoning career in sports media.

Darcy and Mark sat in the first two seats at the front, as coaches always do. Chris Beaudry lived an hour east of Humboldt, so he drove to Nipawin on his own because it was much quicker for him.

I put my suit bag and the box of food I'd picked up at Johnny's Bistro in the overhead compartment above seat 12, four seats from the back on the driver's side, where I always sat. Then I put my knapsack on the floor beside my seat, with the game notes Darcy gave us to review before each game. I leaned back against the window, where my pillow was sitting, to stretch out my legs into the aisle.

Shums sat in the seat in front of me and Joey sat across from him. Lukes was across the aisle to my right. Wacker sat in the seat behind me, across from Fisker. Logan Boulet sat in the row behind Wacker, across from Schatzy. Gomer took his regular spot in the last row, beside the toilet.

We pulled out of the arena parking lot close to three o'clock and made a quick detour to Darcy's house. His wife, Christina—who was kind of like our team mom—had made thirty spaghetti dinners for everyone on the bus to eat before the game. Darcy wanted to make sure that we had enough energy, just in case the game went into triple overtime again. He had also forgotten to wear a belt or bring his dress shoes—a detail too innocuous for my memory to record on just another trip—so he dashed off the bus and ran inside. I don't know if he had a chance to see his two sons, Carson and Jackson, before he left. They were the centre of his life.

Family first.

Darcy came back out of his house and kissed Christina goodbye.

It was just a quick stop. We kept moving towards Nipawin. A little more than an hour after we left Humboldt, we took a right on Highway 3, instead of continuing north through Melfort like we usually did. We headed towards Tisdale, half an hour east. The detour added about another five minutes to our trip, but we still had time to get to Nipawin before puck drop.

At four o'clock, I started to get into game mode. I opened up the box that Johnny's Bistro packed me, to get in my pre-game meal.

It was just another ride—the same card games, the same banter, the same jokes as always. I remember the feeling of how normal it all was, with nothing special to remember. There is so much that I can't remember but wish I could.

I received an email from York University during the ride, outlining what the school was able to offer me to play and attend school there the following season. I forwarded it to my parents, who had already arrived in Nipawin, and asked them what they thought. We exchanged a few messages back and forth.

We passed through Tisdale and turned north on Highway 35, forty minutes from Nipawin.

I looked over the game notes that Darcy had given us. After about ten minutes I stood up in the aisle, opened the storage compartment above my seat, and brought down my dress clothes. I got dressed, pulling on my green dress pants, buttoning up my black dress shirt, and slipping my gold tie, already tied in a double Windsor knot, over my head. I tossed my track suit into the box above my seat, put on my grey wool peacoat, settled into my spot, and looked out the window. I understood that we were getting close to where Nick Shumlanski lived. He'd mentioned it earlier on the trip, but I couldn't quite remember.

"Shums, your house is on this road, right?" I asked him.

Shums looked back.

"Yeah," he said. "It's coming up. I'll tell you when it is."

We drove for a little while. The guys in the seats around me were laughing and joking around. A few started to get up to get changed into their suits, getting ready for our arrival in Nipawin. We were so close.

I leaned forward, took my headphones out of my backpack, and plugged them into my phone. I turned on a playlist called "#16," closed my eyes, and visualized myself making plays on the ice.

I dreamed about a game that would never happen.

A few minutes later, Wacker leaned over the seat behind me and tapped me twice on the left shoulder. I paused the music and looked back at him leaning his head through the gap between the two bus seats.

"What song are you playing?" he asked.

And as hard as I try—and I've tried many times—I'm never able to remember what that song was. I remember Wacker saying thanks and I turned back in my seat and put my headphones back on, thinking about the game ahead.

At 4:43 p.m., Morgan Gobeil texted the team group chat, asking if anyone had extra dress socks. I didn't.

I overheard Shumlanski talking louder than my music, so I paused it to listen in.

"Boys, that's where a fucking legend was raised."

He pointed out the window to a house surrounded by trees among the wide-open fields just as we passed by.

"Oh, cool!" I said.

Tobes—two rows ahead, on the right—saw an opportunity for a light-hearted jab.

"Nobody cares where you live, Shums!" he said.

"Well, I care!" Jaxon replied.

We all laughed, and I'll never forget that sound. It was just typical road trip jokes. So forgettable, really—but unforgettable now.

There were several other guys standing in the aisle, getting dressed. Some of the players were eating, others were still sleeping. Some were looking out the windows, watching the fields pass by. I leaned back into the aisle seat and pushed play again.

We were seconds away from the crossroads at Highway 335.

I put my head down and closed my eyes.

CHAPTER 12

—

April 7, 2018

April 8, 2018

April 9, 2018

April 10, 2018

April 11, 2018

2:20 p.m.

I opened my eyes and everything was white. It took several blinks before the curtains came into focus.

Curtains? I thought. *Where am I?*

It felt like a dream. Maybe it was one, I thought. I closed my eyes and tried to make myself wake up. I couldn't.

White light and curtains. They didn't go away.

I could feel a gripping sensation around my neck, like I was being held in a headlock. Something was pushing my chin up, and I couldn't push it down. It hurt to turn my head.

Why am I here? What happened?

My consciousness crept into focus, the way your eyes adjust to the light. There was a game that night, I remembered. It was Friday. We were playing the Hawks in Nipawin.

We had to win or we were finished. But I couldn't remember anything about the game.

Did we lose? Is it over?

I blinked some more, and the white light started to fade. My parents sat in the chairs beside me. I raised my hand to my neck and felt the brace. Then the fear hit me.

This is a hospital, I realized. *Something is wrong.*

I must have been hit from behind into the boards. Why else would there be a brace around my neck? I tilted my head as much as I could to see my mother and father. They didn't seem surprised to see my eyes open. They acted as though I had just woken up from a nap.

"Is this a dream?" I asked.

They said no.

"Is this a hospital?"

Yes.

"Did we win our game tonight?"

"Kaleb," my father said. "There was no game."

It didn't process.

If there was no game, then why am I injured? I ran through every option I could think of: *Did the refs not show up? Was there an ice malfunction? Did our bus break down?*

"There was a crash," Dad said.

He said it in a way that sounded like it was something I'd already been told. They both started to tear up.

They never cry, I thought. *Something very bad has happened.*

"What's going on?" I asked. "Where is everybody else?"

"Kaleb, we already told you," Dad said. "Don't you remember?"

Their eyes welled up.

I didn't believe them. I still thought I was dreaming. I closed my eyes again and tried to wake up. Again, I couldn't.

"Give me my phone," I said. "I need to see if this is real."

Mom handed me a phone that was sitting on a small table beside us. It did not look like my phone. It was brand new and it had a default iPhone screen saver. My number had been transferred to it. There were more than a hundred notifications on the home screen. I unlocked it and opened up Twitter.

It was everywhere.

#PrayersForHumboldt

#HumboldtStrong

#SticksOutForHumboldt

There were endless posts about the Broncos. I couldn't believe it. It still felt like a terrible dream. Then I saw the date at the top of the screen.

It was Wednesday, April 11. It was 2:25 p.m.

It's been five days.

My parents told me a story that they had already walked me through several times, but I had no memory of it.

It was a cold day—minus-nine degrees Celsius. There was snow on the ground, but it was beautiful out, Dad said. He went to Costco to get gas and picked Mom up at home, and they left Saskatoon for Nipawin in mid-afternoon. During the drive, Mom was texting with me on the Broncos bus about the information I was getting from York University. They took the regular route, which heads straight through Melfort and cuts east along Highway 335. They turned at the crossroads with Highway 35, heading north to Nipawin.

As they got close to town, Dad asked Mom if she was still texting with me. I'd just told her I was going to get dressed and start getting ready for the game. The bus was heading towards Tisdale at the time.

They pulled into Nipawin and stopped at the Hawks office across the street from the arena to pick up their tickets for the game. They were a glossy metallic blue, with the Nipawin Hawks logo detailed on them, and they looked like NHL tickets. Mom slipped them into her purse. Then they went to Gieni's, their favourite restaurant in Nipawin, which is right on the main street as you drive into town. (Dad has a favourite restaurant in every town I've played in—as he says, as much as he loves driving, he loves food.)

They asked for a seat by the window, so they could see when the bus arrived in town. They ate supper and waited. The bus was late, but they didn't think too much of it.

"I must have missed it," Dad said to Mom around 5 p.m. "They'd be here already."

Sirens wailed in the background and a couple of fire trucks rushed pass the window. They didn't think anything of it. Royal Canadian Mounted Police cars followed. Then numerous ambulances. All seconds apart.

"That doesn't look good," Dad said.

A woman came through the doors of the restaurant.

"There's been a terrible crash," she said to the lady at the till. "A semi T-boned a bus."

Both of my parents overheard her. They felt a knot in their stomachs right away. They looked at each other as their faces went white.

"Did you say a semi hit a bus?" Mom asked.

"Yes," the lady replied. "At Armley Corner."

Other customers in the restaurant saw my parents' reaction.

"Do you know someone on a bus?" one asked.

"Our son is on the Broncos bus," Mom said.

It was Easter break, so school was out, which meant no buses were running for students. There weren't Greyhound buses running in the region anymore.

There was an audible cry and gasps as, one by one, the realization hit. Everyone knew.

Mom and Dad couldn't remember if they paid for the meal or not. In the blur, it seemed like they were on the road right away— heading south on Highway 35 towards Armley Crossing. In the faint hope they still held out that it might not have been our bus, my parents thought they might be able to help out at the crash site as nurses. On the drive out, my Mom started getting texts from others, as well as a phone call from Erykah that confirmed their fears. The Broncos bus had been in a crash—and it was bad. An ambulance ripped past them, headed towards Nipawin.

"Kaleb can't be dead," Dad said to Mom. "It can't be that bad."

Dad did his best to convince himself: *He's our only kid. There's no way. He can't be dead.*

More information trickled in via text. The bus was on its side, they learned. There was no word on fatalities.

The shock rushed in. They were both quiet as they drove. It was only about twenty minutes, but it seemed like twenty hours. Every hill was a mountain.

Why is this taking so long?

They reached the top of a hill and saw the flashing lights ahead and then dipped into another small valley before arriving at the intersection. Ten cars were lined up, stopped on the highway.

"This isn't the way it's going to end," Mom said. "As a mom, I should feel if my son is gone. I don't feel it."

Dad pulled off the road into the ditch and drove along it to get as close to the upcoming intersection as he could. He parked—and they ran. As they got closer to the scene, it was hard to tell what was going on at first. They couldn't distinguish between the bus and what was the semi. It quickly came into focus. The roof and the cowling that covered the back of the bus had been ripped off and were lying upside down. The bus was lying on its side, its motor exposed. There were no windows—just rows of exposed seats. There was no front of the bus. There was no driver's seat. The first few rows were missing, too. It was all gone. Green and gold hockey bags were scattered among bags of peat moss that seemed to stretch as far as they could see. Among the bags there were shoes, clothing, and jackets. A trainer's bag.

"There is no way that anyone could have survived this," Mom said to Dad.

They ran closer and stood at the crossroads, trying to make sense of what they saw. It looked like a war zone. It was about 5:30, a little more than half an hour after the crash.

The tractor part of the semi was in the ditch, on its side. The trailer was flipped upside down, surrounded by peat moss.

In a clearing between the bus and the semi and everything else, bodies were lined up in a row, covered with sheets. There were feet sticking out from the sheets. Mom tried to see if any of the pairs of shoes were mine. She saw one brown leather dress loafer that she recognized and she broke down, crying.

She didn't know whether I'd worn black shoes or brown that day, so she tried to hope that she was wrong.

Dad found an EMT.

"We're nurses," he said. "We can help."

"Do you know anybody on the bus?" she asked.

"Our son."

"No," she said. "Just stay here."

"Was anybody taken out of this alive?" Dad asked.

"Yes," she said. "Three people."

"Was Kaleb one of them? Kaleb Dahlgren?"

"I don't recognize that name."

There was a Logan, an Xavier, and a Bryce, the EMT explained. She wasn't sure of anyone else. It was quiet. Eerily quiet. There were no voices, no sounds, beyond the emergency workers moving debris, looking for bodies. Another was found, and my parents watched as another sheet was laid on top. With great dignity, the two first responders gently lifted the body and respectfully laid it beside the others in the row. A paramedic knelt at each body and softly lifted the sheet. He shone a light, searching for life in their eyes, and listened for a heartbeat with a stethoscope. One by one, he covered each body back up and moved to the next.

The row kept growing.

My parents stayed at the scene for nearly half an hour. There were three ambulances and paramedics waiting with stretchers, waiting to be summoned to take somebody away from the scene. They never got called in the whole time my parents were there. It was still sunny, but cold—and getting colder. Dad ran back to the car and drove it closer through the ditch, so they could be warm. While he was gone, Mom answered texts from Tyler Beatch, a friend of ours who used to run the score clock in North Battleford. The world was learning about the crash.

I heard the bus was in an accident. How bad is it?

I'm standing right here. It's bad. It's really bad.

Well, how's Kaleb? Is he there?

I haven't found him yet. There's so many bodies.

Please don't say Kaleb's dead.

I think they're all dead.

When Dad got back, he walked up to Mom, who was still standing there, watching the row get longer.

"Look at all the bodies."

They didn't count the bodies, but the row seemed to stretch forever. A crane arrived to lift the bus, because there were more bodies pinned beneath it.

"You need to go," another first responder told them. "There are families meeting at the leisure centre in Nipawin. You'll get further direction about your son and his condition."

There were other people there, searching, too. My parents ran into Kelly Fiske, Bryce's father. Bryce had survived the crash,

Kelly said. He had been taken to the hospital in an ambulance.

"Have you seen Kaleb?" Dad asked.

"No, I haven't," he said. "I'm trying to figure out who's here and who's not here. They are asking me to identify people that they've taken."

"Have they taken Kaleb?"

"I haven't seen him," Kelly said, again.

My parents got back in the car and realized there was nothing more they could do there. They had to get answers. Dad pulled out of the ditch. Mom called her brother and asked him to go and tell their elderly parents about the crash in person before they heard about it on the news. Then they drove back to Nipawin in a fog of resignation.

How could anyone survive this?

If he's gone, there's nothing we can do.

They contacted more people. My old billet from North Battleford. My dad's co-worker, who had been calling and calling. Erykah, who was at the south side of the scene, got sent on an alternate detour route with girlfriends of some of the other guys on the team because the highway was closed. My parents texted and called her to let her know they had been at the scene.

When they arrived at the community centre in Nipawin, no one there knew anything about the crash. They didn't know why my parents had gone there. It was the wrong place. My parents told the people at the community centre what had happened, and everyone started to panic and cry. People started to make calls, trying to find out where my parents were supposed to go.

My parents broke down there, unable to get answers—not knowing where to find them. Someone at the community centre brought them water and sat them down at a table. Others tried to console them. Finally, a lady hung up her phone and told them they were supposed to go to the Apostolic Church. They wrote down directions and rushed out the door. As they left, they ran into their friends Calvin Hobbs and Scott Thomas, whose son Evan was on our team. Calvin's son Declan was the goalie for the Hawks. They hugged and cried together. Calvin whispered to my father, "I don't know if this is true, but Declan texted me and told me Kaleb was seen at the hospital in Nipawin."

"What do you mean? Where was he seen?" my father asked. "Was he alive? Was he dead?"

"I don't know," Calvin said. "It's just some hope."

Instead of going to the church, my parents drove straight to the hospital. There were ambulances everywhere. They drove up to the entrance to the parking lot, but it was barricaded and they were stopped by security.

"We were told our son is here," Dad said. "He was on the Broncos bus."

"Nobody can get in," the security guard said. "We're not letting anybody in."

Momma Bear leaned over from the passenger's seat and glared at the guard.

"If I find out my son is here, not you or anybody else will stop me from getting into this hospital," she said.

They went to the church to see if they could find some answers there. My girlfriend was already there with some friends and girlfriends of the other players. The entire Nipawin Hawks team was at the church as well—along with the pastor who supported the team throughout the season. Some of the other parents started to arrive. Mom asked everyone she saw what they knew. There had been some survivors, she was told. They were taken to the hospitals in Nipawin, Tisdale, and Melfort—but no one was certain who had survived or where they had been taken. Mom learned that Sean Brandow, our team pastor, was at the Nipawin hospital. She got his number from a Broncos fan, Werner Klinger, who had made the trip out from Humboldt for the game.

When Mom got through to Sean, he told her he wasn't sure if

I was at the hospital or not. He said they were having a hard time determining who was who.

"I'll go see if I can find Kaleb and will get back to you," Sean said.

My parents sat with Xavier LaBelle's family.

"They said that Xavier was one of the players that had been taken to the hospital," Dad told X's father, who is an emergency room doctor. "They said that Xavier was alive."

That's all he knew, though—a vague message relayed from an EMT. Everyone tried to piece together the same fragments of hope.

Mom's phone rang a few minutes later. It was Sean.

"Kaleb's here," he said. "You need to get here right now."

It was now after nine. It had been four hours since they'd first learned about the crash.

Just as Mom hung up, Kurt Leicht—Jacob's father—told my parents he had also heard I was at the Nipawin hospital. More fragments to cling to.

As they rushed out the door, Mom and Dad felt a pang of guilt. They knew that a lot of the families that had gathered were not going to be getting news that their child was alive.

"I feel like we shouldn't be leaving," Dad said. "What about Jacob? We should be waiting with you."

"No," Kurt told him. "We'll find out about ours. You need to go."

This time, my parents and girlfriend had no trouble getting into the hospital. It was chaotic but organized. Everyone was busy, rushing around. Sean met my parents amid the rush.

"I'll take you to Kaleb," he said. "But I have to warn you, he's very ornery."

"What do you mean?" Mom asked.

I was never ornery, so it seemed like a weird comment to make. They brushed it off, just wanting to get to me.

144

The hospital in Nipawin is a small facility. An office had to be cleared of a desk so they could put beds in the rooms, because there wasn't enough space. Sean led my parents into the office room, where I lay on a stretcher. They heard me as they walked down the hallway. A nurse stood next to me. I was covered in blood and had a neck collar on. There was a large bandage wrapped around my head.

I was shouting.

"Fix my fucking head!" I yelled. "It's not rocket science."

My parents had never heard me like that before. It was completely out of character.

They rushed to me.

"Mom, Dad, and Erykah are here, Kaleb," my mother said, putting her hand on me.

"My fucking head," I said. "It hurts."

"Can you move your arms and legs?" Mom asked.

"No, I can't fucking move my arms and legs!" I yelled.

The nurse stepped in.

"Kaleb, you can move your arms and legs," she said. "Show them."

I thrashed my limbs around.

"My fucking head," I said.

My parents asked if I could be given something for the pain, but they were told I wasn't able to take anything yet. The STARS air ambulance was on its way. They were triaging all of the crash victims at the hospital, assessing where they needed to be airlifted to.

My mom put her hand on my cheek. I was freezing. She thought I felt like I'd been kept in a meat locker. Every inch of me felt cold. They found blankets and covered me up. They leaned on me, hugging me, trying to keep me warm.

I kept cursing about the pain.

"My head!" I cried. "Fix my head."

Once I got assessed by the STARS flight doctor, Schaana Van De Kamp, I was transferred from the office into a room in the emergency department. After the pain medications—fentanyl, Dilaudid, and Versed—kicked in, I looked over at my parents, confused.

"Did we win the game?" I asked.

Mom looked startled.

"You guys didn't play," she said.

"What do you mean, we didn't play?" I said.

"You never made it to the game," Mom explained.

I went quiet for a few moments, trying to process what she had said.

"Was it my fault?" I asked.

"Was *what* your fault?" Dad said.

"I got checked from behind," I replied. "Did I turn my back?"

"Kaleb," Dad said. "You didn't get checked from behind. You were in a crash."

Another long pause.

"So, we didn't play?"

CHAPTER 13

—

Tell me I'm dreaming.

I still have no memory of the tragedy that has been imprinted on my life forever.

My parents have had to fill in the blanks for me, as they did that day and would have to do for several days to come.

My parents were told that my neck was broken, I had a fractured skull and a possible brain injury, and both of my femurs were shattered. The right side of my skull had an enormous puncture wound and was partially degloved, meaning a large part of the skin and hair had been torn from my scalp. I had cuts all over my body from head to toe. There were tiny shards of glass under my skin, which would remain embedded in me for years. There was a $5C$ marking next to my left eye—an impression from the decal indicating a seat seven rows ahead of mine. But I was breathing. I was talking. My parents felt the relief of realized hope. They knew that I'd not only survived, but that I had a chance of recovering.

However, as those early minutes together passed, Mom and Dad grew increasingly concerned that I had suffered a traumatic brain injury. The bandages wrapped around my head covered the extent of the physical injury, but my erratic speech, mood, and memory were enough for them to know something was wrong. I was not my normal self—I never swear and for sure don't speak to people in that harsh tone. My face was flat, almost blank. I mostly kept my eyes closed. No expression of emotion on my face. I wouldn't smile or frown. I just was stoic—until another rush of pain would hit, and then I would start excessively cursing again. My parents had never heard me like that. I continued to ask why I was there—and kept believing I had been hospitalized for a game-related injury. As nurses, my parents knew enough about brain injuries, and specifically the issues that can arise from bleeding and intracranial pressure, to know that things can go south very quickly.

A nurse finally gave me something for the pain, which would settle me down for about twenty minutes until I'd need another dose. Once some people had been airlifted to Royal University Hospital in Saskatoon, I was moved out of the office and back into the emergency department at the Nipawin Hospital. A doctor and a nurse were assigned to stay with us the whole time.

Dad's phone kept buzzing. It seemed like everyone we knew was trying to reach us. Word had spread on social media that I had died, and people were sending their condolences. My parents' answering machine was flooded with messages from people who thought I had died. One of my good friends, Wyatt Tyndall, who was at Penn State, called. So did my old roommate Michael Korol, who was studying in Vermont. Wyatt Grant, who was in Phoenix; Connor Ingram, who was in upstate New York State; Jarrett Fontaine, who was in Langley; and Evan Weninger, who was in Omaha, all texted. They were already looking for a flight home, they said. Other good buddies like Adam Ehrmantraut, Brody Doepker, and Josh Roberts were in Saskatoon, trying to find a way to get to me. As we waited for an update, Dad stepped away to call back as many people as he could. While he was away, his phone rang again. The person on the other end of the phone was sobbing. At first, Dad couldn't make out who it was. When the caller composed himself, Dad realized it was Clint Mylymok, the head coach and general manager of the Notre Dame Hounds.

"Please tell me Kaleb's not dead," he said.

"He's not," Dad told him. "But he has lots of injuries."

Clint cried again, unable to hold it in.

"I've got people from the community lined up at my door, asking me how he is," he said, through tears. "I don't know what to tell them."

Dad told Clint about the injuries they knew about. He asked him to share that I was alive and that they were hopeful I was going to make it.

"We don't know the extent of his brain injury, and fractured femurs can create a lot of internal bleeding," Dad said. "We just don't know."

Dad also took calls from other parents on the team, still trying to find out if their sons had made it to the hospital. As those conversations continued, it started to become clear who had survived the crash and who might have died at the site.

"No, I'm sorry," Dad had to keep saying. "Your son is not here."

At that point, though, it was still impossible to know the toll the crash had taken. In the chaos of those first hours, people connected to the team—assistant coach Chris Beaudry, team pastor Sean Brandow, and parents like Kelly Fiske—tried to help identify players who were unable to identify themselves. It was harder than you might expect. We all had bleached-blond hair and were similar in size, and most of us had patchy playoff beards. We were all covered in blood. Some of our injuries were worse than others', further complicating identification. Hospital staff put up signs with the names of the players that they were able to confirm, or believed they had. My parents learned I'd been misidentified several times—and other players had been identified as me, until Kelly Fiske corrected it. All of this added to the confusion for family members trying to figure out what had happened to their loved ones. There was a sign on the door across from us that had *Parker Tobin* written across it. It would take days to confirm that the person they thought was Parker was actually Xavier LaBelle.

My parents waited beside me for two hours until an air ambulance arrived from Medicine Hat, Alberta, because all available emergency air transportation in Saskatchewan was being used. The pilots brought blood from Alberta, because we were in short supply of that, too. They told my parents they would take me to the Royal University Hospital in Saskatoon—which came as a relief, because my parents knew there was a neurology trauma unit there. They would have to take a different route back to Saskatoon, heading west to Prince Albert and then south home, because the crash site had roads in that area closed down. The paramedics took my parents' cellphone numbers and told us they would call if anything happened while we were in the air. They hugged me goodbye, but I was still too dazed to really understand the tears in their eyes.

As they left, Dad saw first responders cleaning out the ambulances that had taken us from the crash site and would now be used to transport the survivors to the airstrip, so we could be taken to the specific trauma centres across the province. He stopped one of the first responders and gave him a big hug, thanking him for taking care of us.

LaBelle—still mistaken as Tobin—and I were flown on the same Alberta air ambulance plane to Royal University Hospital. Xavier was in much worse condition than I was, so he received most of the paramedics' attention as we flew. The paramedics had told my parents they were excited to take the first flight in their brand new "bird." During the flight, I lost control of my bladder and peed all over their bird, so I guess you could say I christened it. When we arrived at Royal University Hospital, I had a catheter in.

My parents were on the road to Saskatoon at the time. They continued to get calls from parents. Now they were starting to confirm the worst—that their sons had passed away. My parents felt an overwhelming sense of survivor's guilt, while still wracked with constant concern about *my* state. At least they had been able to see me—touch me, hug and kiss me—and to tell me they loved me one more time. None of those families had been given that gift.

Minutes from Prince Albert, Dad's phone lit up with a number from Alberta. My parents knew it was one of the paramedics on the air ambulance. Their hearts sank into their stomachs. Fearing the worst, they didn't want to answer. They had to, though. There was no escaping.

The voice came over the speakers in the car. The paramedic told them that they had landed safely in Saskatoon and it had been an eventless trip for me. I was en route to Royal University Hospital.

Another brief rush of relief as they drove through the night.

M y parents went straight to the hospital when they arrived in Saskatoon. Security at the front desk told them to go to the cafeteria, where the families of others in the crash were also waiting. Everyone had to wait together until a doctor was able to come and provide an update on their loved ones' condition. Mom and Dad were close to several of the families of players on the team, but not all of them. They introduced themselves, while trying not to impose. Everyone carried the same look of horrible fear and concern. There were so many tears.

An emergency doctor would come in and ask for each family, taking them off to the side to speak with them alone. Sometimes, they would take the family to see their son. Other times, they still weren't able to go. My parents waited and waited their turn.

They were there for about an hour and a half when a doctor came and led one of the families away to go see their son. They came back into the cafeteria a few minutes later, sobbing.

"That's not our son," they said. "Where is our son?"

They were in obvious distress, breaking down. The person had been misidentified. They'd been given hope, then had it stripped away.

"Where is he?" they cried. "Is he still lying in the field? Why don't you know where my son is?"

A social worker explained that all of the people in the crash had been accounted for. It was just that in some cases, they still were not sure who was who. There was one "John Doe," she said.

But now there were two. At least.

The mother collapsed on the floor.

"This isn't our son," she said again.

There was a discrepancy about the number of people on the bus. The RCMP had been given conflicting information about whether there were twenty-nine or thirty of us. That night, officers returned to the scene with spotlights to do another sweep of the field to make sure no bodies had been missed.

The doctor came and got my parents next. They had to walk past the family on the floor as they sobbed. Another wave of immeasurable guilt hit them. Their son was alive; they were going to see him now. This family had believed that *their* son was alive, too, and now they had no idea. They didn't even know where he was.

I had just been given a CT scan of my head. The doctor confirmed my fractured neck and fractured skull but ruled out the broken femurs. They were led into the emergency area, which had several beds separated by curtains. I still had a flat expression when I saw them.

"What happened?" I asked again.

My parents explained everything to me again, but they didn't tell me about the severity. I didn't yet know that anyone had died.

During a long pause, as they sat beside me, I turned to Dad and told him I had to pee. He said, "Just pee." I paused for several seconds and said, "You want me to pee the bed?" He explained

From the minute I could walk, I was already trying to learn to skate. Hockey was my first love. When I first started playing, I chose the number 16 because it was my dad's number when he played. I wore it all through minor hockey and into junior. I didn't know then how meaningful it would become. [Courtesy of the Dahlgren family]

I didn't grow up with any siblings, but I had friends who were like brothers. We played roller hockey for hours in my basement—and it cost me a few front teeth. But it was much more than just roughhousing. I've been fortunate to forge bonds with buddies that I know will last a lifetime. [Courtesy of the Dahlgren family]

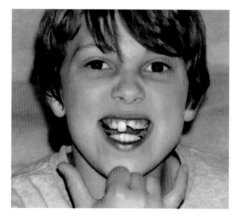

Playing competitive hockey in Saskatchewan sometimes means you have to leave home. I was lucky to find second families in North Battleford and Wilcox while chasing my goals as a hockey player and student. I'll never forget the people I met along the way. [Athol Murray College of Notre Dame]

The smiles in this photo capture what it felt like to be a Humboldt Bronco. As Darcy Haugan always said, "It's a great day to be a Bronco, gentlemen." [Amanda Brochu/Humboldt Broncos]

Growing up with type 1 diabetes, I couldn't find many examples of people with the disease who made it to the highest level of the game, outside of trailblazers like Bobby Clarke. I wanted to start a program to give young people with diabetes the kind of support and inspiration I craved as a kid. One of the main reasons I looked forward to playing in Humboldt was being able to launch Dahlgren's Diabeauties. (Here I am with my first Diabeauty—November 1, 2017.) [Jocelyn Doetzel/Humboldt Broncos]

Bryce Fiske, Stephen Wack, and I took over the Clement family's basement—and became a part of their family. Jaya, Rowan, and Madden were like little siblings to us. In my heart, they'll always be my brothers and sisters. [Carla Clement]

Picking up the "taxi crew"—Morris, Shane, Bernard, and Dallas—became one of the best parts of game day in Humboldt. From our in-depth postgame chats to our passionate Special Olympic floor hockey battles, we all shared a love of the game. I learned so much from the spirit and determination they brought to life each day. [Courtesy of Kaleb Dahlgren]

One of the greatest gifts in hockey is being able to share your love of the game with the next generation. Through our weekly "rec hockey" sessions, my teammates and I were able to pass on the Broncos legacy to kids in Humboldt who were just learning how to play. This kind of connection was central to the community that surrounded the Broncos organization. Giving back fuels the soul. [Carla Clement]

Heading into the playoffs, we carried a simple motto: "Believe." That word hung above our locker room door on a sign with every player's signature on it. To us, it meant we could conquer any obstacle we faced, together. At the time, that meant winning a championship; today, it means so much more. [Mark Cross]

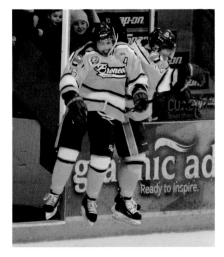

Derek Patter and I always did our "Jump-man" routine after every W, even though short guys can't jump. Whether we played a triple overtime game, volunteered to serve lunch at a local school, or wagered on who would win *The Bachelor*, the Broncos always kept it fun. [Marla Possberg/Humboldt Broncos]

Before we left Humboldt on April 6, our lineup was posted in the locker room. I snapped a quick photo of our names for the game that was never played. [Courtesy of Kaleb Dahlgren]

My parents were among the first to arrive at the site of the crash. The front of the bus was unrecognizable. The field was covered in debris. As they searched for me, my mom took a single photo of the wreckage, still wondering if any of the shoes or clothing scattered in the snow belonged to me. [Anita Dahlgren]

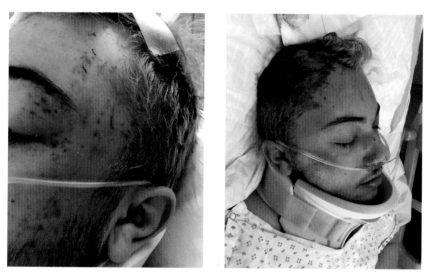

Among all the wounds I suffered in the crash, the most serious was a traumatic brain injury, which wiped out days of my memory—and is something I'll deal with for the rest of my life. I also lost part of my scalp, and the seat number 5C was imprinted next to my left eye. I was sitting in row 12 before the collision. [Left: Erykah Pool/right: Mark Dahlgren]

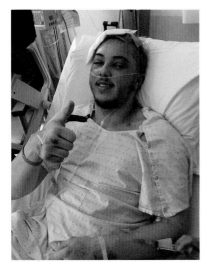

When I first woke up, I tried to be as positive as I could—but the reality of the tragedy didn't fully connect. In the midst of a four-day fog caused by post-traumatic amnesia, my parents had to tell me about the crash several times. Each time, I forgot. [Ron MacLean]

I was wheeled down to the rehab clinic at Royal University Hospital on April 11. Despite being told to take it easy, I kept trying to push my boundaries by doing extra squats and lunges. A short time later, I'd receive a T-shirt from Anze Kopitar and the Los Angeles Kings with their motto: "Enjoy the Grind." It became my mantra throughout my recovery. [Courtesy of Kaleb Dahlgren]

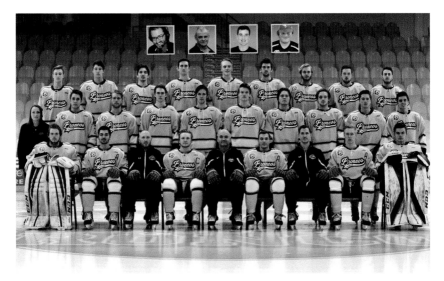

Family first. [Amanda Brochu/Humboldt Broncos]

When my boyhood idol, Joe Sakic, came to visit me at City Hospital, I asked him about the secret to his wrist shot and his approach as a team leader. But the most important message he shared was about his experience as a member of the 1986 Swift Current Broncos team—which was involved in a bus crash that killed four of his teammates—and his advice on how to move forward. [Courtesy of Kaleb Dahlgren]

My biggest supporters in life: Mom, Dad, and Paige. Through thick and thin, they have provided me with unwavering love and guidance. I love you with all of my heart. [Courtesy of Mark Dahlgren]

One of the hardest moments in my recovery was my return to Humboldt for the season opener the following September. We stood in the middle of the ice, as though we were ready to play another game. But the names of the teammates I'd started this journey with a year earlier were now written on banners hanging above the rink. None of our numbers would ever be worn by a Bronco again. [Marla Possberg/Humboldt Broncos]

Even though I haven't been medically cleared to play, I found a new family with the York University Lions while pursuing my education. At York, I follow in the footsteps of Mark Cross, whom I knew as a coach—and who was a leader when he played for the Lions just a few years earlier, leaving a lasting legacy in his wake. [Jojo Yanjiao Qian/York Lions]

A masterpiece for those involved in the crash: thirteen birds in a V formation, carrying on together as one. Sixteen stars, because they shine down on our lives today. I loved everyone on that bus. They will be with me forever. [Calvin Truong, Golden Iron Tattoos]

At the crossroads, I found fragments of the lives of my lost family—reminders of the beautiful lives they lived and the legacies they left behind. It was a chance to say goodbye to the friends that I'll never forget. It was another milestone on the road to healing. [Mark Dahlgren]

that I'd been given a catheter, and that I didn't have to worry about getting off of the stretcher to go to the washroom. I paused again trying to process that, then turned back to him.

"Oh God," I replied, mortified.

Dad smiled, softly—grateful that I was alive, that I still knew who they were, and that we could still share small moments that, one day, we might be able to laugh about.

"Just let it go," he said.

The night blended into morning, like one extended day. Mom, Dad, and Erykah sat next to me. They still hadn't been home, even to change clothes. After a few hours in the emergency ward, I was moved up for close observation in neurology. It was clear that the most serious concern was the trauma to my brain.

During the day, a neurosurgeon gave me an assessment. He poked and prodded me, which pissed me off a bit. I was still quite irritable, according to my parents. I was also still very confused.

"Kaleb, do you know where you are?" he asked.

There was a pause.

"I'm in Toronto," I said.

The doctor looked up at my parents.

"No, Kaleb," he said. "You're not in Toronto. You're in the hospital."

"Yeah," I said. "Okay."

"Do you know why you're here?" the doctor asked.

"Yeah."

"Why are you here?" he asked.

"My penis," I said.

The doctor looked up at my parents again, and they looked at him, startled.

"You're here because of your penis?" he asked me.

"I have other issues," I said. "But mostly my penis."

I was still mortified about the catheter, and for some reason believed that it was the biggest concern at the moment. My parents had to prevent me from trying to pull the catheter out.

During that assessment, the doctor held my leg down and asked me to push up. Then he'd push against my hand and ask me to resist. I was able to do it all, which came as a huge relief to everyone. I wasn't satisfied, though. I was still abrupt and sarcastic. I was annoyed that I was being treated as if I couldn't move.

"I can fucking get up and walk if you want me to," I told him.

"No, no, no," the doctor said. "I don't want you to walk."

"If you just give me ten minutes, I'll get up and fucking walk," I said.

"I just want to see how strong you are," the doctor explained. "I don't need you to walk."

I was still unable to understand the gravity of what had happened. I was frustrated with the way people were talking to me. I was angry about the pain. I was irritated by the neck brace. I was surly because of the drugs.

Everything I said was flat and matter-of-fact, unless I was angry.

I just wanted to play hockey with my team. I just wanted my most important concern to be winning alongside the Broncos. We were supposed to be in Nipawin. We were supposed to win and stay alive. I just closed my eyes—everything went black, and then everything went white—and now I was here, unable to pee on my own and being treated as though I couldn't walk alone, either.

How did this happen?

Later, as I lay there, I grew worried that York University and the other schools I was speaking with wouldn't know that I'd been injured—and that when they did, they would rescind their offers.

Dad told me not to worry about it.

"They'll know that you were in a bus crash," he said.

"How the fuck are they going to know?" I snapped. "They're

out east and in the US—they're not going to know about an accident in Saskatchewan."

I insisted that we reach out to them to let them know I'd been injured but that there was nothing for them to worry about. I'd be back on the ice in time for next season.

"Kaleb," Dad said. "It's okay."

My parents kept trying to change the subject, but I wouldn't let it go until Dad finally agreed to reach out. He connected with the coach at York first. I made him write the email beside me, so I could tell him what to say.

"Tell him I'll be skating again soon," I said. "Tell him that I'll be good for the fall."

Dad agreed to send emails to the other schools as well. He knew it was a ridiculous thing to be worrying about at the time, but it was the only way to appease me.

That Saturday, the day after the crash, my billet mom from North Battleford, Anne Cole, and her sister Donna Weber came to visit. My eyes were closed, but I could recognize them by their voices. It was so nice of them to come, but I was still incapable of showing emotion. Several of my close friends were also able to get into the hospital to see me that day. Adam Ehrmantraut and Brody Doepker, my high school buddies who lived in Saskatoon, came to visit me. They both arranged to FaceTime with Wyatt Tyndall and Michael Korol, who were in the States. We'd all become best friends in Grade 9, and they wanted to reconnect our "Fab Five" high school buddy group. (We thought it was a cool name in high school.) We have remained best friends for ten years now. My old teammate from the Stars, Keegan McBride, stopped by—he'd just returned from a vacation in Mexico—and spent a week seeing me every day. Josh Lilly from North Battleford came to visit as well, dropping off Scooby-Doo snacks for a diabetic brother.

By that time, several of the families of people who had been killed in the crash had learned about their loved ones' fate. It had been a deluge of sorrow. Each visit by the doctor to those waiting in the cafeteria seemed like the revelation of life's cruel lottery. Some of us lived, some of us would never fully recover—and some of us were never coming back. Within the spreading grief, some of the families looked to find comfort in the Broncos who remained. They asked to see the survivors, maybe to find some sense of solace in a connection that could never be stripped away.

When my parents learned that some of those family members wanted to speak with me, they knew they had to give me the most complete picture of the tragedy as they could.

For the first time, they told me about who we lost.

The truth was, at the time, my parents had no idea how widely the news of the crash had spread across the country and around the world. After answering so many calls from people we knew, they stopped looking at their phones. They didn't check the internet. We remained in our own small bubble, trying to figure out how the rest of our Humboldt family had been affected.

Some of the families of the other players started to visit the hospital on Saturday afternoon, wanting to connect with us as they grieved the loss of their sons.

I had kept asking about the others, but my parents and Erykah were still trying to get information about everyone else. Even they didn't know with certainty who had survived and who had passed away. By then, there was confirmation that at least half a dozen people had been killed, but the feeling was that the number was likely higher. The picture was much clearer—although there was still a lot of uncertainty.

"I'm dreaming, right?" I said. "Tell me I'm dreaming."

"Kaleb, you're not dreaming," Mom said.

"No, this has to be a dream. I've just got to wake up," I told her. "I'm dreaming."

They told me that Stephen Wack had been killed. Logan Schatz was also gone. Jaxon Joseph didn't make it, either.

The list just grew.

Darcy Haugan and Mark Cross had died, they told me. Tyler Bieber and Brody Hinz, as well. Glen Doerksen, our bus driver, was also killed. They knew Dayna Brons was in critical condition.

There was still so much pain to come.

They knew that Nick Shumlanski had survived the crash. None of it made sense to me.

"He was right in front of me," I said. "How did we survive?"

I kept piecing together who was sitting where on the bus, realizing how random it all seemed. It couldn't be true. It had to be a dream. I couldn't make sense of it.

My parents kept telling me that it was real.

Then it hit me: I'd never know the reason. It was simply impossible to find a purpose for such a horrific tragedy. It was not, however, hard to find a sense of duty in the aftermath. We were a team. We were family.

Family first.

If I was here and they were gone—if that was the outcome that couldn't be changed—then it was my responsibility to carry on for them. That was the only thing I could do.

"I need to live big, because they can't live their lives," I told my parents. "I need to live *my life* big—for me and for them."

CHAPTER 14

—

I t was difficult to keep track of who had lived and who had died. My mind kept erasing the facts.

After my parents told me the extent of what they knew, the names faded in and out. Stephen Wack, I remembered. My roommate, my good friend. We had made plans for me to visit him in St. Albert that summer.

But Stephen didn't make it. I knew that. It was stuck in my mind.

I'd ask how others were or make a comment about them in conversation, and then catch myself: *Wait, are they here—or are they gone?*

The magnitude of the deaths was difficult to process. I'd ask my parents again, and they'd gently run through the growing list of the living and the deceased.

The brain injury must have affected my ability to retain the information. Or maybe it was the strong pain medications. Or the shock of it all. Maybe it was my mind subconsciously resisting the truth.

There was little time to reflect in those early days after the crash, and maybe that was a good thing.

To complete the night, I had one last check-in. This is what the nurse wrote in my progress notes:

April 7/18 23:10

Numerous visitors this evening. Pt [patient] chatting—some inappropriate conversation with some. Accident hasn't sunk in yet. Conversation is about university, playing hockey + why Nipawin isn't going to play them. Has been told by family + friends re: fatalities + pt spoke of it but no emotion shown. Very thankful for people coming to see him—Very appreciative of care. Lacks some insight. LOC [level of consciousness] name, Saskatoon, when first woke up at 20:00 hours asked pt if in hospital or in shopping mall. Pt picked mall. April 11, 2018, off [on] exact day. Still asking when playing hockey game. Asleep @ the time. Girlfriend + his mom @ bedside.

On the morning of Sunday, April 8—two days after the crash—I was moved from close observation in neurology into a room with three of my teammates—Graysen Cameron, Derek Patter, and Brayden Camrud. It was great to see them again and be in their presence. I was thrilled because I just wanted to be together with my Broncos family.

We were surrounded by pictures and gifts. We were sent tons of food and platters from restaurants, like boxes of pizzas and burgers and fries. We were sent baskets of other necessities, like shampoo, soap, razor blades, and shaving cream from local pharmacies. It overflowed into a spare room next to the area the four of us were staying in. It was absolutely remarkable. We didn't really know where it was all coming from, because we didn't yet understand the magnitude of how the world beyond the walls was reacting to news of the tragedy.

Security was posted at the entrance to the hospital unit on our floor and outside the door of our room, keeping out the media and making sure there weren't too many visitors disturbing us. Even with guards, there were between twenty and thirty people in the hallway almost constantly. It was lovely of everyone to want to see us, but it was also overwhelming. My parents and Erykah had to politely ask people not to visit me, because I was getting too much stimulation from all of the visitors. Even so, there was a line of chairs in the hall, filled with people waiting for a chance to see us. It meant the world that all of my good buddies who had contacted my dad had flown back to Saskatoon to see me. It just goes to show how strong of a bond we all have. Even my friends in Saskatoon would make the effort to be there daily. There was no way I was going to turn them away.

Our area constantly had people coming through. There were so many people coming in and out of our room that I dubbed it the "trap house." Technically, we were trapped in a room, lots of people would come in and out, and we had security at the door— sounded like a trap house to me in my delusional state. It was our little Broncos community.

Some people just peeked in and left, without waking me or disturbing me. They just wanted to see for themselves that I was okay. Sometimes, hospital staff who came in to take care of us would break down in tears.

The only problem was that it still wasn't clear that I *was* okay. I had an MRI done, but I couldn't stay still, so the images were poor and there was no definitive word on the extent of my injuries. We knew I had a fractured skull, fractured vertebrae in my neck, a puncture wound in my head, and degloving of the right side of my head. At the time, I think everyone knew I had a severe brain injury; it just hadn't been medically proven. I was clearly not myself. I didn't really rest, and the more tired I became, the more agitated I was.

One of the players I know on the Nipawin Hawks came by to see me. After we chatted for a bit, I brought up the series that we hadn't finished.

"Are they just going to put you guys through to the finals?" I asked.

"I'm not really sure, Kaleb," he said. "Everything is on hold now."

"They're probably just going to put you through," I said. "You guys are so fucking lucky that we didn't make it, because we were going to beat you that night—and then we would have won the next game, and you guys would have been done."

The poor guy shifted in his chair, not knowing what to do.

"You're right, Kaleb," he said. "That last game was so good. That overtime—it could have gone either way."

"If you guys get put through, you better fucking win it," I said.

"For sure, Kaleb," he said. "We'll do it for you guys. If I brought you a jersey, would you wear our jersey if we made that run?"

I looked at the poor guy like he was nuts.

"Fuck, no," I said.

A few of my former Broncos teammates—guys like Antonio Di Paolo and Sam-Jaxon Visscher, who had been traded during the year—also came to the hospital and stayed with us. They'd end up coming back several days in a row, staying for hours—still part of the family.

I'd always tried to connect with my teammates after a trade, to encourage them and let them know how important their contribution had been. It's a tough situation for any player to deal with. Now I was glad that they took the time to be with their old family.

The hockey world, I learned, extended way beyond former teammates. Hockey is the kind of sport that connects people even if they've never played together. It really is a unique community, and the tragedy had been a devastating reminder of that. We didn't realize it yet, but thousands of people across Canada and many around the globe had placed sticks outside their doors— as a tribute to the people killed and injured in the crash. Social media was flooded with love and support using the hashtags #HumboldtStrong and #SticksOutForHumboldt. Ribbons were worn, stickers were produced, bracelets were made, shirts were created to honour those who passed, and messages were sent. The whole nation was grieving. The world was with us.

Sadly, ours wasn't the first tragedy involving a travelling sports team in Canada. Our tragedy recalled others. The "Boys in Red" van crash in New Brunswick in 2008 killed eight people on their way home from a high school basketball game and left an open wound in the small community of Bathurst. I was visited by Lauralee Davidson, a survivor of a bus crash involving a women's hockey team in Windsor, Ontario, in 2005, which killed four people. Two decades before that, the Swift Current Broncos were involved in a crash that killed four members of the team. That collision—on December 30, 1986—is still remembered by many in Saskatchewan.

The Broncos were en route to play the Regina Pats when the bus they were riding in hit a patch of black ice and skidded off the road, collided with an embankment, and flipped on its side. Trent Kresse, Scott Kruger, Chris Mantyka, and Brent Ruff were killed. Future NHL players Sheldon Kennedy and Joe Sakic were both members of the team.

On Sunday the eighth, Kennedy and a few of his former Swift Current teammates—Peter Soberlak, Bob Wilkie, and Pat Nogier—came by the hospital to visit with us. They told my parents that we could not work through this alone; we need to speak with counsellors or just talk to others about the crash and how we were feeling. Don't ask why it happened, they said; you will never find an answer. Focus on moving on. Wilkie talked about how, after the Swift Current Broncos accident, they were told to go home for a couple of days and get their heads together and come back ready to play. He said most of them just went on an alcohol bender when they were home and then returned and started playing. No one offered to talk with them, no one offered counselling. He said many of the survivors suffered from alcoholism, mental health concerns, and relationship issues, including divorce.

Later that day, we were visited by Glen Gulutzan, then the coach of the Calgary Flames, and Todd McLellan, who was coaching the Edmonton Oilers at the time. They both spent time visiting with us and brought along boxes of Flames and Oilers apparel—T-shirts, hoodies, and toques. Before he left, McLellan told me that if I managed to get to a point where I was able to skate, he'd bring me out to the Oilers' fall camp.

"I'm going to put you on a line with McDavid," he said, "and you can do some reps with the guys."

I looked at him in disbelief.

"You're shittin' me," I said.

McLellan laughed.

"No Kaleb, I'm not shittin' you," he grinned. "You rehab to the point where you can skate, and I'll bring you out."

I nodded.

"You bet, Coach."

It didn't stop there. There was a vigil for the team planned at the rink in Humboldt that night, with several prominent guests from across the country. Many of them came through Saskatoon to see us first.

That afternoon, Erykah told me that we had a mystery visitor coming.

"Who?" I asked.

"I can't say," she said. "It's a surprise."

"I hate surprises," I snapped. "Tell me who it is." I was still irritable and difficult to reason with. It wasn't worth it for her to keep it from me.

"Well, Ron and Don are coming," she said—meaning Ron MacLean and Don Cherry, of *Hockey Night in Canada* fame. That seemed pretty cool to me.

Erykah continued: "And the prime minister is coming."

There was a long pause while I processed the news.

"Trudeau?" I asked, finally.

"Yes!" Erykah said.

"I don't want to fucking see him," I barked. "I'll see Ron and Don—but I'm not seeing Trudeau."

"Kaleb," Dad said, "come on. He's good enough to come. The least you can do is be civil to him"

I dug my heels in.

"No," I said. "What has Trudeau done for the West?"

My parents looked at each other, shocked. Neither knew that I held such strong political views—but everything was coming out now. Dad backed off because he could see how agitated I was getting and he didn't want to get me worked up.

A short time later, a group of security officers came into the room and asked everyone except for parents and the boys to leave. When the room was clear, Trudeau walked in with his son.

The prime minister seemed a bit out of sorts, as though he wasn't quite sure what to do. He had just visited with some of our other teammates who were being taken care of in the intensive care unit. It was clear that the tragedy had affected him.

Dad worried that I was going to go off on a political rant while the prime minister came to greet me. As Trudeau spoke with the others, Dad tried to prep me to meet him—urging me to remain polite.

"You can just stay quiet," Dad said. "I'll talk to him. You don't have to say anything."

Trudeau greeted Brayden, who then spent some time chatting with Trudeau's son about all of the positive things that hockey brings. As the boy turned to leave, Brayden called after him from his bed.

"Hopefully your dad is a better coach than he is a prime minister," he said. That brightened up the room, even though Brayden wasn't really himself when he said it.

Trudeau came over to us next. Dad stood between the prime minister and the bed, trying to shield me from him, just in case

I got going. As they made small talk, Trudeau's son went around him to the foot of my bed. I introduced myself to him.

"Do you play hockey?" I asked.

"Yeah, I play hockey," he said.

"What position?"

"I play defence."

"Oh yeah," I said, nodding. "How many PIMs do you have?"

"PIMs?" he asked.

"Penalty minutes."

He told me he had one penalty, but that he'd scored a few goals and added a few assists.

"I don't care how many points you have," I said. "It's the PIMs that are important, because that means you're standing up for your teammates—and *that's* what matters."

Dad overheard as he tried to make small talk with Trudeau.

Oh no, he thought. *Kaleb just told the prime minister's son to be a goon.*

The group decided to mark the occasion with a photo, which made Dad even more concerned about how I would react. Trudeau stood next to the bed with my family. I remained completely quiet as Trudeau's security detail stood there, watching us.

"Is it okay if I put my arm around you for the picture?" Dad asked him.

"Sure," Trudeau said.

Dad put his arm around the prime minister. I lay there with my eyes closed and no expression on my face as the photo was snapped. In the end, I didn't say a single word to Trudeau. In hindsight, politics and brain injury aside, it was pretty nice of him to visit.

Late that afternoon, there were several periods of apnea when I stopped breathing. My parents had to shake me to get me breathing again, as the nurses rushed over to help. It turned out to be a reaction to the narcotics that I was on, but considering everything that had already happened, it raised even more concerns about my situation. That evening, I was moved out of the shared room with my teammates to undergo close observation because of the episodes.

While we were in the separate room, the vigil was being held for our team back at the Elgar Petersen Arena in Humboldt. Media had come from all over to cover the event. Hundreds of community members and family members of my teammates gathered inside for a service that was broadcast live across Canada. Erykah had set up the laptop for us and streamed the service. I slept through most of it, still dealing with the effects of my medication and finally getting a chance to be in a quiet space.

Standing at a podium above photos of every person involved in the crash, Pastor Sean Brandow spoke passionately about the tragedy—addressing everyone in the arena and watching across the country. He shared that he attended every game and sat behind the bench, where he could see the names on the back of the jerseys. But so much about this team, this community, was the name across the front.

"It's huge, this team. This group of guys that rally together all around this one thing," he said. "I like to look at the names on the back of the jerseys, and I think it's really fitting now. I just want you to know that we hurt with you. Each name represents a family."

Brandow spoke of the enduring pain that the community would face.

"Do you know how Jesus was who he said he was? His scars," the pastor said. "A scar is something that is healed, but still there. This isn't going to go away. But it's not going to be as raw. Can we heal? Yes. Will the scar be there? Yes."

During the service a call went out over the hospital intercom calling for a social worker to come to the ICU right away. My parents' hearts sank. It sounded like another person from the bus had passed away.

In the end, though, it was another heart-wrenching twist in the chaos that follows a tragedy of this magnitude.

The person who was initially believed to be Parker Tobin had regained consciousness and identified himself as Xavier LaBelle. At the same time, Xavier's photo was displayed beneath the podium at the vigil in Humboldt. His father, Paul, was at the arena. He answered his phone at the vigil and learned that his son was alive.

At the same time, tragically, the Tobin family learned that Parker was gone.

That evening, I was alone in the hospital room with Dad. He'd managed to get home for a quick shower during the day, so Mom and Erykah were able to do the same at night. None of them had really slept in more than two days.

As I lay there, I began to fidget. I looked over at Dad and told him I had to use the washroom. I had been so annoyed by the catheter that I kept tugging on it until the nurses gave up and removed it. They would bring a urinal bottle over for me to pee in. Dad picked it up and brought it over to me.

"I'm not peeing in that," I snapped.

"You have to," Dad said. "You don't have your catheter."

"I'm not fucking peeing in that," I repeated. "I'm going to the toilet."

"Kaleb, you can't walk," Dad reasoned. "You're not cleared to walk. You're injured."

I glared stubbornly.

"Well, I'm not peeing in *that*."

Dad called for a nurse, who wheeled in a portable toilet, called a commode, for me to use. I'd have to shimmy out of bed and sit on it. They sat me up and went to slide me over.

"I'm not fucking pissing sitting," I said.

"You have to, Kaleb," Dad said.

Finally, the nurses agreed to wheel the commode into the bathroom. A male nurse stayed with me, holding me up while I peed in the toilet. It was a brief compromise.

But I woke up again in the middle of the night, having to pee again. This time, there were no nurses around.

"Dad, I have to piss," I whispered.

"Okay, I'll go get someone," he said.

"I can fucking walk," I replied, frustrated. "Why won't anybody let me walk?"

Again, Dad tried to explain how serious my injuries were and that the doctors worried that I could make everything worse if I tried to do too much on my own. He wouldn't budge, so I relented and let him call for help. While we waited, I asked if he could help me sit up on the bed, so we'd be ready when the nurses arrived. He got up and helped move me so that my legs dangled off the bed as I sat on the edge. Dad went to help the nurse as she brought the commode into the room. He had his back to me.

In a flash, I pushed myself forward off the bed and started walking towards the bathroom.

Dad saw me and ran to grab me, worried that I might fall. He twisted my gown and held me from behind as I kept moving as fast as I could. I was determined to piss alone.

I walked into the bathroom with Dad still hanging on, and flipped on the light switch. I turned and looked at myself in the mirror. My head was wrapped in bandages, which were blotched with blood, pieces of my matted blond hair sticking out and small pieces of glass still embedded in my scalp. My face and hands were covered in marks and scratches. I was bruised and pale.

"Fuck, do I look like shit," I said.

Dad helped me over to the toilet, still holding on to me. I stood there.

"Are you going to piss, or what?" he asked.

"I'm not going to piss with *you* here," I said.

He sighed.

"Kaleb, I'm not leaving. If you fall, you're going to get seriously hurt," he argued. "I'll turn my head. Just piss."

I pushed back.

"I'm *not* going to piss with you standing here," I said.

Dad threatened to get the nurse, but he knew he wouldn't be able to get me to agree to her being in the room. He gave in and stepped outside, terrified that I was about to hurt myself. As soon as he heard the flush, he rushed back in and tried to help me again. I stopped at the sink and gave my hands a long, proper rinse with soap and fiddled around with my hair—all out of stubbornness. Dad followed me back, arms poised in case I slipped. When I got to the edge of the bed, I realized I just didn't have the strength to pull myself back up.

"Okay," I said to Dad. "You're going to have to help me now."

On Monday morning, I was moved back into the same room with my teammates. We each had our own section, which was divided by curtains that could be moved so we could hang out. The other guys had various injuries, but none of them had serious brain trauma. They all conversed with ease. They were actually very concerned about me because I was acting so out of character. Patter and Cameron even commented to Dad that they hadn't heard me swear all season.

During this time, my blood glucose levels were running very high because of the trauma and stress on my body from the injuries, lying in bed with no physical activity, and eating poorly. The hard part was that my parents did not know my insulin-to-carbohydrates ratio to administer insulin. They had to trust me and my brain-injured state of mind to tell them the correct dosage, which was a recipe for disaster.

It was truly humbling to see how many people wanted to reach out after the crash. It was clear that the tragedy had impacted anyone who'd travelled on a bus with a team or with school—or for whatever reason—and they felt the magnitude of what had occurred.

Perhaps the most impactful visitor, to me, was Hayley Wickenheiser. She came to visit us on the Monday, after the vigil. She had played on Team Canada with Fiona Smith, who was the sister of one of my Midget AAA coaches in North Battleford, Martin Smith. Hayley reached out to them to see if she could arrange a visit with me and the other players. She is an absolute hockey legend. Trudeau and his office had actually reached out to Hayley before he came to visit us and told her that he wanted to come to the vigil, but wanted her advice on how to do it. She advised him to keep a low profile and blend in quietly, which is what he did, sitting at the very back of the rink and avoiding all press.

Imagine the prime minister calling you up for guidance. That's how much respect Wickenheiser has earned.

Hayley grew up in Saskatchewan, so the crash had a personal impact on her. Her presence had a huge impact on us. She'd end up coming back to see us several times while we were in the hospital and later visited my house. She even took a photo in my number 16 jersey. Of all the influential people who came by to see us, I have to say that I think meeting Hayley was one of the biggest honours.

"I can't believe you're here," I said to her at the end of that first visit. "Can I just give you another hug before you go?"

Four days after the crash, I was cleared to begin some light physio—which meant I could get out of the trap house and take a walk around the floor. It put me in a better mood. I wore a turquoise gown with yellow pyjama pants, with a wide black belt tightened around my lower back for support. I wore the brown slippers my parents had brought me from home. There was still a white bandage across the right side of my head.

The physiotherapist quizzed me as we walked.

"Can you tell me what day it is?" she asked.

I looked down at my hands, trying to count the days on my fingers.

"Is it the eleventh?" I asked.

"Close!" she said.

"Is it the tenth?"

"It is!"

"I thought that was *yesterday*," I said. "Oh my goodness. It's been the tenth every day for the past six days."

In the moment, it didn't even register that the accident had happened only four days earlier.

"It's like *Groundhog Day*," she joked, referring to the movie in which Bill Murray keeps repeating the same day.

"Honestly, it doesn't change," I said. "It's the tenth *every* day."

As we continued down the hallway, the physiotherapist asked me to walk in a straight line, across a pattern on the floor.

"This is going to suck," I said.

My entire body ached and I laboured as I moved my legs. But the pain was much worse in my neck and across my shoulders, and my lower back throbbed. A CT scan revealed two fractured ribs and a broken vertebra, which I'd sustained while playing and which hadn't yet been discovered. Two weeks later, another MRI would reveal four more fractured vertebrae.

An X-ray was taken to see if I needed surgery to stabilize the fractures in my neck. It turned out the fractures were stable because of the muscle in my back and neck, so I didn't need the neck brace any more. I was told that the muscle likely prevented me from being paralyzed. I have to thank Chad Martin for laying that foundation.

Despite the pain, it felt good to be up and moving. After passing the sobriety test, she had me place a hand against the wall and lean forward and balance on one foot. I passed that test, too—but I was still a long way from recovery.

The thing is, I still have no memory of any of this. Not a *single* moment. These are all just stories that have been told to me, filling in the blank pages of my mind.

I have no memory of cursing about Trudeau. I can't recall chatting with Sheldon Kennedy and learning about the Swift Current crash. I don't remember asking Hayley Wickenheiser for a hug. I don't remember the first time I learned about who had died.

Or the second time.

Or the third.

I don't remember the first time I wondered why it had happened to *them* and not *me*. Or when I vowed to live big in their honour. And I don't remember the deep sobs coming from outside our room, in the hallway. I didn't hear Dad consoling the weeping man he found standing there—or asking him who he was.

"I'm a first responder from Tisdale," the man replied. "I was *there*."

"Are you okay?" Dad asked him.

"I'm sorry," the man said. "I'm sorry. I just can't seem to get over this. I can't sleep. I can't eat. I just can't control my emotions."

Dad put his hand on the man's shoulder.

"I just thought that, maybe, if I came to see some of the guys it might help me," he said.

"Well, do you want to meet our son?" Dad asked. "He's not himself. He's quite vulgar—but he *is* kind of funny."

The man smiled through his tears and said he would like that.

Dad led him into the trap house and opened the curtain around my bed. The man took one look at me and began to weep.

"Are you okay?" Dad asked, cradling him.

"That's *Kaleb*," the man said.

Dad was startled.

"How do you know Kaleb?" he asked.

"He was the first one I helped when I got there," the first responder cried. "I'll never forget Kaleb."

I can't remember that, either.

I was awake when the first responder arrived at the crossroads. He found me on my hands and knees, trying to help my teammates on the ground. I'd taken my jacket off and placed it on one of them.

"Are you hurt?" the first responder asked me.

I turned to him. My face was scratched and there was blood running from my head where a large piece of debris punctured the side of my skull.

"Where are you hurt?" he asked me again.

"My head, my neck, my back," I told him.

"We're going to put you on a backboard," he said.

"No, I'm fine," I said. "We have to help everyone."

I was shaking.

"We're *going* to help them. But let's get you help first." He got me to lie on the ground. "Wait here."

He ran to get his partner and a backboard. I lay there, shaking in the cold. I was trying to get back up when he returned.

"You have to stop moving," he said.

They placed me on the backboard, gently, secured the straps, and lifted me up.

"Make sure I'm on tight," I said. "Don't drop me. I think I've had enough today."

The first responders smiled back and managed a small laugh—and for a moment, they felt light and calm. As they carried me to the ambulance, I introduced myself.

"My name is Kaleb Dahlgren," I told them. "I'm twenty years old and I'm a type 1 diabetic."

They loaded me into the ambulance.

"Thank you," I said. "Take care of everyone else."

He smiled softly, closed the door, and turned to his partner. "I'll never forget Kaleb," he said. Then he turned back to the chaos of the crash, to save whatever lives remained—and to feel the agony of the ones that didn't.

A s the first responder told the story through his tears next to my bed at Royal University Hospital, my parents realized they had arrived at the scene shortly after he had first arrived and that I was actually inside one of the ambulances next to them as they searched for me.

We visited for a while—and I'd forget the entire thing. But the first responder would come back many times over the course of my stay in the hospital and even later when I returned home. He'd tell me the story about how he met me in the field and fill the blanks of the memories I couldn't see. I think it was cathartic for both of us.

I had so many questions for him. I still have tons of questions that will never be answered.

CHAPTER 15

—

On the morning of April 11, our family doctor, Richard Leakos, called Dad. He'd been sent the results of my latest MRI. We learned that the impact had caused bleeding in ten different parts of my brain. The bleeding had stopped, which was a positive sign. But the damage was potentially catastrophic.

"I'm so sorry," he said when Dad answered the phone. "It's terrible."

At first, Dad thought Dr. Leakos was just talking about the collision, but he continued.

"I'm so sorry about Kaleb's injuries," he said. "Is he awake?"

Dad told him I was.

"Does he remember who you are?"

"Yeah," Dad said. "Why are you asking me this?"

"I'm just looking at his MRI," Dr. Leakos said.

"Is it bad?"

"Yeah. It's really bad, Mark—I'm so sorry."

"Well, *how* bad?"

"Is he talking?"

"Yes, he's seeing the physiotherapist today."

"No," Dr. Leakos replied. "He *can't* be."

"He's up, he's walking, he's talking," Dad said. "He knows people."

"That just can't be," he said.

"Well, you've got to come and see him."

Later that morning, Dad surprised me with a new iPhone that had been given to us by SaskTel. We still didn't have our personal belongings from the scene, and as a joke, Dad had given me a flip phone and said it would have to do for now. I was okay with that, and I thanked him, but then he laughed and handed me the brand new iPhone 10 from SaskTel. Now I could connect to Instagram, Twitter, and Facebook, where thousands of messages from people were waiting for me. I fiddled with the new phone for a bit, ate lunch, and took a long nap.

When I woke up a few hours later, my parents were sitting beside the bed. They looked broken. Something terrible had happened. I was confused. I didn't know where we were—or why.

Is this a dream?

Is this a hospital?

Did we win our game tonight?

"Kaleb, there was no game. There was a crash," they said as tears started to flood.

My mind was completely blank. My parents saw the confusion on my face. They looked very concerned. "What's going on?" I asked. "Where is everybody else?"

"Kaleb, we already told you," Dad said. "Don't you remember?"

I didn't remember and still thought I was dreaming. "Give me my phone."

As I unlocked a random iPhone 10, my nightmare became a reality.

"Kaleb," Mom said, "Dayna passed away today."

"What?" I said.

Dayna had been cared for in the ICU, in a medically induced coma, and had undergone two surgeries. Sadly, her injuries were too severe to overcome. Her death raised the number of fatalities in the tragedy to sixteen.

But when I woke up, I didn't know that *anyone* had died. I didn't even remember that we had been in a collision.

I learned about the horror all over again. This time, I'd never forget.

I only had a few minutes to try to process the news. I had to be wheeled over to my first legitimate physio session in the gym at the hospital. I was a bit indignant about the wheelchair, considering that I was about to work through a series of squats and lunges.

The physiotherapist kept asking me to slow down and take it easy, but I kept pushing myself to the limits of what I was able to do. I hopped on a stationary bike, until she told me to get off. Then I stepped onto the climber—and again, she had to tell me to stop. I wanted to work as hard as I could to get back on the ice. I felt like I had to do it, for me *and* for the team.

Later that day, Dr. Leakos came to the hospital. Even though I'd blanked out, I was functioning well again. He asked me questions about my life, and I had answers for everything. He couldn't believe it. When Dad walked him out, Dr. Leakos teared up.

"With his injuries, Kaleb shouldn't be functioning like this," he said. "It's a miracle."

In those first hours after being told about the accident again, I wasn't able to comprehend the gravity of it. It hit me later that night.

I picked up my phone—which *wasn't* my phone—and again I had to fight to remember that Dad had brought it to me earlier that day.

I opened up Instagram and scrolled through the photos of my teammates. I visited each of their Facebook and Twitter pages. As I lay in the hospital bed, exploring the happy moments of their lives, remembering the unique points of their personalities, the reality that they weren't coming back settled in. More than all the physical pain and cognitive confusion I endured through those first days after the crash, this was by far the hardest moment. The enormity of this loss was overwhelming. It rushed at me and I was overcome with emotion. Tears ran down my cheeks. I realized that I had another fracture—my heart.

In that fog of grief, I went to text Wacker. I typed out a message—and then I remembered that he was gone. I deleted the message and put down my phone. The room was quiet. I looked around at my two teammates and thought about the others who hadn't survived.

How can this be real?

Why am I still here?

And why aren't they?

We were so fortunate. So lucky. It was all so random.

Amid that fog, I felt full of gratitude. I was fortunate to have known every person on that bus—the sixteen who were gone and the twelve others who were still here.

We arrived as strangers but will forever be a family.

For my parents, each day blended into the next, as though they were stuck in a constant haze. It was overwhelming. They just kept moving through the days, grateful that I was alive but uncertain about my condition—and broken over all of the deaths and the families that would be forever altered by the crash.

The funerals began the week after the crash. I wanted to attend each one, but I couldn't get clearance from the specialists. My brain injury still had the doctors concerned, and they didn't want me to be overstimulated.

It broke my heart not to be able to attend any of them.

My parents also wanted to be at each funeral, but they didn't want to leave me alone at the hospital, so they alternated—one would go to a service while the other stayed with Erykah and me.

Those were among the toughest times for them. There was

pretty much a different funeral every day. Going to that many in such a short time was shattering.

A few were in Humboldt, at the Elgar Petersen Arena. Throughout the hour-long drive, Dad saw green and gold signs, balloons, and hockey sticks displayed on farm laneways and along the side of the road. When he arrived in Humboldt, every tree, fire hydrant, and lamppost was decorated with green and gold ribbons. At the rink, he walked by the home bench and looked up at the seats where he and Mom sat. A week earlier, they'd been there to watch a triple-overtime game where everyone was on the edge of their seats, cheering, without any concept of what lay ahead. It was heavy.

Other funerals were in Saskatoon. Evan Thomas's was at SaskTel Centre, where the Saskatoon Blades of the WHL play. The weight of each of them—of being among thousands of people in shared agony—compounded and compounded. There was no way Mom or Dad could each have attended all of them. It was just too much. There were too many lives stripped away. Too many questions that could never be answered.

Several more took place in Alberta, where a bunch of the players were from. The Broncos chartered a flight to Edmonton so that families of the team could attend a group of services there. Dad and Erykah made the trip. My family also arranged for Antonio Di Paolo, a former Bronco who had been traded that season, to come on the flight.

When they landed in Edmonton, they were greeted by fire trucks lined up with their ladders high in the air, adorned with massive Canadian flags. The families were loaded into SUVs that followed a police escort to Rogers Place, the Oilers' brand new arena. A service was held for Stephen Wack, Parker Tobin, Logan Hunter, and Jaxon Joseph. Conner Lukan's funeral was in Slave Lake the next day.

Even though the grief felt like too much to bear at times, the support from across the country helped provide a lift. Whenever Mom and Dad drove down the road from the hospital, there were green and gold signs for the Broncos, everywhere. Every business with an automated sign had a message of love for Humboldt. They'd already seen pictures of the thousands of sticks that had been left on porches across Canada. One day, as Dad was driving, he heard people calling in on the radio, talking about how they could support us. They weren't even playing music. Everyone just called in to reminisce about people they knew who were on the bus and shared happy memories of them. It was a station Dad always listened to, so he called in, too. The hosts were so surprised to hear from him that they spoke on the air for a while, with Dad thanking all of the listeners for their love and support.

It felt like the whole country was hugging us.

On April 12, Dad went home just long enough to get changed, then he stopped in at a Tim Hortons to grab some coffees before returning to the hospital. When he walked in, every person in the place was wearing a hockey jersey. Across Canada that day, people had worn their favourite jersey to work or school in a show of love for Humboldt. Dad's eyes welled up as he stood at the cash, ordering his coffee.

"Oh my goodness," he said to the person taking his order. "I think you guys are doing this for us." He turned and walked up to one of the other customers.

"My name is Mark Dahlgren," he said. "My son was on that bus and he survived. *Thank you.*"

Then he went up to every single person there, shaking their hands. There were a lot of tears in that Tim Hortons before he left.

A few days later, on April 15, Hayley Wickenheiser returned. This time, she brought her friend, Canadian country music star Paul Brandt. He sat in the middle of the trap house, pulled out his guitar, and asked if we had any requests. Derek Patter, Graysen Cameron, and Ryan Straschnitzki were all there. We each had our Broncos jersey hung above our hospital beds. Brayden Camrud, who had been discharged, came to visit. It was incredible.

I asked Brandt to play "Convoy," an old classic about a trucker's life on the road and one of my favourite songs. Later, during his song "Alberta Bound"—a love letter to his home province—Brandt paused in mid-verse to make sure Camrud and I knew that a chinook was a warm wind. I laughed and assured him that I did. The other guys, all from Alberta, had a chuckle at our expense.

Brandt also played us a moving acoustic version of one of his best-known songs, "Small Towns and Big Dreams," turning the lyrics into a tribute to rural communities like Humboldt where giant hockey dreams are born.

I grew up in a small town, Brandt sang. *A hockey night in your hometown kind of place . . . That's where I come from, that's who I am . . . I've been around the world, no matter anywhere I go—even out in Humboldt—I found my kind of folks . . . That's where I come from, that's who I am.*

It was a touching concert for just the five of us and our families, sitting in a small hospital room, living through a nightmare, but still clinging to beautiful dreams.

The outpouring of support continued. My Notre Dame jersey sat vigil in the church at the campus in Wilcox the entire time I was in the hospital.

My spirits were lifted when Shumlanski, Gomercic, and Camrud came to visit us in the hospital. The Vancouver Canucks' Derek Dorsett and Derrick Pouliot, two Sask guys, also stopped by to visit. I received touching personal messages from Steven Stamkos and Patrice Bergeron (one of my favourite current players). Mike Fisher called. Brayden Schenn connected with me through his sister Madison, who is a good friend of mine. Sidney Crosby sent signed pictures for each of us and a Pittsburgh

Penguins jersey signed by every player on the team. The NHL sent us the Stanley Cup, which I posed with—giving a thumbs-up—in my hospital bed. Bobby Clarke, the Flyers legend who also has type 1 diabetes, called me with a personal message of support and had his daughter Jody send me a tonne of Flyers gear. (I received so much gear from NHL teams that people might think I attended an actual training camp.) A segment on *Hockey Night in Canada* spoke about the call from Bobby and the show wished me well. Max Domi, whom I'd spoken with in the past because of our mutual experiences with diabetes, also sent me a signed jersey. George Canyon, another Canadian country star—and a diabetic—called to say he was thinking about me. John Chick, a CFL star and another diabetic, called to wish me well, too. I told him I was living the hospital lifestyle and that the trap house was "pretty bumping," and that we had security at the door and sometimes they would have to ask people to leave. Chick laughed, then asked Dad if I was "out of it." Dad chuckled and told him it was just me and that everything I said was completely accurate.

Then, on April 17, Connor McDavid and Ryan O'Reilly dropped by to meet with us. They had both visited the people in the ICU first, which clearly had impacted them. They brought signed hockey sticks and offered their support.

The other guys in the trap house were being released to hospitals in Alberta so that they could be closer to home as they recovered. I still wasn't cleared to go home, though. I needed to be constantly monitored by neurologists. Other patients would soon be admitted into our room—and I didn't like the idea of that at all.

I felt trapped in the trap house. I wanted out.

After some discussions about my care, my parents made arrangements for me to be moved to City Hospital, another facility in Saskatoon, which focuses on rehabilitation.

Before I left, I made one last round of visits with everyone who was still recovering in the Royal University Hospital. I would often go and visit teammates who were dispersed throughout the hospital to see how they were recovering and check in on them. For me, this would be one last farewell as we all started to go our separate ways. Then I returned to the trap house and grabbed my belongings.

Life started to become a bit more normal with the move to City. My parents and Erykah no longer stayed the night in uncomfortable chairs beside me. Instead, they'd come first thing in the morning and head home for supper. Erykah was still with me all day every day, and she helped with things like cutting my nails, picking glass out of my head, and washing my hair. She was a constant support and never left my side the whole time I was in the hospital, which I am thankful for. Erykah's parents, Chris and Danielle, and her brother Nikhil came from Swift Current to spend a week with us at Royal University Hospital—and other members of her family came to visit as well.

While I received so much support, I saw that many other people in the hospital were not as lucky. They looked lonely and depressed, just trying to survive the day. One elderly lady who was in my room at Royal University Hospital for a time did not receive any visitors at all. It broke my heart.

I began a serious regime of daily rehab, with the doctors trying to get me to a place where I could just function on my own—while I was working to get back to the ice. The rehabilitation unit was on the seventh floor and overlooked Kinsmen Park and the South Saskatchewan River, which flows through the centre of Saskatoon. The unit has thirty-five beds and cares for patients with numerous injuries, including spinal cord injuries, acquired brain injuries, and strokes. There was a gym and lots of exercise equipment, as well as a kitchen where they would assess your ability to make meals and perform household chores. The days were jam-packed with assessments and physical rehabilitation.

Things went well. I broke several records in various testing, like reaction and organization. While at City, I had my first haircut since the accident, from my dad's hairstylist, Collin, who came in to see me. Aidas, my massage therapist, also came into the hospital to get the blood flowing to different areas that might have had less circulation. While he was giving me a massage, the portable table he brought collapsed and I fell to the floor. It became a huge ordeal, with nurses rushing to the room to assist me and incident reports, even though I was totally fine. Poor Aidas messaged my dad for days afterwards, making sure that I was okay.

In the end, I stayed at City Hospital for ten days before I was finally allowed to go home. A total of three weeks in the hospital. The day before I was released, a benefit concert was organized for Broncos families. A few dozen current and former NHL players, like Shea Weber and Brendan Gallagher, were in attendance, too. The night before the concert, there was a special dinner for all of the families. I really wanted to attend. I was so sick of being cooped up in a hospital and frustrated that I hadn't been at any of my friends' funerals. The doctors knew that it was important to me, so they granted me a day pass. I was able to go home, shower, and change there for the first time since the crash.

While I was away from the hospital, Joe Sakic—my all-time favourite player—stopped by City Hospital to visit with the Broncos who were there. I missed him.

At the supper that night, there were probably 250 people. It was a huge event. Right away, I told my parents that I needed to go and speak to all of the Broncos families in attendance. First, it was important to me that I see each of the sixteen angel families and offer my condolences. I spent about twenty minutes chatting with Darcy's father, Leroy.

Soon, we were called to sit down for dinner. I started to get angry. I wanted to keep talking to the families. I wanted to speak to each one before dinner began. I was determined.

"I'm not sitting down," I told my parents. "Now that I've

started, if I talk to one, I've got to talk to them all." I was worried that the families I hadn't spoken to were going to think I didn't care about them. I didn't want anyone to get that idea.

"Kaleb, it's okay," Dad said. "Just come and sit down."

We argued briefly before I agreed. But as we ate, I kept thinking that all of the families were looking at me—that they were angry that I hadn't come to see them.

I'm here and their loved one is not, and at the very least, I owe it to them to speak with them before I sit down to eat.

Then I started to worry more.

If it takes me twenty minutes to speak to each one, it's going to take me a lot more than three hours to speak to all the families here. We don't have time for that. The event will be over. And I still have to talk to all the families of the other survivors. There just isn't enough time. Why am I eating?

I stood up again. I was going to keep talking to the families.

"Kaleb," Dad said, "it's okay. Please sit down."

"Look at them looking at me," I said. "I won't be able to talk to them all."

"If you don't get to talk to them, don't worry about it," Dad said. "It's all right."

"What do you mean, don't worry about it?" I snapped. "It's not right. That's not right. The *right* thing to do is talk to them all."

"Let's go into the hallway," Dad said.

The four of us got up and left the table. In the hallway, we decided that it was best if I just left. I felt I had let the sixteen angels down and that I wasn't a good leader that night. I worried that the families would think less of me. I just wanted to offer my condolences and love to each of them so badly. Erykah drove me back to the hospital before dinner finished. Once we got in the vehicle, I settled down immediately.

I wasn't able to be rational because of the weight of the emotion of being with all of the families at the same time. It was way too much for me that soon. After I left, though, the NHL players who were in town came into the dining hall to mingle with everyone. Mom and Dad chatted with several of them, telling Todd McLellan and Glen Gulutzan the story of how I'd forgotten that they had visited and that when they told me, for the second time, that I might get to skate with McDavid, I said, "You're shittin' me." They had a good laugh, because it was exactly what I'd said to McLellan when he told me I could come to training camp.

Later, Dad felt a tap on his shoulder. He turned around.

"Hi, are you Mr. Dahlgren?" the person asked.

Dad looked him up and down.

"Oh my God . . . Joe Sakic," he said.

"Yeah," Sakic said. "It's Joe."

He asked if I was still around. He'd heard that I was a big fan—but he'd missed me at the hospital and wanted to chat. Dad told him that I'd had to leave early. He offered to bring Sakic to meet me in the morning, but he had to catch a flight first thing.

"Is there any way you could take me there tonight when this is done?" Sakic asked.

Dad knew security at City Hospital was pretty strict about visiting hours, but this was Joe *frickin'* Sakic.

The event ended shortly after ten. Sakic found Dad and asked if they were still on. They went out to the car—to *our* car. Mom sat in the back seat, but Sakic insisted that he take the back seat. She fought back and said no way—and they went back and forth until Dad finally said, "Joe, you're not going to win this."

So, Joe Sakic relented and rode shotgun as they drove to City Hospital to see me.

They arrived after 10:30 and the door was already locked. Dad pressed the buzzer, and an older lady came to the door.

"We're here to see Kaleb Dahlgren," he said. "He's on the rehab floor. I know it's past visiting hours, but we really need to see him."

The lady pursed her lips.

"I'm his dad. He was with us earlier, but he had to come back early," Dad pressed. "I'm a little worried about him."

"Visiting hours are over," she said.

Dad continued. He was with Joe *frickin'* Sakic, and he wasn't going to let me miss this.

"He's a Humboldt Bronco," Dad said. "And, you know, it would just be nice—"

"Well," she said. "We're really not supposed to . . ."

Dad moved aside so the lady could see his guest.

"This guy beside me is Joe Sakic—a Hall of Famer," he said. "He wants to see my kid, and if *Joe Sakic* wants to see my kid, we're gonna see my kid."

The lady looked closer.

"Oh my God," she said. "You're Joe Sakic!"

That changed everything.

"My husband's not going to believe that Joe Sakic was here," she said. "Well, okay, if you guys go in, and are quiet, I'll let them know you're coming straight into the room."

And that's how I came to be sitting next to my boyhood idol.

I asked Sakic about the secret to his wrist shot, and he gave me a few tips. We spoke for a while about leadership. I wanted to know what it took to be the kind of leader that he was.

Then Sakic told me about being a member of the Swift Current Broncos—and about losing his teammates in that horrible crash three decades earlier.

"I've been through this," he said. "You cannot change what happened."

I nodded.

"What you've got to do is still be a leader and lead by example," Sakic said. "Be strong for those who aren't here. Live your life to the fullest for them."

That night, after Sakic, Mom, and Dad left the hospital—and

after the lady at the front desk got a photo with a Hall of Famer for her husband—I lay in bed and thought about what he had said. I thought about all the pain I was in. I thought about my brain and the uncertainty around the extent of the damage I'd endured.

I would have taken on so much more, I thought, *if it meant the sixteen could still be alive.*

I couldn't, though. There was no way to change what happened. The only thing to do now was to remember each of the sixteen who died—and be thankful that I had had the chance to be part of a family with them. To carry them with me every day.

As I'd told my parents when I first woke up: I need to live, *now*, for them.

CHAPTER 16

▬

After you survive a tragedy, it's amazing how much more you notice the little things in life. Everything takes on new meaning.

In the weeks after I was released from the hospital, I started to find beauty in places I hadn't before. At the time, I couldn't walk down the street in Saskatoon without someone wanting to stop and talk to me. I'd become a celebrity for all the wrong reasons. It was a lot to deal with, so I sought a quiet place where I'd be able to take a deep breath and reflect.

I found it next to the Broadway Bridge. The Saskatoon landmark stretches over the South Saskatchewan River. There's a nice spot on the bank next to the bridge where you can sit and look across the river at the city as cars pass by overhead. It's a calm and peaceful place—and I found solitude there.

This quiet spot gave me space to think about the crash alone. It was an escape, in a sense—even though there was no escaping the reality of what had happened. Maybe it was about finding perspective, more than anything. It was about noticing the beauty in the small things.

The Broadway Bridge is a beautiful piece of architecture, with arches that hop across the river like a skipping rock and trusses that reach up to support safe passage above. It was built during the

Great Depression to provide employment. It was created to help people through difficult times.

There are birds on the Broadway Bridge. They perch on the rails along the roadway, resting together until it's time to fly away. Each time I'd return to the bridge, the birds would be waiting there. And each time, I'd watch them soar into the sky.

These are the things I noticed after the tragedy stripped everything else away. The birds, the sky, the breeze on my face, the stars at night, and the stillness of the dark. I noticed the way that light cuts through clouds and scatters in glistening specks across the water.

I'd sit there and think about all the small things that make life's big picture so beautiful. I'd think about the twenty-nine lives that sat together on a bus on a cold April afternoon—and about all the lives that were connected to us. The people in the front office, the workers in the rink, the fans in the stands. I'd think about the people of Humboldt—the parents, the kids, the lives that shared the weight of this pain.

We were all a team. We were one.

I'd watch the birds fly away and think about the lives that remained—wondering where they'd go and what they'd do with their chance to soar away. I'd look up at the stars and see them sparkle against the endless dark. They were so far away, yet we could still see their constellations, still trace their light—still be guided by their presence.

Those images connected with me. They helped me find some sense of hope and purpose in the wake of a tragedy that should never have happened.

This is a chapter that should never have had to be written. But it has to be. It's the hardest one I'll write.

I wanted it to be the most beautiful chapter ever created. I wanted it to tell the story of the beautiful lives that were taken away. I wanted it to capture every detail of the legacies they left behind.

It's impossible, though. There is no way to bottle up the enormity of a life, just as there is no way to contain the majesty of the stars. You just let their light find you in the dark, and live in their wonder.

I have the Broadway Bridge tattooed on my arm. There's a stick and puck on the frozen ice along the river, displaying our bond shared through hockey. The skate marks signify the game we never played and the scars etched onto my soul. Grass peeks up from the side of the ice, paying homage to the communities we were rooted in. There are thirteen birds flying away from the bridge, into the sky in a V formation. Thirteen lives, given the gift of future days. They move forward with the path of stars radiating just above. There are sixteen of them. Forever glowing.

There's something so beautiful in the way a single life can touch your soul. There are literally eight billion people in this world. I'm grateful for the fact that I was able to have such a great connection with sixteen individuals who aren't here today, and knew them and loved them for who they were. I think it's something so special, and something that a lot of people take for granted.

What follows is just a fraction of a portrait of the people we lost—an incomplete picture, taken from the fragments of their time on Earth, which I was fortunate to briefly share.

Tyler Bieber, 29

Tyler would often travel to our away games and provide play-by-play for Broncos fans when he didn't have other volunteer commitments. At our last game before Christmas break, I had an injured wrist and wasn't playing, so Tyler asked me to join him for an interview during our team warm-ups. I agreed to go up to the booth. It turned into a ten-minute chat, and I had a great time talking with him. Afterwards, we spoke more about his life and what had prompted him to get into sports broadcasting. I ended up staying in the booth for a little bit longer because Tyler invited me to join him as colour commentator, which was a unique experience I still cherish today. I saw Tyler in his element. He was a mild-mannered guy, but when the puck dropped, he became intense. He told the story of the game with such passion and detail, you would feel like you were sitting in the arena while listening at home. He was an amazing announcer. He was one of us—a part of the team. The voice of the Broncos. He showed me how to really love and cherish a different view of the game.

Logan Boulet, 21

I didn't know Logan before the season started, but we quickly became close. Every Monday, we would sit beside each other in the dressing room, practise, work out, and go to Johnny's. Later, I'd pick him up for Special Olympics floor hockey, and then we'd quickly head back to my house for team *Bachelor* nights. He opened up to me and we shared a lot of great conversations. I learned that he was one of the most selfless people I'd ever met. I remember him sticking up for Bryce on the ice—and breaking his hand in the fight. He would never pass up an opportunity to help out a team-mate or a random stranger in need. Before he died, Logan had signed up to be an organ donor. He'd spoken to me about it briefly and we talked about the impact you can have on people, even when you're gone. When I was sixteen years old, I had told my parents that I intended to be an organ donor, but I never registered until after the tragedy. I saw how Logan's selflessness had actually kept other people alive. It's an amazing gift. Today, people talk about the Logan Boulet Effect—and how the lives he saved carry on in his absence. I think about the effect of Logan in my life every day, and I always remind myself to think of others first.

Dayna Brons, 24

The only good thing about getting hurt during the season was that you would have the opportunity to get to know Dayna. As one of the most frequently injured players on the team that season, I had the privilege of getting to know her quite well. There were a lot of wonderful things about Dayna, but the one that stuck out for me the most was how incredible she was at caring for other people. Whenever a player got injured, she would go above and beyond to make sure we were okay. She would send us messages to check in and see if we needed anything. If a player had to go to the hospital because of an injury, she would go with them—and stay there, no matter how late it got. It spoke volumes about how much she cared about us. As a hockey player, you never want to admit when you are hurt. We like to act tough. But Dayna allowed us to feel comfortable around being honest about our pain. Everyone has their own battles, and Dayna was the kind of person who would check in to see how you were doing in yours. It meant a lot to me personally. I've tried to carry that on by being there for people in the same way that Dayna was for me.

Mark Cross, 27

Mark was a big brother to me. The kind you look up to and aspire to be like. Yes, he was my coach, but he was the most approachable and relatable coach I have ever had. He always made other people feel welcome and comfortable. There was an instant warmth to him. I remember connecting with him as soon as I met him. He was just so friendly and we had similar values. At York University, where he played varsity hockey, people still talk about his generosity as a teammate. When the school wanted to bring in potential recruits, Mark was the player they would put the recruit in touch with. He'd let them stay at his house and show them around campus, making them feel like they belonged. I can't think of a better person for that job than Mark. I often hear stories and am reminded daily of the legacy Mark left on the varsity athletics community at York. The impact he had on the campus is remarkable.

His example is one I've tried to emulate in my own life, looking for ways to mentor people. You can make a big difference just by being there for someone who needs it—showing that extra support, with a little bit of warmth. That was Mark.

Glen Doerksen, 59

Glen was a part of our Broncos family. We would have various bus drivers throughout the year, but Glen was definitely a regular on our road trips. Sometimes, bus drivers would stay in their bus during the games or go somewhere to pass the time, only coming into the rink the odd time to watch part of the game. However, Glen would always come inside and watch our games. I remember him up in the stands, cheering and rooting us on. If we won, Glen knew to honk twice as we pulled out of the parking lot to celebrate the two points captured on the road. He loved those little things. I would always chat with our bus drivers whenever I boarded the bus for a trip, and I was able to share several conversations with Glen. I'd ask how his day was or what he had been up to, and he'd always have a funny remark to keep the mood light. Glen had a great sense of humour and loved to make us smile. I would always thank the bus driver when we arrived home from a trip, but on April 6, 2018, I didn't get the chance to thank Glen when I left the bus. That has bothered me ever since. Glen taught me that a simple joke or short conversation can make someone's day better. I try to carry this forward into every encounter I have.

Darcy Haugan, 42

I never had a coach who spoke about family as much as Darcy did. He would do anything for his family. Even when he was on the road with us, away for days at a time, Darcy always put his family first. He also turned the Broncos into a family. Darcy would always say, "It's a great day to be a Bronco, gentlemen." And every day, it was. The culture of that team was like nothing I'd ever experienced before. When Darcy recruited players, the first question he would ask the coach or general manager of the team was "Is the kid a good person?" Darcy was a firm believer that character determines success. Everyone involved with the Humboldt Broncos had character. He did not worry about skill, talent, or hockey IQ. Darcy wanted good character first and foremost. That's why our team was so tight-knit and got along so well. People often talk about a sports team being like a family, but I can honestly say that Darcy created an environment in which that sentiment was actually true. I respected that about him. Family has always been important to me, and it became even more so after going through my father's illness with him. After the crash, the importance of family became extremely apparent. Darcy taught me that the connection we have with the people we love is the most important gift we have. We need to treasure it and take care of it. Because of Darcy, I'll always put family first.

Adam Herold, 16

Adam joined our team late in the season. He'd been captain of the Regina Pat Canadians Midget AAA team and was an incredibly talented defenceman. Adam was quiet and a bit shy, in a tough position as a call-up. He reminded me of what it had been like to go to Notre Dame for the first time—it's a tough situation to be in—so I took him out for lunch to try to get to know him better. I learned that he had a quick wit. He was such a nice, young small-town guy and definitely had the characteristics it took to be a leader. He worked hard on and off the ice. After our lunch, he had to run home to get some course work done for school. On the ice, he was a pretty special player. He was a stud defenceman who was incredibly consistent. He always made the right play, which is rare for a rookie called up partway through the season. Right away, Adam was one of our top players. He let his talent do the talking. He taught me you can make an impression, even if you're new—even if you're young. Experience doesn't dictate talent. Walking into new situations now, I think of Adam and his quiet confidence—and the immediate impact you can make even as a rookie.

Brody Hinz, 18

I think about Brody often. I don't know if I've met anyone who loved sports as much as he did. He had a gift for stats and numbers, and he turned that gift into an invaluable piece for the Broncos puzzle. Brody provided insight into how we could better understand our game by tracking shot locations, turnovers, fly-bys, hits, zone entries, and many other analytics. I didn't have a genuine appreciation for what Brody did until I sat with him one game when I was injured. He could follow the game, knowing who did what while entering the stats, better than I could while just sitting and watching. He was truly impressive. Not only was he great at keeping the stats, he was a great person. Brody was a light on our team. Every time he walked into the arena, he had a big smile on his face. It was his happy place. I thought of him when I had the chance to visit the NHL's war room, where all the big decisions are made. I thought about how amazing it would have been for Brody to be there to experience it. He would have soaked it all up. Brody taught me about the importance of looking at life from different angles.

Logan Hunter, 18

I can still picture Logan giving us a little smirk while slamming on his air guitar before belting out Nickelback with all of his heart at the back of the bus. He was by far the most eager participant in "Rookie Idol," in which new players on the team had to sing a song during one of our road trips. Logan sang "Burn It to the Ground" and put absolutely everything he had into it. The key to success in Rookie Idol lies in being all in—even if you're the worst singer. By no means was Logan a good singer, but he gave it everything he had. That's the kind of guy he was. He was enthusiastic about everything we did as a team. He was there for every *Bachelor* night and for every pre-game meal at Johnny's. He brought energy and fun to the team. He was also a very good player—probably the best rookie on the team, and easily the best we had in a shootout. He approached each shootout the same way he lived his life. He never deked. He always shot glove side. Every single time. And he scored constantly, even though the goalie knew what was coming. He had confidence, whether he was belting out a Nickelback song or scoring a game winner. That's what Logan taught me: always trust your shot, and take it.

Jaxon Joseph, 20

Jaxon had the kind of smile you can't forget. Wherever he was, he always wore a huge grin. It lit up every room. Jaxon took a lot of heat from the guys because he was always carrying on—always up to something. Whether he was jokingly boasting about how many goals he had scored at a party or making a remark about the current Monday night Bachelor, he always had a comment. I loved that about him. Stephen, Bryce, and I often picked him up on our way to the rink, and he was always at Johnny's Bistro with us. We would often talk hockey—who was lighting it up in the NHL, players we admired, or our thoughts on a certain game the previous night. We shared that love for the game, and it was a special bond. Jaxon would never say no to hanging out with anyone and was just a great guy to be around. He always had a story—like joking that his dad was Cujo (Curtis Joseph) when he first got traded, later to tell us that his father was actually *Chris* Joseph, who also played in the NHL. He was so proud of his family. He was the kind of player every team needs—the "glue guy." Someone who was able to cut through the tension and make you enjoy being there. Whenever I think of Jaxon, that's what I think about. The game is fun. Life is fun. So smile and enjoy it.

Jacob Leicht, 18

Jacob was probably the hardest worker on our team—perhaps one of the hardest workers I've ever played with. He just brought this incredible tenacity and work ethic to everything he did. I've always valued teammates who put in that kind of effort. You never questioned Jacob's commitment to the game and to the team. He was also a quiet leader and my go-to person when I wanted something done right. You could always count on Jacob to lend a hand when it was needed. Even when we were skeet shooting, Jacob was the guy who would reload the gun and make sure everyone knew how to shoot safely. It was a small detail, but it didn't go unnoticed. He was born in Humboldt and embodied the spirit of the city. He worked and worked and worked, and never got upset. He was one of the most well-rounded teammates I've ever played with. I never heard him swear. Not once. He would always call me "Momma Bear" or "Mom" and was the first one to start that nickname trending around the team. Even though he was only eighteen years old, he carried a maturity that was rare for someone his age. Jacob always put his head down and kept going. That's something I've tried to emulate in my life. To be steady and constant—and to never stop working, like Jacob.

Conner Lukan, 21

When I think about Conner, the first thing that comes to my mind is sacrifice. In the final two minutes of Game 5 of our play-off series against Melfort, I watched Conner block five shots in a row. I'm not kidding—*five shots*. That almost seems impossible, but I watched it happen with my own eyes. He dove in front of shot after shot. He did whatever it took for us to get the win. He sacrificed his body for us. That really hit home with me. I'd never seen anything like it. It was one of the most courageous things I've witnessed in a hockey game. I was speechless. Needless to say,

Conner was an amazing teammate. Just an all-around quiet leader who let his play and actions do the talking. The type of guy who would put it all on the line for the group without expecting anything in return. You knew he was going to give it his all and lay it on the line every night. He showed me what it takes to sacrifice, not just in hockey, but in life. If I ever consider dodging a responsibility or avoiding something difficult, I think of Conner. I think of five shots—and know that, just like him, I can make whatever sacrifice is needed to get the job done.

Logan Schatz, 20

Our captain was the biggest personality in the room. Wherever we were, you'd always recognize Logan's voice and his contagious laugh. He took the game seriously, but he also knew it was important to have fun. He often told me, "Come on, man, you've got to let loose a bit." One time when we went to a preseason game between the Oilers and the Carolina Hurricanes in Saskatoon together, he told me he was going to call Drake Caggiula over to chat because he knew him. "You don't know him," I said. Logan replied, "Yeah, but I bet I can still get him to come over." He called out Drake's name like they were old buddies—and he actually came over. We spoke to Caggiula, a complete stranger who played for the Oilers, for a while in the tunnel. Logan spoke to him as though they were old friends. I still remember his "DRAAAKE!" yell vividly. But that's the kind of guy Logan was. He was easy to get along with and charming. A natural leader. Your instant best friend. He taught me the importance of enjoying the moments while we have them and to make memories that will last a lifetime. I've tried to carry that forward in my own life. I push myself to do things I might not feel comfortable doing. To enjoy the small things that are essential to life's bigger pursuits.

Evan Thomas, 18

Evan was another Saskatoon guy on the squad. He was a couple of years younger than me, so we never had the chance to play together until Humboldt. Evan was a natural leader and a great team guy. He was a genuine dude and loved to spend time with the guys. Just a natural athlete, too. He had a competitive edge to him and never wanted to lose. It wasn't until we started up our team fantasy hockey pool that I realized he was quite the competitor. He made all of these obscure picks, going way off the board to piece his team together. In the end, he had a stacked team that dominated for most of the season and gave him bragging rights. Before our games, we would play "sewer," in which you try to keep the ball from hitting the floor without using your hands. Evan was a regular and competed hard. He would always come close to winning, but never did, and would get heated before we even stepped on the ice. Everyone loved giving him the gears, which was all in good fun. When I think of Evan, I think of the important lesson of giving your all in everything you do.

Parker Tobin, 18

Parker was one of the most interesting teammates I've had. He was our team's *NBA 2K* legend. He always bugged me about playing him. I would try to talk big, even though I sucked. He had a good sense of humour and it became a running joke, so one day I finally gave in. I lost by forty points in both games and he had bragging rights for the rest of the season. In the new year, we had a practice out of town, and he and I drove together. We started discussing politics, which is a topic that does not come up very often on a junior hockey team. We even explored global issues like climate change, war, and poverty. We had only a few differences in our perspectives, but we engaged each other with genuine curiosity. I honestly don't remember having a conversation that intellectual in my entire hockey career. Parker was a very smart guy. His aspirations reached way beyond the rink. He always had questions. He always wanted to learn. In hockey, it's not always easy to show your nerdy side. Parker didn't care about that at all. We are very similar in that regard. I always wanted to do well in school and didn't really care what others thought about that. Parker took it a step further, though. He made being nerdy cool. He taught me to embrace that part of my personality even more—and to always ask questions and learn more.

Stephen Wack, 21

One night during the season, Stephen and I drove out to a field to look at the stars. We were both into astronomy, and he had a new app on his phone that mapped out all the constellations and the location of all the planets. We were excited to check it out. It was a foggy night. We drove out to the middle of the prairie to get the best view we could. It was incredible. We stood in a field, looking up at an endless sea of stars. We stayed there for a while, getting lost in the galaxies. Stephen was really into videography and photography. He asked if he could take a photo of me beneath the stars to capture the moment. Then I asked if he'd let me take a photo of him, too. They both turned out so well—each of us standing beneath the dark sky on the open prairie, with billions of stars above. Stephen and I would share so many fun times as roommates that year. But when I think about the one that epitomizes our friendship the best, it is this one. Stephen taught me to capture the moments while we can. I didn't know then that, one day soon, I'd be staring up at the stars, thinking of him.

PART
THREE

CHAPTER 17

▬

I left the hospital on April 27 and spent weeks adjusting to the new normal of my life back in Saskatoon.

I returned to Humboldt for the first time a couple days after my release, on Monday, April 30. The entire time I was in the hospital, I had a longing to go back to the city that had meant so much to me.

It was a difficult but important trip for me to take. We drove down the streets where so many of my memories of the season had been made. I wore my jersey to honour those who weren't here, and to carry them with me through the challenging journey.

I surprised the Grade 5 class I had worked with that year. The students were super excited to see me, but I also felt the pain they harboured. I spoke to the class about the tragedy, answered some questions about my recovery, and visited a bit. I spoke with Celeste Leicht, Jacob's mom, who is the school's vice-principal. It was an emotional conversation. But it was comforting to speak with her and the rest of the staff I'd become good friends with.

I went to the local radio station to offer my condolences for the loss of their friend and co-worker, Tyler Bieber. I also went on the air and thanked the community of Humboldt for all the love and support we had received.

At Futuristic Industries, where many of the taxi crew and Special Olympics floor hockey players worked, I walked through

207

the door and Angelica (who was my floor hockey girlfriend) yelled, "THERE'S MY BOYFRIEND!" with the biggest smile on her face. Everyone was jacked to see me, and I had to keep reminding them not to hug me too tightly because of my broken vertebrae. When I found Shane, he started sobbing. He ran up and gave me a big hug that seemed to last for minutes. He and so many others who played Special Olympics took the crash extremely hard. He was so surprised to see me. He asked why I wasn't in the hospital. I told him that, since day one in the hospital, I had wanted to come back to Humboldt to see the community I fell in love with. He looked at me with tears running down his cheeks and said, "I love you, Kaleb."

I met Chris Beaudry at Elgar Petersen Arena to collect my belongings from the dressing room. This was one of the toughest things I had to do. Memories flooded my mind like a tsunami, wave after wave crashing in. My stall was still marked with my name on the plate above it. My gear had already been retrieved from the crash site to be professionally cleaned and had been sent to my home.

The room was eerily quiet, but it felt loud at the same time. It was filled with energy. I felt shivers down my spine and the hair on my neck stood up. I looked around the room. We never made it back. Stalls were empty. The room was exactly the same as we'd left it that afternoon. There were still two rolls of tape in my stall. There were backup sticks on the stick rack.

It was crushing. I looked at all the stalls where each guy sat. I remembered all the moments we shared. All of the laughs, the cheers, the chirps—and the bonds we forged in that room each day. I smiled as my eyes welled up with tears.

I signed my name on the bottom of my seat, officially passing it on to the next Bronco: *Kaleb Dahlgren* 2017–2018.

I collected my belongings from under my stall, grabbed my backup stick, and left the room.

At the end of the day, I returned to the Clements', my billets, to pack up the items from my room and load them into the back of my vehicle to take them home. I did a full sweep of the basement one last time, entering Bryce's room, then the furnace room, the bathroom, and then Stephen's room. All that remained were memories—a collection of forty-five empty bottles from our *Bachelor* nights, along with a plastic flamingo we used as a beer funnel, which Bryce, Stephen, and I planned to sign at the end of the year and pass on to the next billets.

After some hugs and tears, we headed back to Saskatoon. I was physically, mentally, and emotionally exhausted, but happy that I'd returned. It was a weight lifted off my shoulders and one step forward in my long healing process.

A little more than a week later, my buddy from Notre Dame, Brayden Richards, came from Calgary to visit me for a week. It was the first time I went to the Broadway Bridge. Brayden and I ended up going together three nights in a row, and I would continue to visit the spot throughout the summer. He was one of the many friends who visited and spent time with me after I was released from the hospital. I'd always cherished the relationships I was lucky to have, but just like the many small things that took on new beauty after the crash, I found myself even more grateful to be able to spend time with good friends. They were always there for me before, and they remained by my side after the crash.

I returned to City Hospital to visit with Jacob Wassermann and Xavier LaBelle, both of whom were still recovering there. I also went to Royal University Hospital to visit with Layne Matechuk and Morgan Gobeil. It was never easy seeing your buddies in pain and discomfort and not their normal selves. Jacob and Xavier were doing physiotherapy exercises daily and developing strength quickly. Layne and Morgan were still in rough shape. It absolutely killed me, seeing how badly they'd been hurt.

That *should* have been me.

I wished I could have traded places with them, or that they could have been as lucky as I was. However, each time I went, I could see that there had been major improvements in their abilities. This made each visit more hopeful than the last. I went to see them as often as I could. It was nice to sit and connect with the guys who were on their own journey to recovery. Watching all of them continue to progress and come out of this tragedy stronger inspired me. All of the survivors are warriors in their own special way.

The bond that we shared as Broncos will never go away.

While I was at City Hospital, York University's coaches, Russ Herrington and Jesse Messier, and several players came out to Saskatchewan to attend Mark Cross's funeral. His legacy with the Lions was enormous and carries on to this day. During their trip, a group of them drove to Saskatoon from Regina to meet with me and my parents for breakfast. Coach Herrington handed me an official letter of intent to attend York and join the program.

The Lions knew that my future was uncertain. I had not been cleared to play. It wasn't clear when—or *if*—I would be. They told me to take it one day at a time. There was no rush for me to be at York in the fall, although I was welcome if I was ready.

"I think that you would enjoy being with our team and with our group," Herrington said. "But this is your decision, and we want to support you no matter what. As long as I am still coaching, you will always have a spot with us."

If it took a year or two—or four, or more—I had a future with the York Lions. If I wanted to just take one class online and stay at home to start, they were completely fine with that.

It meant the world to me.

"I'm going to be in Toronto by September," I told them. "I'm going to be there."

Again, they said, there was no pressure and to take my time. My health and well-being were the most important things.

"I'll be there," I said.

I knew right then that I would be accepting the offer, but deep inside, I knew I couldn't guarantee when I'd be showing up to campus.

Living my life with diabetes, I was used to being told, "You can't do this" and "You can't do that." I was used to being told that the odds were against me. That I had to be careful—and realistic about the challenges I faced. And all of my life, I'd ignored the doubters. Even as a short hockey player—five foot eight—I thrived in a shutdown role and was net front on the power play, which is something you almost never hear of.

My parents were supportive, as always, but told me to not put pressure on myself to attend York in the fall. They asked me to wait a couple of weeks before officially committing. They knew I was still dealing with many things—physically, mentally, and emotionally.

They were right. I still wasn't really in a condition to go to school. Over the long term, we still didn't know how my brain was going to recover—or how I would react to the demands that university and hockey would put on me.

My parents wanted to know what the doctors in the hospital thought. They wanted to make sure I wasn't making a rash decision or putting pressure on myself unnecessarily.

"Why don't you wait and see how you recover?" Dad said. "You may never be able to play again."

I was adamant, though.

"Don't take this away from me," I said. "I've worked all my life for this. At least let me sign. If I never play, at least I'll have achieved what I wanted to do."

I was never the best hockey player, but I'd always believed that if you put your mind to something, you can achieve it. A decade earlier, I'd set a goal of playing university hockey. After all of this hard work, I'd finally earned it. I wasn't going to let this chance slip away.

I waited a couple of weeks, and then on May 2, I officially signed my commitment to attend York. We celebrated with ice cream cake and took pictures to remember the day. It was a huge moment in my journey to recovery. York announced my decision nine days later. As soon as the news was out, I received a bunch of messages from students at the school, welcoming me. It helped reaffirm my belief that I'd made the right decision.

Despite the commitment, though, a lot of uncertainty remained about my future in the game. My focus at the time was getting myself back into good enough health to play. That was the only thing I was able to control. If my body was able, I was going to play again.

Since the crash, it felt like most people were trying to make my situation seem worse than I felt. Every time I said I was feeling good and doing well, the nurses on the neurology floor would look at me suspiciously. They told my parents that people with brain injuries are masters of deception—they find ways to compensate for what they're lacking; they'll do whatever it takes to give correct answers so that people don't know they have a brain injury.

The nurses kept trying to stump me during the testing but weren't able to. My cognitive ability didn't correlate with what the images of my brain suggested it should be.

By this time, all of my injuries had been assessed. I had a traumatic brain injury, a fractured neck and nerve damage, a fractured back, a fractured skull, a puncture wound, and partial degloving of the right side of my head. There was blood behind my right eardrum and a large blood clot in my left forearm. I suffered from post-traumatic amnesia. And later, I'd discover that my head had actually increased in size. I was one hat size larger, which I remain to this day.

When I left the hospital, I was told by the neurologist to get tons of sleep and fresh air and eat lots of greens. She also told me to not drink alcohol, do drugs, or listen to very loud music, and to eat healthy. That was pretty much the prescription for dealing with a brain injury.

I stuck to it religiously. If sleep was the best thing for my brain, I was going to commit to sleeping as much as possible. Most of these things I was doing already, so it wasn't a drastic change. I'd schedule two naps every day and would go to bed at night and wake up eleven to twelve hours later. I tried to be outside as much as possible and drank special drinks full of green vegetables from Thrive Juice Company, a local juice shop in Saskatoon that gave them to me free of charge.

It was really nice to finally sleep in my own bed, but I had to take precautions when I slept. I wasn't allowed to sleep on my side or stomach. I had to sleep strictly on my back because of my broken vertebrae. I'm a side sleeper, so this was easier said than done. It was a challenge, but something I was going to have to get used to.

The truth, though, is that the mental pain was much worse than the physical pain I was in during that time.

Even though I didn't show it outwardly, I felt the anguish of everyone we lost that day. As I thought more and more about where everyone was sitting on that bus and how random the outcome seemed, the more I realized just *how* lucky I had been. Conner Lukan and Jaxon Joseph were sitting right beside me. Stephen Wack and Logan Boulet were behind me. It just doesn't add up.

It was hard because the majority of those involved were so young. Death is easier to accept when it involves someone who is much older and has lived a complete life, but every single person who died because of the crash should have had much more time. This was sudden and unfair. I was raised to never ask why about matters that have no explanation. Events happen, but life is about how you perceive the event and how you choose to react. It is a simple concept. You have to accept that sometimes there will never be a reason why.

Even with that foundation, I found myself facing those unavoidable questions. I tried to push them to the back of my mind, but they were always there.

Why am I here? Why did they *die?*

Those questions carry a great deal of survivor's guilt, even though there was nothing I could have done—or can do—to change the outcome.

There is an anguish that comes with the absence of the people on that bus. The only thing to do is face it. The truth is, I was lucky. And that luck sometimes comes with pain and guilt, which weighed heavily on me through that first month.

After the crash, some people told me it just wasn't my time to go. I know they were just trying to comfort me. But I don't believe that, because it implies that it *was* time for those who died to go. It wasn't. Everyone on that bus had a purpose in life. And there are sixteen purposes that won't be fulfilled, even as their legacies carry on after death. Their lives were taken. It wasn't fair. It wasn't right.

CHAPTER 18

—

I spent many of my waking hours in May doing physiotherapy, enduring dry needling, getting massage therapy, and receiving chiropractic treatments. Physically, I started to feel much better. I had more energy, too, which meant the naps started getting harder. I just wanted to move. I wanted to get back on the ice. Soon, after I kept pushing, my doctor cleared me to resume some physical activity. I got the same green light from my physiotherapist.

I realized that I needed to get on the ice as soon as possible.

We knew Darren Schroh, who owned Schroh Arena, a local hockey rink. He offered to get me ice time whenever I needed it, without anyone else around.

Mom and Dad drove me to the rink on June 1, because I wasn't cleared to drive. I still couldn't turn my head fully to check over my shoulder.

I felt it as soon as my skates hit the ice. I dropped a puck at my feet as I stepped out, cradling it with my stick—back and forth, and back again—gliding towards centre ice. I cut across the blue line and looped through the far end, near a large "Humboldt Broncos Strong" mural that was painted on the wall beyond the glass. I turned and sent a soft pass across the empty rink.

It had been nearly two months since I'd felt the weight of a puck on my blade and listened to the crunch of ice beneath my skates. I wore my green Broncos helmet, green Broncos gloves, and my charcoal-grey Humboldt Broncos track suit. Mom and Dad watched from the players' bench. It was just the three of us, together.

But I felt it, right away. They were with me—all sixteen—as real as you or I have ever been, or ever will. I could sense that they were there with me, watching me—either in spirit or as living memories that will never fade. They were happy to see me back on the ice. I could feel them with each stride and every time my stick touched the puck. I skated with them, weaving around them, passing through them.

The crash had changed me in many ways I could see—and in many ways I knew would take years for me to understand.

My life was completely different. I was working through the grief of losing family that I loved, mentally and emotionally. Rehabbing from injuries. Doing cognitive exercises to strengthen my brain. Following all the steps to achieve a full recovery. Supporting the survivors, the sixteen angel families, and the Humboldt community. Planning the move to Toronto for university. Having a romantic relationship of three years come to an end. Working to get back into game shape. On top of all that, trying to spend time with my family and friends.

But as June came around, there wasn't much time to process anything. I think the busyness helped me start to feel like myself again.

The very next day, my parents and I hopped on a plane and flew to Washington, D.C., to attend the Stanley Cup final between the Capitals and the Vegas Golden Knights. I finally was cleared to fly and could watch my two favourite teams play. The NHL invited us out.

During that trip, I climbed aboard a bus for the first time since the crash. When we were told that we'd take a shuttle from the hotel to the arena, we didn't even think about it. It didn't hit me until I sat down in the front row. It was a full-size coach bus.

I looked over at my parents, sitting across from me.

"I'm sitting in Mark's seat right now," I said.

They suddenly realized what I meant. I could see their faces flush with concern.

"And you're sitting in Darcy's spot," I told them.

They asked if I was okay—and, truthfully, I was. We were on a bus, but it wasn't *that* bus and it wasn't *that* time. We were going to be okay.

I nodded at them.

"I'm good."

My parents seemed a little shaken when we got off the bus, concerned about how I'd be affected. But everything was fine. I wasn't going to live my life in fear of the things I can't control.

At the game, I was introduced in the arena to all of the Capitals fans and was on the video board. I wore my Humboldt Broncos jersey as I waved to the crowd, and then lifted it up to reveal a Capitals jersey underneath. The fans, who were already giving me a standing ovation, went even more wild. It was absolutely electric. It felt like an overwhelming rush of love.

It is difficult to put into words all of the different emotions surrounding these events. I received ovations at several events that I attended. On the street, I would have strangers walk up to me and ask for a hug. Or an individual might start crying when they talked to me. People would even stare, like their eyes were glued to me.

I knew that those who approached me meant well. You could see it in their eyes. It was overwhelming to consider just how far the impact of this disaster had spread. For example: a woman from Iraq met me at Royal University Hospital on my way to physio one day. She said she had been back home when the crash happened, and it was all over the news there. That just doesn't happen every day.

I am beyond grateful for the support that poured in from around the world. I don't think people realize just how far a little gesture can go. These conversations, messages, and boxes of mail, putting sticks by the front door, and so many other small signals of love helped repair me.

It still leaves me speechless.

The NHL brought us out to Las Vegas to be part of the NHL Awards ceremony on June 20, 2018, where the Willie O'Ree Community Hero Award would be awarded to our coach, Darcy— and accepted by his wife, Christina.

Ten survivors made the trip, as well as Reagan Poncelet and Blake Berschiminsky, who played with the team throughout the season but didn't make the trip to Nipawin. It was the second time we'd been together as a group since the crash. Not even a week before, a bunch of us had met in Edmonton for a weekend together. We were able to reconnect, have some deep discussions, and just enjoy each other's company.

Las Vegas presented the opportunity to get away with the guys. We stayed at the Hard Rock Hotel and hung out together, like old times. We went to see the famous raunchy comedy show *Absinthe*. We chilled by the pool, tried our luck at blackjack, and cruised the Strip. Being in Vegas was a blast and something all of us needed. We were long overdue to have that kind of quality time together. In a strange way, it felt like our year-end bender. But it also felt incomplete. I was constantly wishing that *everyone* could be back together—those who were unable to make it and those who weren't here anymore. There was a void. We did our very best to enjoy it, just like everyone would have wanted.

It was fun, but it wasn't an escape. The NHL followed me around with a camera for one of the days. We got to hang out with NHL players and had some good visits with Nate MacKinnon,

Pekka Rinne, and Connor McDavid, and we took a group sel-
fie with P.K. Subban and Anze Kopitar. The whole time, I
thought about how Morgan Gobeil, Layne Matechuk, and Nick
Shumlanski and the sixteen who passed away in the crash would
have loved this experience.

I was asked to speak on behalf of the team during the ceremony. It was a role I'd been encouraged to assume by the media
relations people the Broncos brought in after the crash. Others
were getting bombarded by requests, while I had experience
speaking to reporters and was in a good state of mind. It wasn't a
role I sought out, but I hoped it might take the pressure off others.
In Las Vegas, I was really "volun-told" more than anything—but
again, I felt a sense of responsibility. I didn't want anyone else to
have to go through this.

During the NHL Awards show, we waited backstage, ready to
be introduced. Before we were announced, we could see a video
playing on a monitor, showing us what was being broadcast to the
world. It recounted what had happened and showed scenes of the
tragedy. We weren't expecting it. It threw us off guard, and several
of us were in tears before we walked onto the stage. It was still
awfully raw.

I swallowed hard, trying to fight back the tears. I knew I had
to hold it together for all of us. Wearing our gold Humboldt
Broncos jerseys, pinned with green and gold ribbons, we entered
to a standing ovation from the NHL's stars. My speech was written
out and displayed on a teleprompter. During rehearsals, I couldn't
make out the words clearly, so I had to put on Camo's glasses to
read the words. I ended up having to wear my own for the speech,
which I rarely do. Everything was supposed to run smoothly, but I
wasn't expecting everyone to stay standing. When I looked out at
the teleprompter, I realized that six-foot-five Pekka Rinne's head
was blocking the screen. I couldn't see a word of it.

My eyes widened and I felt a rush of panic. I lowered my head slightly, then looked up again, hoping people might have taken their seats. They hadn't. I couldn't ask them to sit down, so I completely winged it.

"Thank you very much," I said. "We really do appreciate this."

I mentioned the three players who were unable to make the trip with us and how proud we were to represent them.

"We want to thank everyone around the world who has given their time, donations, messages, and even the little things—like putting a hockey stick on their doorsteps. A very special thank you to the NHL for everything they've done for us and their support to the Humboldt Broncos organization every way they possibly can," I said.

"We are very privileged to be here tonight to support Darcy and those fifteen others who are not here with us anymore, for they will always be loved in our hearts and cherished forever.

"We are extremely thankful we get to present an award that means a lot to the hockey community."

Applause.

"We love you!" someone in the audience shouted.

I took a deep breath. I turned to join my teammates, while Willie O'Ree came onto the stage to present the award named after him.

Christina walked up from the crowd to accept the honour for Darcy. She gripped my hand briefly as she passed, greeting us before taking the podium. Her speech was strong and beautiful, sharing the Broncos' Core Covenant displayed outside Darcy's office:

Family first . . . Be thankful for the opportunity to wear the Bronco jersey . . . Understand that we are building foundations for future generations with our words and actions . . . Always have hope that everything is possible . . . Always give more than you take . . . Strive for greatness in all areas of life.

"It does not mention wins or championships, because Darcy's purpose as a coach was to impact lives and develop strong character," Christina continued. "His legacy is far more than what's recorded on the stat sheets. It is measured by the lives and communities that are better off for having Darcy in them. It is now up to those individuals to pay forward his legacy onto others . . . the torch has been passed."

CHAPTER 19

▬

E njoy the grind.
Among the many NHL players to reach out to me to offer
words of inspiration and support in the wake of April 6 was
Anze Kopitar, whom I looked up to and modelled my style
of play after. The LA Kings forward is captain of his team and
one of the best two-way forwards in the game. He's twice won the
Frank J. Selke Trophy as the league's top defensive forward.

Kopitar sent me a signed game jersey and some other Kings
gear, including a T-shirt that read "Enjoy the Grind" on the back.
It was the Kings' slogan—and a mindset that helped the team win
two Stanley Cups in the past decade. Everyone faces their own
grind in life, but the goal is to find the positives in the process.
It's a frame of mind that became critical to me in my recovery and
a slogan that I've carried with me ever since. My life has been a
grind for as long as I can remember, and I've enjoyed it.

For me, the summer following the crash was another grind.

After trauma, everyone heals differently. There is no single
answer when it comes to dealing with that pain. For me, it was
hockey and training. It was pushing forward, towards a new goal.

Determined to join the York Lions on the ice in the fall, I
worked as hard as I ever have—pushing through three physio sessions a week in the clinic and exercises every day at home.

All of my injuries were healing and progressing tremendously.

The fractured vertebrae had healed, my range of motion in my neck and back had returned to normal, cuts and bruises had healed, and, surprisingly, I was able to grow back some of the hair I lost to the degloving. I still had some pain and discomfort from the nerve damage in my neck, and my traumatic brain injury was the main lingering concern. In all of this, I was gaining more strength every day.

I was on the ice three days a week, working at a hockey skills camp for kids and teenagers. The job was incredibly important to me. I did not want to sit around all summer and feel sorry for myself. I knew that going back to hockey was the perfect fit.

I absolutely loved it. Coaching elite young hockey players offered me a new vantage point on the game and allowed me to celebrate the bonds the sport provides. Giving back to the game that had given me so much felt rewarding. It became a key part of my healing process. Helping the players helped *me*.

I also worked out on my own. I practised my stickhandling and balance. I did a tonne of push-ups, because I wasn't cleared to lift weights. I also improved my strength by doing isometric holds, which are basically static body-weight exercises. Mark Cross had designed some for us, and we often did them throughout the season. Unexpectedly, without lifting weights I actually got stronger than I had been before the crash. Maybe it was the grind—my relentless desire to prove I could make it back to the ice. Or maybe it was just a more efficient way to train.

That summer, I also went back to Next Level Training Centre to work out with my buddies who played in college and professional hockey. A couple of the guys were doing bench presses to see how they were progressing through the summer months. I decided to hop in at the start, just to see how much I had *regressed* from previous years. I lay down on the bench and took a deep breath, pushing all I had into the bar. The bar lifted off the rack and it was all me. One rep, two reps, three reps . . . *thirteen* reps . . . *sixteen* reps. Then I racked the bar. The guys looked at me in disbelief and questioned how I had just done that—while lifting weights for the first time in four months. I looked at them and laughed.

"It must be the one hundred push-ups I do before bed every night."

I joined them again a bit later into their bench press as the weight increased. I did the most reps out of them all.

How the heck is this happening? I wondered.

The truth is that I was never worried about whether I'd physically be able to play hockey again. My legs were good and I knew that the vertebrae in my back and neck would fully heal. Whenever I stepped on the ice, I felt as comfortable and ready to play as I ever had. The problem wasn't my physical ability. It was the unknown damage to my brain.

Throughout the summer, despite the success of my recovery, I carried one constant worry: *What if I'm never able to play the game again?*

I am in a "miracle bubble"—meaning that, according to the experts we spoke with, the injuries to my brain should have been enough to permanently limit and disable my cognitive ability. Based on the results of my MRI, I shouldn't have been able to remember my parents' names. I shouldn't have been able to remember the Humboldt Broncos. I shouldn't even remember how to skate. But, months after the crash, I was still able to do all of those things. I was able to function, for the most part, as I had before the tragedy happened. Even my personality had returned. I started to regain my social filter. I no longer blurted out whatever I was feeling— and I cursed *a lot* less. (My mother was happy about that.)

I was getting back to being my old self.

That summer, I went into a store to buy a new pair of shoes. I came out with the phone number of one of the most beautiful girls I'd ever met. Her name was Paige Watson. The next evening, we went for a walk down by the scenic South Saskatchewan River that runs through Saskatoon. Paige was an absolute sweetheart and we connected instantly. It felt like a new beginning, which was exactly what I needed. I quickly discovered that we both had a love of ice cream. So, the next night, we grabbed a scoop from the famous Homestead Ice Cream shop. Our connection did not stop there—we had pretty much everything and anything in common.

At this time in my life, I wasn't looking for anyone. I wanted to focus strictly on my recovery and respect my past. I actually was planning on being single for my whole undergraduate degree in Toronto, and then consider looking for a life partner. But there was something about Paige that made me feel like she was in my life for a reason. Feelings developed rapidly, and I spent most of July and August getting to know her better. She was from a small town of four hundred people called Neilburg, Saskatchewan. She grew up on a farm, the youngest in her family of five. She was a country girl at heart and enjoyed the golden glow of the prairies.

I was still extremely busy throughout July and August, but Paige and I were able to make time for each other and go on some fun dates. Many nights, we would chase the sunset and then go down by the Broadway Bridge and look up to the stars.

Chandler Stephenson, a Washington Capitals player and a Saskatoon boy, texted me before the playoffs started and said that when they won the Cup, he was bringing it to Humboldt and I was coming with him. Chandler stayed true to his word and brought the Stanley Cup out to Humboldt during his day with it after the Capitals finished off the Vegas Golden Knights in the Stanley Cup final. I joined him there that day. The Cup, in so many ways, symbolizes hockey dreams. It embodies the history of the game—the passion at the heart of hockey towns. It was a beautiful moment for Humboldt.

226

I took part in several Broncos events over the summer, spending as much time in Humboldt as I could. I looked for ways to give back to the community that had given so much to me. I began doing elementary school speeches for my Diabeauties in mid-May and crowned four more Diabeauties in the next month. I attended the JDRF Walks in Humboldt and Saskatoon, sharing my diabetic story at both of them. I went to my old high school, Holy Cross, and gave a presentation on diabetes and the impact the crash had on it. After that I went to Winnipeg with Matthieu Gomercic and volunteered as a coach at the Mark Scheifele KidSport camp. This felt natural to me, and it brought back memories of the weekly recreation hockey camp in Humboldt that I'd run with Mark Cross. I spent a day at Parkridge Centre, mingling with the residents and staff of the long-term care facility, and spent many evenings watching my Diabeauties at their local baseball and hockey games.

Some of these experiences were challenging and emotional, but it was what I needed.

When I reflected on my life at the end of the summer, I realized that, through helping others, my own wounds had started to turn into scars. I stopped asking why and started asking myself, *How can I make a difference? What can I do to turn this absolutely horrific reality into something that helps people?*

At the same time, I faced a lot of pushback against my plan to attend York in September.

The doctors in Saskatoon were flat out against the idea. I was advised to take a year off from school completely. Maybe I could try one class remotely and see how it went. But moving away from home, in the doctors' opinion, was out of the question. They were concerned that I would be overstimulated and would overdo it. I still needed time to recover, and I'm not the type to slack off, even if the doctor prescribes it.

There were also concerns that moving to Toronto would be overwhelming for me. It's a huge, fast-paced city—a much different environment than Saskatoon. The move alone could be overwhelming, and they were unsure how the stress might affect me. And, of course, I would be living on my own for the first time, away from home, without a billet family. That's a reality that most young people heading to university have to grapple with, but it's another story when you're dealing with a traumatic brain injury at the same time. On top of all that, there was school itself. The jump to university can be difficult. I had not taken a full course load in three years. Professors demand a lot right away. There is *a lot* of freshman burnout. Even though I was crushing all of the cognitive tests I was being given, we weren't fully aware of how the brain injury had affected my ability to learn.

The odds were stacked against me. But that just made me want to go even more.

Don't get me wrong. I believe that health and well-being are paramount. The reality of my diabetes has a tremendous amount to do with that. It was impossible for me to ever *not* be aware of my health. As I lay in the hospital bed after the crash, all I could focus on was hoping to make it to another day—and maybe be able to get up and move around again.

That's when it really hits you: health is number one.

I think it can be hard for people who have not had to deal with disease or a life-threatening injury to realize just how important health can be. Once you've experienced something like that, it becomes an absolute priority. You can have many aspirations and goals, but if you don't take care of yourself first, you're unlikely to achieve them.

After the crash, I had to be aware of my physical health—but also my mental and emotional well-being. All of those work together. It's not just physical, but the psychological, too.

Despite the honest questions I fought with, the experts kept suggesting that I should be showing *more* distress about the crash. They were concerned that my demeanour had remained relatively level-headed and that I hadn't broken down the way they thought I should.

The provincial insurance company, Saskatchewan Government Insurance, sent me to a psychologist for an assessment to determine whether I had any deficits and to see how I was coping with the tragedy. As psychiatric nurses, my parents were both very aware of the emotional effect a tragedy can have. We would discuss our feelings throughout the weeks after the crash and check in with each other daily to discuss sleep, dreams, mood, and feelings. They knew the signs to look for. They felt certain that I wasn't concealing any damaging issues like depression, anxiety, or post-traumatic stress disorder. I wasn't suicidal. Aside from my vulgarity and lack of a filter, they didn't think I was exhibiting concerning behaviour as I worked through the grieving process. Still, they knew there were signs they might not be able to see and were happy I was going to see the psychologist.

From the start, the psychologist I visited was skeptical about how I was coping. He felt I was hiding behind a facade and strongly recommended that I not go to school in the fall—and that if I did anything, it should be to just take one class online.

Obviously, I disagreed with him completely.

"I think you have this wrong, honestly," I said. "Personally, I feel the best I've ever felt. And you telling me I can't do something isn't going to work."

I told him my perspective on life and death—and the process of grieving. I told him about my belief that we should feel gratitude for having known these people at all, instead of just being angry that they are gone. If I were not here today, how would I want the survivors to live their lives? I explained how that concept is the base for how I am living *my* life.

The psychologist didn't buy it. He just sat there, disagreeing.

"There's got to be more," he said.

"No," I said. "There's literally not."

Dad came with me to get my results, because my parents wanted the psychologist to know that my personality had changed after the crash. When we first met, he hadn't asked my parents for a history of my personality to use as a baseline to assess whether something had changed. During our meeting, Dad outlined some of the specific changes they had seen in me. The doctor kept saying he felt he wasn't getting the entire picture from me.

"There's got to be some more grief and trauma there," he said, "because I'm not getting from him the level of grief that somebody would feel in an incident like this."

He felt I was suppressing and hiding my emotions because I didn't want to deal with the tragedy.

"That's not how he's wired," Dad said. "He looks at the world in a different way than other people. He doesn't grieve like other people."

The psychologist continued to claim that I was just saying words I thought he wanted to hear. He believed I probably had more issues than I thought. If I went to Toronto, I'd get swallowed up—change my lifestyle, possibly resort to alcohol or other substances.

Dad assured him that this was my actual perspective and that I'd been sharing it for years.

"That is how he feels," Dad said. "It hasn't changed."

I was still battling grief. You do not just snap your fingers and it's all gone. It came in waves, which would continue to crash in the days, weeks, and months to come. It would hit me with every reminder of the Broncos. But this was something I embraced and could handle by finding the positives in these emotions, which is something I've learned to do at every crossroads I've faced in life.

When I was sixteen, I began adding a little plus sign over a negative sign on the tape on the top of my stick, to be a constant reminder of that philosophy.

Despite that mindset, all of the doubts compounded and I'd be lying if I didn't contemplate them myself. I questioned my own ability—and worried that my brain injury would severely affect my capacity to excel in school the way I had previously. When you have doctors who study the brain basically tell you that you're going to fail, it does a number on you. It's one thing to take a single course at home, but it's another to take on several courses while joining the varsity hockey team in the country's biggest city.

I still believed in myself, but there was certainly doubt. Of course, there was also a burning desire to prove everyone wrong.

I tried to explain that to my parents, who were also apprehensive. We sat down multiple nights to talk about it. We weighed all the pros and cons of going to York University that fall. I understood why they were both worried. They had gone from thinking I might be dead to learning I had a traumatic brain injury, and now I was planning on getting up and leaving for Toronto. It was all a *little* much. I know it was particularly hard on Mom. From their perspective, there was no need for me to rush. The best-case scenario was for me to take it easy for a year and maybe do a class—and work with a hockey team, doing something I loved. York wasn't pressuring me at all and my offer was set. I could defer without question.

I disagreed. In my mind, I had nothing to lose. If I went and it didn't work out, at least I'd tried. If I didn't go, I'd always wonder how I would have done if I had.

Everyone expected me to stay home. But that felt like the easy way out for me. I wanted to be independent and keep growing as an individual. I wanted to do it for me—but I also wanted to do it for the Broncos. I wanted to do it for those who were no longer here to pursue their academic or hockey dreams.

And I wanted to be part of a team again. A new team. I wanted to be a Lion.

If school was a concern for the doctors assessing me, then hockey was out of the question. In their view, the risk was far too immense for them to sign off on clearing me to play. I was told to not even think about it. I asked if I would ever recover and was told that there was an awfully slim chance. If I did, it would take a long time and the progress would be slow.

The thing about bubbles is that they pop. It's difficult to determine when or why they pop, but we know that can happen.

I passed every single test I was given through the summer of 2018, and even broke records. I actually did better in my ImPACT testing—which measures memory, attention span, and visual and verbal problem solving—than I did while I played for Humboldt. I showed few signs or symptoms of my cognitive ability being diminished by the injuries I'd sustained.

The doctors were unsure why I hadn't been affected the way they thought I should be, other than that some people are very lucky and end up being way ahead of what their prognosis should be. On the other hand, some people can suffer very minimal damage to their brain—a small concussion, for example—but end up being severely impaired by the injury. There are so many unknowns. Everybody's different.

When the experts reviewed scans of my brain, they saw all of the areas where I'd suffered a bleed—ten spots in total. The bleeding stopped shortly after the crash, but the injuries were still severe. Each section remained altered, visibly distinct from the rest of my brain.

It was pretty hard to take in. I didn't really believe it. Many of my teammates had died from their brain injuries. I tried to convince myself that the hospital had mixed up the scans. There was no way that was my *actual* brain. But at the same time that it was frustrating—and despite my disbelief—I still had to listen to what the experts were saying.

After I was cleared to skate, I knew that if I tripped and fell headfirst into the boards, I could pop the bubble. I get that. That's the risk I would have to accept every time I stepped on the ice, even to skate.

There isn't a straightforward way to heal my brain, so I have to do whatever I can to facilitate healing and maintain my health—but also accept that it might never get back to 100 percent. There was nothing else I could do. I had to accept that my dream of playing again was actually out of my hands. I could only hope for a second chance.

It was humbling for me.

I can't ask why. I just have to take it for what it is. I'm just grateful and thankful for the situation I have. It could have been *much* worse. All I can do is make the most of it. And that meant preparing as though the faint hope I carried of being able to play again would come true. I trained as though I had every intent of stepping on the ice in a full-contact game again.

I was lucky to be able to grind at all. I was sure as hell going to enjoy it.

In the end, my parents came around to my way of thinking. They knew how important going to York was for me, and they knew I was too determined to let it slip away. Even though I was only cleared to skate, I had a spot on the Lions roster and I was invited to take part in the team's preseason camp. There were still many questions that would have to work themselves out, but I was going to be in Toronto—I was going to be part of a team—hoping for a miracle that might allow me to play the game I love again.

So, we did what we always did as a family. We drove.

We packed my life into my SUV. The three of us pulled out of the driveway, en route to Toronto. We drove south to the border, through North Dakota and across Minnesota, and stayed the night in Minneapolis.

My parents watched a little more closely as they passed on-ramps where cars merged into traffic, or as the semis roared by in the lane beside us. Echoes of the crash were everywhere, but we kept moving.

I read a Jon Gordon book that had been assigned by the men's hockey team before the semester began. It was an inspirational book called *The Energy Bus*—how fitting.

We listened to music. We rode in silence, together.

We hit a flash flood in Wisconsin, passed through Chicago, and stayed in Kalamazoo. Then crossed the border into Sarnia, Ontario.

"Jeez," Mom said. "You're such a long way from home."

It was just under three thousand kilometres in total. There was no looking back.

We saw the skyline of Toronto rising in the distance. It was the first time any of us had been there.

As journeys go, it was a grind. We enjoyed it.

CHAPTER 20

—

The next chapter didn't start exactly as I'd planned: I took one step on the ice and biffed it hard.

When we arrived in Toronto, I had to go straight to the campus for an equipment fitting for my Lions gear. We didn't even have a chance to get settled. The team set me up with brand new shin pads, pants, shoulder pads, gloves, and a helmet. It was all stiff and bulky—and I wasn't used to it all. They also gave me a new stick, that wasn't the same curve as my old one.

Russ Herrington, the head coach, asked me if I was going to skate with the team that afternoon. I was welcome to join if I wanted to, but there was no pressure.

Of course I wanted to. I was eager to make a strong impression on my new teammates, and missing the first skate just wasn't an option.

However, it was a recipe for disaster.

Aside from trying to play in brand new equipment, my skates weren't sharpened and I didn't have an edge on one of the blades. I tightened them up and pulled on my practice jersey, figuring I'd be fine.

I walked towards the rink with a group of players who had competed at some of the highest levels for their age in the country.

I stepped out—a member of the York Lions—and tumbled to the ice. I mean, I *completely* ate it. Everyone stopped and looked at me. It was humiliating. They must have thought I belonged in a different league—like, *Can this guy even skate?*

They didn't even know me yet, even though they knew all about me. I was the new guy from Humboldt. A Bronco who had survived the crash. Everyone knew I was coming, but no one knew how to react.

As I slid on the ice, they didn't know if the fall had something to do with my injuries. They didn't know if it was okay to laugh or chirp me, which would have been the appropriate thing to do. Instead, there was just shocked and concerned silence.

I pulled myself up and kept going.

"Rough start," I said.

The ice time ended up being a "captain's skate," which meant it was a "gentlemanly scrimmage." This was the closest thing to game action I'd seen since April 4. I kept falling every time I tried to turn, and my shin pads were rubbing uncomfortably on my skates with every stride, so I kept fidgeting with them. It was amateur hour. I was bad.

My parents watched from the stands. They were nervous every time another player approached me. I wore a yellow jersey indicating that I was a no-go for full contact, but hockey is a fast sport, so every close call made them wince. At the same time, it was a moment of quiet pride for them. They didn't think I was as bad as I felt I was, but even Mom admits that my timing seemed off. They saw the smile on my face as I stickhandled the puck and shot on net. They saw the joy coming back as I balanced without an edge. Dad thought back to when I was young and told him I loved hockey because of the cold air on my face and the breeze in my hair. It was like I was that kid again, innocent and carefree, chasing a puck down the ice. But now I wore brand new York Lions gear. Now, I had reached the goal I'd dreamed of achieving.

It was a much less glorious moment for me. On the ice, I was nervous. The Lions were a very good team. They'd won the Queen's Cup—the championship of the Ontario University Athletics conference—in 2017 and lost in the OUA bronze-medal game the season before I arrived. I wanted to make a good first impression, but instead made what was probably the worst impression possible. My performance was embarrassing.

After practice, I got undressed and quietly vowed to be better next time. The locker room was a bit awkward. Many of the guys didn't know how to approach me. To be fair, they were in a difficult position. Should they bring up the crash? Should they ignore it? Would I be upset if they did—or didn't?

Honestly, I wasn't scared to talk about the crash. I'd discussed it in several articles and on television, and I'd spoken to random people on the street and to others who lost loved ones in the crash. I was comfortable and open about the topic. I knew that my new teammates would be coming with the right intentions. Plus, talking about it helped me heal.

A few of the Lions at the skate who were in their graduating year had played with Mark Cross. They opened up to me about it that day. I felt terrible for them because I could see the hurt in their eyes. I knew that pain, too. It really drove home to me just how huge of an impact Mark had had on his teammates at York. I then thought about the fifteen others who had made similar impacts on people in their own lives. It's sad, yet beautiful. For the short time they had, my sixteen family members made a difference in the world in their own special way. That's pretty inspiring.

My parents stayed on for a few days to help me get settled—and maybe to prepare themselves to leave me behind.

We unpacked everything at the mature student apartment complex on Assiniboine Road and met my new roommate, Jeremy Lucchini. He was from Trail, British Columbia, and was also on the men's varsity hockey team. We were both looking for roommates at the same time, so Coach Herrington connected us to each other. We chatted a bit, and he seemed like a compatible roommate. It was his first time moving away from home, so this was a big adjustment for him, too, but he was ready.

Coincidentally, our apartment was on the top floor—the *sixteenth* floor. However, the elevator only went to the fifteenth floor, so you had to take one flight of stairs. Our apartment over-looked the beautiful York campus. We had two floors in our pent-house—a main floor with the living room and full kitchen, and a second with two bedrooms and a bathroom. It wasn't a massive apartment, but it still had lots of room for the two of us.

When Jeremy and I met in person for the first time, we went out with our parents to grab things we'd need for the school year. One of the golden rules for living with diabetes is that you should always have a snack handy. This time, I didn't—my snacks were in the car—but we were planning on getting lunch right after a quick stop at Dollarama, so I figured we'd be fine.

I was wrong.

I began to feel a little bit shaky as I walked down the aisles with my parents, Jeremy, and his mother, Sandy. I mentioned it to Mom and she told me to grab a piece of candy and eat it instead of going out to the car. We'd pay for it at the cash before we left. I grabbed a Lucky Charms chewy bar from one of the shelves and opened it up.

The next thing I remember is waking up in a hospital bed, with my parents sitting beside me.

What just happened?

Where am I?

I've been here before.

When you have extremely low blood sugar and don't treat it in time, you can have a seizure. It had only ever happened to me once before, when I was four. I'd been extremely diligent about monitoring my glucose levels, so it had never happened again.

238

Mom and Dad had been right behind me. Mom saw me stumble and grab hold of a shelf, which I took down with me as I fell. Dad lunged forward just in time to grab me so that my head didn't hit the floor. Boxes toppled on top of me. I shook and convulsed in the aisle as Mom cradled my head and Dad called for help. There was foam coming out of my mouth. Everyone in the store started to freak out. People were grabbing blankets off the shelves to lay my head on, sugary drinks, and packages of sugar, while others just stood there, wide-eyed, staring—Jeremy was one of them. I cannot imagine what he was thinking about his new roommate.

When the paramedics arrived, Dad informed them I was a survivor of the Humboldt Broncos crash and that I'd suffered a traumatic brain injury. That got everyone in the store even more worked up.

My parents told me the story as I lay in the bed at Etobicoke General Hospital.

"You had a seizure," Dad said.

I didn't believe him, again.

"No way," I replied.

I looked down and saw the IV in my arm. Here I was, exactly five months after the crash, joining a new team, going to a new school, living in a new city, and it felt like I was all the way back to square one.

Everything came into focus quickly, though. I still had my clothes on. I didn't have a neck brace. I didn't feel pain all over. I took a deep breath, closed my eyes, and shook my head, laughing. *Are you kidding me?*

The doctors were concerned about my brain injury, so they had given me another CT scan before I could be released. We waited around in the emergency room, which was a pretty sketchy place. It was definitely an eye-opening welcome to Toronto. I wanted to get out of that hospital as soon as possible.

Thankfully, I was released later that evening and didn't have to spend another night in a trap house.

The incident was scary, and it certainly jolted my parents, but they quickly realized I was in good hands at York. The school was very careful and thoughtful about what I needed. They committed to continuing my rehab and making sure I had all the resources I needed for my ongoing recovery. They even have a premier diabetes lab on campus.

The first day we arrived, when I did the equipment fitting, Russ introduced us to the team's athletic directors. They took us on a tour of the campus and the athletic centre. Everybody knew we were coming and was waiting to greet us. We met the head of the varsity athletics department and everyone in the athletics office. We met the university's lead athletic therapists, who would be in charge of my continued rehab. They already had a customized plan laid out for me. The school had all the resources I would need to succeed physically, mentally, emotionally, and academically. It really helped ease my parents' concerns and reaffirmed that I'd made the right decision.

York was also very cognizant of the psychological burden I might be carrying. That first week, the team had organized a series of physical and mental tests. Russ told me everyone on the team had to undergo the same evaluations, but they did not want me to participate until I saw the athletic therapists. Once again, I passed all of the physical testing. I was in very good shape. My vertebrae had healed, and while I still had nerve issues in my neck, for the most part I felt really good.

Russ mentioned that he had booked a meeting for me with one of the school's psychologists and that I should check in with her. I knew that this was to check in about the crash—an extra precaution to make sure that I was doing okay and that I knew there were resources I could reach out for in case I wasn't. I appreciated the support.

When I met with her, we had a nice conversation about everything I had endured in the last year. She was a lovely lady, but she had a hard time believing I was doing okay. Much like the last psychologist I had seen, she seemed to think I was keeping something from her.

She asked if I would be travelling with the team by bus—and if that concerned me. I told her that I'd already taken a bus trip. We sat in the front row, where my coaches had sat, and I was okay.

"The circumstance was super rare and I'm willing to take my chance to go on the bus again," I assured her.

She looked at me, concerned.

But I honestly felt okay. I think she realized that by the end. I had my moments, for sure—I'd always carry that scar—but I was not going to let them get in the way of the next step in my life.

My parents left a few days after the seizure, when they knew I was okay and getting settled. I drove them to the airport, hugged them goodbye, and watched the two of them leave to catch their flight back to Saskatoon. There were no tears; we all knew this was the right decision for me.

As I walked around York's enormous campus that first week, I felt people staring at me. It was the same thing that had happened in Saskatoon, but I guess I hadn't expected it to happen in such a large place, with over 50,000 students. Sometimes, people would come up to me and ask where they recognized me from. I'd have no clue who they were.

"I'm not sure," I'd say, while knowing exactly why they thought that. Without a word of exaggeration, it happened hundreds of times.

I always tried to avoid the question and was evasive. But if they persisted, I'd let them know I was a Humboldt Bronco, and immediately the conversation would get even more awkward.

They'd either tear up or apologetically backpedal out of the conversation. I didn't mind it. I knew they meant well. But it was something I had learned to accept—it would always be there. No matter what I did in life, I would always be labelled as a Humboldt Broncos survivor.

But I just wanted to be part of the team—another player, another rookie—trying to move forward beyond the spotlight. It was going to be difficult.

After my first debacle, I switched back to my old gear and got my skates sharpened. I took a deep breath. I was much faster on the ice. I could actually keep up. In fact, I was beating some of the veterans during our skating drills. All of the physio, chiro, and isometric training was continuing to pay off.

Still, it felt like there was a disconnect between me and my teammates. Through those first few skates with the team, no one really knew how to talk to me. It ended up being just a lot of awkward small talk—"Hey, how's it going?"—and nothing more. There was an elephant on the ice with us. They knew I wasn't cleared for contact and that they had to be careful around me on the ice. They all knew about the crash but had no idea how to talk about it.

During our first team meeting, I decided I had to address what I knew everybody was already thinking. After the coach was done speaking to the team, he asked if anyone had questions. I piped up. As a first-year student and incoming recruit, it's a pretty tough thing to do, but I knew I wouldn't be fully part of the team until I did.

"I've been wanting to say this for a while now. I'm sure everyone in this room knows what I've been through in the past," I said. "I'm healed from my injuries—mentally, emotionally, and physically—and I'm all right to talk about it. If I wasn't, I wouldn't be here. I want you to treat me like a normal teammate. You can chirp me, have fun. I'm here to have a good time. I'm here for university. I'm here to be an incoming student-athlete. I want to be a *York Lion*, not a *Humboldt Bronco*. So, please, treat me like a York Lion."

When I was done, everyone in the room started to clap. Afterwards, several teammates came over and expressed to me how they needed to hear that talk.

From there on out, everything shifted. My teammates started to joke around with me more. I told them I wanted to be treated like every other incoming freshman—and they did.

It felt good to be part of a team again. It felt good to be a Lion.

CHAPTER 21

—

Ireturned to Saskatoon on September 12, 2018, just a couple weeks after moving to Toronto.

My parents picked me up at the airport with Paige—who became my girlfriend in late August—and we headed out for Humboldt to attend the first game of the Broncos' new season.

The team's return was a huge media story, even though only two players from our team had been able to return. I was super proud of Derek Patter and Brayden Camrud for recovering from their injuries and going back to Humboldt to play another season. I know it took an enormous amount of resilience and mental toughness to do that.

Almost all of the survivors from our team made the trip to show thier love and support in that opening game, which was broadcast live across the country on TSN. As we drove up to the front entrance of the Elgar Petersen Arena, there was a large picture of each of the individuals who had passed away in the crash. Each was in a black iron frame that had legs sticking into the grass in the centre boulevard. They were all decorated in green and gold ribbon. Dad commented that he was thankful my picture wasn't on the boulevard, then caught himself and said, "I wish there were no pictures on this boulevard."

As we walked up to the entrance, sixteen hockey sticks adorned with green and gold ribbon stood in a line against the outside wall of the arena. We went through the side entrance to the banquet hall, which was full of lights, cameras, and microphones. Once again, it felt uncomfortable to be answering questions for a scrum of reporters. But I was pushed into it, and there was a sense of obligation and duty, so I did it.

Before the game, the survivors in attendance went down to the locker room, and each of us addressed the current Broncos players. I walked up to Patter and Camrud and told them both how proud I was of them. It was the first time I'd been in the room since returning with my family after being released from the hospital. Everything had been left exactly as it was when we walked out to the bus that April afternoon.

The space was the same, but so much different.

Even though I'd moved on to York, part of me wished that I had another year of junior eligibility. After everything that had happened, I wished I could pull the Broncos jersey over my head again and play another season in Humboldt. The entire organization was, essentially, new. I recognized only a handful of faces. I worried that, with just two guys remaining, the culture that had been built—that Darcy had envisioned—would be lost. I wanted to help Patter and Camrud carry that forward, to make sure that the Broncos would always demand the same character and spirit we had forged that year. I wanted to be a leader in that room again.

But I couldn't. As much as the Broncos would always hold a place in my heart, they weren't my team anymore. We were already the past. So, I tried my best to encourage the future. This team was about to play its first game under an incredible spotlight, with an enormous amount of pressure and scrutiny. I kept it short and sweet.

"This is just one game out of fifty-eight," I said. "I know you guys are going to play your hardest. I know you're going to wear the crest proudly. But just have fun. This should be the most fun game of your life."

In the end, that's all hockey is. It's about having fun. And if you're not having fun, then you shouldn't play the sport. Just like in life—if you're not having fun doing what you're doing, then you shouldn't be doing it.

This was going to be a heavy game for all of these players, especially Patter and Camrud. I could sense that they had put immense pressure on themselves. You could hear a pin drop in the room and see the tension in their bodies. But the truth was, win or lose, the game wasn't going to matter. The only way they could truly honour the legacy of the crest they wore was to have the time of their lives playing the game—just like we had the year before.

Minutes later, we stepped out onto the ice for the first time together since our morning skate on April 6. This time, we were in our shoes. We went out through the tunnel, the same way we always had, and walked towards a red carpet on the left-hand side while the crowd cheered as each of our names was announced.

As soon as my foot touched the ice, I went numb. Emotions hit me like a brick wall. This was the biggest hit I had ever taken in my life. I put my head down to watch my feet—focusing on just putting one foot in front of the other. The ice seemed overly slippery. I don't know if it was my boots or the emotions ripping through my body, but I had trouble gaining my balance. I was scared of waving to the crowd because I thought I was going to fall. I finally got to the mat and looked up.

I'm safe now, I thought. Then I gave a little wave.

After we were all announced, the crowd gave us a standing ovation. I could feel my body start to shake as I felt the love of the community.

The Nipawin Hawks were announced after us. Memories flooded back. It was all too similar to our last meeting on April 4.

We stood there together as everyone throughout the arena paused for a moment of silence to pay our respects to the players and staff who were involved in the tragedy. The arena went quiet. I tried holding myself together, but I started to cry.

I looked over to my left and saw Tyler Smith collapse. I put my hand on him and started to rub his back for comfort. Even though we felt exposed and alone out on the ice, we were still in this together. I felt a camera staring us down. I raised my head for a split second to look around—sure enough, it was on us. I put my head back down and tried to blink my eyes to make the tears stop.

The minute felt like an eternity.

When the moment of silence ended, we walked along the rink boards to centre ice for the ceremonial opening faceoff. Patter and Camrud lined up to take the faceoff against each other, and we all spread out across the ice for a picture. There were no smiles—everything was raw. Tyler Smith dropped the puck, and then we took another photo. I grabbed Camrud and Patter, gave them each a hug. As we embraced, I said, "I love you, brother. Have fun."

Then we all lined up on the mat across the red line for the national anthem. It felt good to see the guys again, even though we weren't all there—we weren't complete.

Everyone grieves differently. That's something I learned throughout my recovery from the crash. There is no *right* way to do it. We carry our pain in unique ways and ultimately have to grapple with it on our own.

The survivors who were able to text, along with Poncelet and Berschiminsky, all joined together in a group chat to support each other. We'd reconnected in Edmonton and Las Vegas in June. I knew everyone would heal in their own way, so I reached out often to see how they were doing. I just wanted to check in and make sure they were okay. Some of them were doing really well and progressing. Others, understandably, were having a difficult time.

I can't comprehend what some of my teammates have endured. Not being able to remember anything about the crash has been a blessing in disguise for me. Doctors think that, one day, I will remember the crash—or that I *should* be able to. But for the time being, I don't. I feel absolutely terrible for the guys who live with such haunting memories. They must carry an enormous burden. I can't fathom it.

No one should have to go through that. Even the first responders—the paramedics, firefighters, and RCMP who helped at the scene. No one should have to go through that ever. My heart aches for them all.

We all have our own physical and psychological wounds. I respect that there is a different healing process for each of us. Healing is not a linear path and it never will be.

I tried reaching out to all of the survivors to make sure that everyone was okay, but I quickly learned that everyone needed their own space to heal emotionally and physically. We had different perceptions and perspectives on the crash and the aftermath. We all had different journeys to take. We all had to mourn in our own unique ways and still love each other among the differences.

Camrud and Patter had progressed well enough that they were actually playing for the Broncos, which was unbelievable and amazing on their part. Matthieu Gomercic and Bryce Fiske had both committed to the University of Ontario Institute of Technology, where they played for the men's varsity hockey team. Nick Shumlanski was on his way to play for the University of Prince Edward Island. I was excited for them because they had all been interested in taking the university route after playing in Humboldt.

Tyler Smith was working hard on his recovery and seeing progress that would get him back to Humboldt a couple months into the season for game action. Graysen Cameron had been told he'd never play hockey again after suffering a broken back, so he decided to take up coaching and give back to the game—but still held out hope that he might play again. Xavier LaBelle had suffered serious injuries, including spine fractures, brain trauma, and nerve damage, but he was also putting in tons of work and was on the road to a remarkable recovery.

It was terrible to see the seriousness of the injuries some of my teammates had suffered in the crash. It was life-altering in ways that we can't fully understand. There would be huge adjustments for them and their families.

Jacob Wassermann and Ryan Straschnitzki were adapting to serious injuries, which included paralysis—and were both in the midst of inspiring journeys, while having to endure so many difficult changes in their lives. Jacob was taking on competitive water-skiing and Ryan was transitioning into competitive sledge hockey.

Layne Matechuk and Morgan Gobeil were both still in the hospital at the time, bravely fighting through debilitating injuries. We stopped in to visit them before we left Saskatoon for Humboldt that day. I'd made sure to stop in to the hospital every other week through the summer to show them love and support. They are younger than me and both had better futures in the game than I ever did. It was hard to see how all of that had been taken away from them. They were so inspiring, though—with every visit, you could see how much they'd improved. They stuck to the slogan that we used to govern our playoff identity, written on a piece of yellow rink board that we all individually signed and hung over our dressing room door as a constant reminder: "Believe."

They did. The amount of progress over the months was incredible. Absolutely incredible.

All of my teammates inspire me—they're my heroes. They helped me keep on pushing and moving forward.

During the game, there were more things to do and more people to greet—and little time to reflect. The game was a blur. From what I did see, the Broncos played their hearts out.

When the game ended, we all ended up going down to the ice with Christina Haugan, her boys, and Chris Beaudry. Camrud and Patter joined us on the red carpet at the north end of the rink. Reagan Poncelet, Blake Berschiminsky, and affiliate player Mitchell Girolami came to be with us as well. We stood in a line while the packed arena watched on—sombre and quiet. To honour the twenty-nine on the bus, they read each name out and displayed photos of the individual on the video board. As each name was read, a gold and green banner was unfolded in a circular formation around centre ice. The numbers of all of the players on the bus were retired, and the banners will hang in the Elgar Peterson Arena forever, as a remembrance of those involved in this tragedy.

They started with the sixteen who had passed away.

I felt overcome with agony and just wanted to get off the ice as soon as possible. I just wanted to go somewhere alone and weep. But there was no point in hiding it. Everyone there was already in tears. I thought about all of the families affected by the crash, including those who had died and those who had survived. I thought about each parent, brother, sister, significant other, best friend—everyone whose life would never be the same.

We put our arms around one another and consoled each other. We remained there, linked in our pain for a while. You could hear the echoes of sobbing throughout the arena. My face was red and wet. We all succumbed to the gravity of that place, in that moment.

Each name pierced my heart as it was read, and my body filled with pins and needles from head to toe. The pictures were the hardest part. They captured their lives. Their happiness. Their energy. Then you turn your head to ice level and see a banner unfold in front of your eyes, reminding us of their death. Then the next name was read, piercing my heart again.

My flight back to Toronto left first thing in the morning. I had a test that afternoon—and another in a couple of days. My university career had just begun, and I needed to put in my best effort. Commerce wasn't going to be an easy subject, but I was determined to succeed.

I wouldn't stay away for long, though. In fact, I returned to Saskatchewan a week later with the York Lions for the Mark Cross Humboldt Strong Remembrance Tour. The team had set up three exhibition games against other Canadian university teams in the Canada West conference. We also visited a number of schools, ran hockey clinics, and hosted community events. It was just one of the ways the Lions honoured Mark's life and legacy. That season, the acronym CROSS—the initials stand for character, respect, optimism, sacrifice, and selflessness—was painted in the Lions' locker room in his memory, reflecting the values that he'd lived his life by, so that every player in the seasons to come would be guided by his example.

That day, we took a coach bus on the way to the airport in Toronto. No one on the team said anything to me about it, but once again, I knew they were looking at me, wondering how I'd react. Everyone was super nervous about the situation. They didn't know what to expect.

I walked up the stairs and said hi to the bus driver. I sat down in the eighth row and put on my seat belt. The engine rumbled and the bus lurched forward. We pulled out into the road. I closed my eyes for a moment and thought about the sixteen. I hoped that if they could see me now, they'd be proud.

I pulled a book out of my red Lions backpack and opened it up. My new courses had already started, and I wanted to get a head start on the readings that were due the next week. I leaned back against the seat and turned the page.

We played against the University of Regina in Strasbourg, where Mark grew up playing minor hockey. The next game was back in Humboldt, at Elgar Peterson Arena, against the University of Calgary.

Forty minutes before the game started, under pressure from my Lions teammates, I took a solo lap of the rink. Fans had already started to fill the seats. When they saw that I was back on the ice, they started pounding on the glass and cheering. I could feel the breeze on my face as I smiled back at them. It was a wonderful moment.

I joined the Lions for the warm-up, wearing a custom-made white jersey with the words "Humboldt Strong" on the front and the last names of the sixteen deceased on the back.

For the warm-up, I requested that the arena staff play the warm-up mix from the 2017–18 season, which Wacker and I had put together for the Broncos. There was a bit of rap and EDM, with some remixes and beats from 2 Chainz, Deorro, and the Weeknd, and it finished off with "Jumpman" by Drake and Future. It was a minor detail, but a tribute to the team that I felt was needed.

As the Zamboni cleaned the ice, I switched into my red Lions jersey.

When we came back out on the ice, both teams lined up on the blue lines. We had arranged to announce my first York Diabeauty at that game. I had also brought out all of my Saskatchewan Diabeauties to be a part of the event. I had custom jerseys made for each of them. They were York red, with green and gold lines on the sleeves to display the Humboldt roots. It had my remodelled Dahlgren's Diabeauties logo on the front, with the number 16 and my last name on the back. On one shoulder, the patch was a York Lions logo, while on the other there was a Humboldt Broncos logo. Inside the jersey, when you flipped up the bottom edge, was the phrase "Enjoy the Grind," and on the collar it said, "Property of Dahlgren's Diabeauties." I wanted the children to feel like they were part of a family.

The little boy I crowned as a Diabeauty that night was from Regina. He was four and had been diagnosed with type 1 diabetes when he was only fourteen months old. He walked out to centre ice. I skated up to him and gave him a fist pump and asked, "Hey buddy, how are you doing? You doing all right?" He looked at me and nodded. The arena was full and he was so shy. I went down on one knee to get a photo with him.

My old teammates Patter and Camrud joined us at centre ice, while Wassermann watched on from the stands. All the other Diabeauties were introduced. I took the ceremonial faceoff with the captain of the University of Calgary Dinos. I was honoured to carry on a program that had meant a great deal to me and was an integral part of my reason for coming to Humboldt to begin with. It was special that I was able to announce my first York University Diabeauty back where it all started, in Humboldt.

Before we returned to Toronto, we put on a hockey clinic in Lumsden. During the session, one of the kids we were instructing accidentally got his stick caught in my skate. I lost my balance and fell awkwardly on the ice, feeling a snap in my ankle.

Thankfully, the fall didn't cause any further concern for my brain injury. When we arrived back in Saskatoon that night, Paige and Dad met me at the bus and took me to Royal University Hospital. Mom was working, and she was worried sick when she heard the news.

With crutches and a makeshift cast wrapped around my ankle, and Paige helping me, I stumbled into the emergency entrance while Dad parked the car. The waiting room was packed. I thought, *Uh-oh, we will be here until sunrise.*

As I approached the triage nurse, she had this strange look on her face and went white. I started to introduce myself.

"I know who you are, Kaleb," she said. "I was working the night of the Broncos bus crash and looked after you and your teammates."

I felt sick. I thanked her for all of her help that night. I told her what had just happened, and they hurried me into a room.

The doctor came in as soon as I sat down. She had also been there the night of the crash. She told me my visit this time had rekindled some difficult emotions in some of the other staff who were on shift that night. A lump settled in my throat. The last thing I wanted to do was bring back horrific memories from that night.

I was back from the X-ray quickly. The doctor came in shortly afterwards and said there was no fracture, but it was likely that there was severe tendon or ligament damage. In the end, an MRI confirmed I had completely torn a ligament in my ankle. It would have been a season-ending injury, if I hadn't already been unable to play full-contact hockey because of my head.

A few days later, we flew back to Toronto. I had a Tensor bandage and a boot cast around my ankle—and another injury to add to the list.

CHAPTER 22

—

W *hat a way to start . . .*
Throughout my first semester at York University, I was
known as Scooter Boy.

With a torn ligament in my ankle, I had to spend those
first few months in school zipping around campus on a red scooter.
I called it the Red Rocket. It had a basket on the front, so I could
carry my backpack from class to class.

Even for Scooter Boy, that first semester was a whirlwind. I
was there to prove my doubters wrong. It was an innate reaction.
As soon as the doctors said I was going to fail, I was determined
to succeed.

Because of my injuries, York helped accommodate me in that
pursuit. I took a lighter course load in my commerce program at
first, just to make sure I could handle the work. That first semester, I took four courses.

The only effect the brain injury had on my ability to learn,
as far as I knew, was that it was harder to retain information by
reading alone, and my reading speed had slowed down. To help
with that, I was given access to a special software called Kurzweil
3000, which would actually read my textbooks to me while I followed along. It was very helpful, but also kind of annoying. There
are dozens of voices and accents you can choose from, but in the

end they all sound like the same robot reading to you. However, I found that by listening and reading along, I was able to retain much more information than if I had done either alone.

At the same time, I was putting in over twenty hours of training and rehabilitation a week to recover from my injuries. I would go to the student-athlete injury clinic to work on my neck and back for an hour, then would have another hour-long appointment right after that for my ankle. Following that, I would head over to our gym in the rink and do more rehab exercises, along with our team workout. This happened five times a week.

On weekends when we played, I would work out with the scratches before the game and stay around another thirty minutes to focus on rehab. Massages, mobilizations, ice tubs, chiropractic treatments, and resistance band exercises became my best friends. I was still getting ten hours of sleep a night and eating well. I was doing all the things recommended. I wanted to be *healthy*.

Not only did I have to face the demands of academics, hockey, and physical rehabilitation, but I had to deal with the psychological aspect as well. Mental health is just as important as physical health. There wasn't any single thing I did that helped me heal from the trauma; it was a multifaceted approach.

First, I acknowledged that everything I felt was normal and okay. I was okay with not being okay. These feelings were natural.

I was vulnerable and opened up to people, which is something that's hard to do as a male. I shifted my perception to find the positives arising out of this tragedy. I couldn't control what happened that day, so I focused only on the things I *could* control—like my own actions, attitude, integrity, values, and work ethic, plus how I treated others.

I was grateful and thankful for the bonds formed with every individual on that bus. I had gratitude that I was here today, for all of those who aided in my recovery, and for support I'd received from the world. I put myself in the shoes of those who are not here—*How would I want the survivors to live their lives? What would I want them to do and how would I want them to feel?*

I saw challenges as opportunities to grow. I found my passion to give back and followed through with it.

But still, I can't say that I am 100 percent healed. I never will be. I will carry these scars forever.

Even though I wasn't cleared for contact, I loved being a part of the Lions family. I got to know my teammates well. We practised every day, with games on the weekends. It was nice to be back into the rhythm of going to the rink, working towards a common goal as one.

It was also difficult, though. I had to adjust to not being able to play, and I had to figure out where I could best contribute to the team. I worked hard in practice, wearing my yellow jersey. I was vocal in the locker room, which is normally not a role that most freshmen take on, but it was something I was used to as a leader on my junior teams.

It was still hockey, but everything felt just a little different.

The commute, for starters. I learned that our team took public transit to games against our city rivals at the University of Toronto and Ryerson University, both of which have arenas right off the subway lines. For those games, we'd load all of our gear into a van and then walk across the street to the subway station to head to our game. It was a neat experience for me, having never lived in a city so large. Subway riders are an eclectic collection of personalities. It was one of the small things about life away from home that I came to appreciate.

I would have given anything to have been able to suit up and play in an actual game again, but there was nothing I could do to rush that process. I just had to deal with the frustration of watching from the stands. I felt like I couldn't contribute to my full potential or really be able to lead fully, since I did not go to battle with the guys when game days arrived. And I knew that if I had been able to dress, I could impact the team in a positive way. What didn't help was the fact that guys were telling me that I was looking good in practice and looked like I could play. On one hand, it was awesome to hear that. But on the other, it ripped me up on the inside. I would have dived in front of a 140-kilometre-an-hour slapshot if it meant I could play one shift in a game.

Despite that, I had plenty of goals off the ice, too, and came to terms with the fact I could still be a leader.

In November, I announced the first Diabeauties in Toronto. Three of the kids we'd been able to connect with came out to a Lions game to be honoured, just as I'd done in Humboldt. It was great to get a chance to carry the program forward and to make these kids feel special. The smiles on their faces were worth all the meetings with the varsity athletic staff and the York marketing team to make the event happen. York promoted the event to all the students, and it turned out very well. I was grateful for all of the effort the school put in to making it a big event. It was a big moment for the Diabeauties program—but also, it meant a lot to me, personally.

Afterwards, I connected all of the new Diabeauties with everyone who had already gone through the program in a Facebook group. Celebrating these kids was important, but the hope was to also help build a community of support for them for years to come.

The work I put into rehabbing my ankle was so successful that I was back on the ice in just a few months. No more Scooter Boy.

The quick recovery, along with the continued improvement of my neck and back injuries, lifted my hopes that I might be able to join the Lions' regular game roster sooner than anticipated.

Unfortunately, as good as I felt, there was still one enormous obstacle that I had to get past.

Since the crash, I'd held out hope that the prognosis I'd received from the doctors in Saskatoon was wrong. I desperately wanted to be able to play contact hockey again. I wanted to play for the Lions.

When I committed to York, they told me I would have access to some of the top services in the country to help my recovery. They didn't lie. I asked them to get me in front of the best neurologists available, and they did.

In January, York arranged for me to see Dr. Charles Tator, one of the country's most renowned neurologists and an expert in traumatic brain injuries. I looked him up online. I was excited but instantly nervous because he was *the* man. His opinion would be probably the best I'd ever get. It could be very bad or could be positive, but his assessment was likely to dictate my future.

I took the trip from York with Tracy Meloche, the assistant manager of York's athletic therapy program, who had set up the appointment. I was incredibly anxious during the subway ride downtown and as we sat in the waiting room of Dr. Tator's office.

There are many hockey careers that end because of concussions and brain trauma. The transition to not being able to play hockey again is always difficult. I don't think many people really understand just how hard it is to have to give up something you've dedicated so much of your life to, just like that. Especially when the injury is hard to see and understand. It takes an emotional toll—and I'd be lying if I said I hadn't experienced that. As much as I wanted to make the most of my time at York academically and through my volunteer work, I wanted to make an impact on the ice.

I looked at Dr. Tator as my only hope.

He opened the door to his office and walked over to greet me. He was short, an older man, and the fringe of white hair on the sides of his bald head matched his white lab coat. Add in his thin, wire-rimmed glasses and he sure looked the part.

After we introduced ourselves, he asked me to remember three random unrelated words. Dr. Tator then ran me through a series of tests in his office.

He held my head and rotated it from side to side, tested my reaction to quick movements, monitored the mobility of my neck and arms, and put me through a series of motion tests. He studied my balance and functional movements in a series of exercises. He had me stand on one foot while raising my opposite knee, and then I had to reach up to touch a point above me and then back down to touch my toe.

The entire time, Dr. Tator wrote down observations that I couldn't see in his notebook. He kept shaking his head as he wrote, and I couldn't figure out why. It was driving me crazy.

Then we ran through a series of memory tests, with him asking me to repeat random sentences that he said to me. Some were very easy, while some were very hard. There didn't seem to be any pattern to them.

When we were done, he asked me to tell him the three words he'd asked me to remember at the start of our session. I knew them all—I *nailed* it. (I'm pretty sure that one of the words was Lithuania, but I can't recall the other two now.)

Dr. Tator shook his head again.

It made me even more nervous.

Okay, I thought. *What's going on?*

I sat there in Dr. Tator's office, waiting for him to speak.

"Come here," he said, sitting at his desk. "I want to show you this."

He opened up the scans of my brain on his computer screen. He pointed to the spots that I'd become all too familiar with.

"These are the ten areas of bleeding," he said. "Normally, people in this situation can't remember their name, or walk, or talk."

I'd heard that before.

"I'm flabbergasted," he said.

Dr. Tator explained that he had never seen anything like my case before. Based on the brain imaging, I shouldn't have been able to perform the way I did during the tests he administered.

"You have no symptoms that tell me that you can't play hockey," he said. "If I didn't look at this scan, I think you'd be playing university hockey right now."

But . . . ?

"I can't clear you to play hockey," he said.

My heart sank.

I was happy that I had done so well in the tests, but this was not the news I wanted to hear. For the first time, I felt a pang of resignation.

"You need to count yourself lucky," he said. "Very lucky."

He told me he didn't want me to do anything that could compromise the situation I was in. That meant no drinking or smoking cannabis, which was fine with me. It also meant constant sleep—never less than eight hours a night. I already knew that sleep was the best way to recover from a brain injury.

And it also meant no running or jogging, he said.

That was probably the hardest recommendation to accept. No running? That meant no ball hockey. That meant that so much activity would be limited. As he explained, running would create motion that could further damage the vulnerable points in my brain. He was concerned that I might develop chronic traumatic encephalopathy, better known as CTE. He suggested that if I wanted to continue high-level athletics, I might consider taking up swimming.

I chuckled at that.

Swimming? I can't even float!

Dr. Tator explained that everything comes with a risk, and I needed to decide which risks I was willing to take. Would I be willing to live with the consequences of a night of binge drinking or a game of pickup hockey that got a little too rough?

The truth was, I wasn't.

A semester of school had helped solidify the goals that I already had beyond hockey. All of the rehabilitation I had done since the accident had made me realize I wanted to become a chiropractor. I planned to attend chiropractic college after completing my commerce degree. I'd start my own practice. Settle down and have a family of my own. I would teach my kids about the game I loved, taking them on imaginary NHL road trips as we carved out dreams together on the basement floor.

That future seemed as beautiful to me now as any I could have imagined before.

I thanked Dr. Tator and left his office, still clinging to one last hope. Part of me believed that my test had been mixed up after the crash. There had been so much confusion within the results, there could easily have been a mistake. We still only had the results of one MRI.

I asked Dr. Hemen Shukla, one of our varsity sports medicine physicians, to arrange another MRI for me about a month later. I thought it might reveal that the first scan had been wrong all along. I continued my classes and worked with the York Lions while waiting anxiously for the results to come back.

Paige flew out from Saskatchewan to visit me that February, and I showed her around Toronto. We took the subway downtown. We went to a Raptors game—the one in which former Raptor star DeMar DeRozan returned to Scotiabank Arena for the first time since he'd been traded to the San Antonio Spurs. We stood courtside as the fans erupted for him, inspired by everything he had done for the city and the team—gifts that would live on, even though his time in the city had come and gone. It was about more than what DeRozan had done on the court; it was about what he meant to the city off of it.

Paige and I left the arena that night surrounded by fans who were revelling in the memory of what DeRozan had meant to them, even though the team had never won a championship while he played for Toronto.

In early March, Dr. Shukla took me into his office to show me the results of the latest MRI. He knew what I was hoping for. He knew that I wanted to be told there had been a mix-up all along—that, sure, I had suffered a concussion, but nothing nearly as bad as the doctors had said. I wanted him to tell me I could play the game again, and realize the dream that I had been following.

He opened an image on his desktop and pointed to what I could already see. There were ten white spots on my brain. The new scan was identical to the original.

"There are ten lesions," he explained.

I already knew that, too. It was me all along.

Scars never go away—you just learn how to live with them.

I am a miracle. There is no way around that fact. I am not supposed to be able to do the things I can do—to go to school and excel in class, to speak to large crowds about diabetes or resilience, to write my story to help others. I'm not supposed to be able to fall in love, to imagine a family in my future, to have the ability to change the course of my dreams. I shouldn't be able to become a chiropractor. I shouldn't be able to open my practice back home in Saskatoon, where I can set my own hours so that I have the time to take my kids to the rink. I shouldn't be able to do any of that. But I've been given a gift. I don't know why or how, and that will always be something that I grapple with. That thought is as constant as the other scars I carry. All I can do is live every moment as fully and completely as I am able. To make the most of this time, while I have it, because you never know what tomorrow will bring.

After Dr. Shukla showed me those results, I accepted just how fortunate I am to be here at all. I knew it was incredibly unlikely that I'll ever be able to play competitive hockey again. But what's more important: the quality of my hockey career or the quality of my life? It was something I just had to accept. This bubble I've found myself in is precious, and I owe it to myself and my family—and to the Broncos—to be careful with the gift I've been given, and to make the most of it.

That spring, as the first anniversary grew near, I spent more time looking at the stars.

The Broncos had been on my mind and in my heart all year, and they weighed on me even more in the weeks leading up to the anniversary. I decided that the best way to remember them was to relive the happiest memories. I flipped through the photos and videos of us goofing off as a team—wrestling for seats on *Bachelor* night, doing fully clothed cannonballs into hotel pools, playing pre-game "sewer," belting out tunes during Rookie Idol.

I let my mind drift back and thought about how fortunate I was to have been a part of a family in Humboldt. I was grateful to have snapshots from our past, so that I can always return to the memories.

On the first anniversary of the crash, I woke up thinking I was dreaming—that all of this was a year-long nightmare. I was wrong. I marked the day by writing a letter to the team, which I posted online and which was read aloud by my billet sisters, Jaya and Rowan Clement, during an emotional anniversary memorial on the ice at the Elgar Petersen Arena. It was about the way I felt as I thought about the sixteen watching over me and the other twelve who continued to inspire me with their remarkable resilience.

Unforeseen 16—April 6, 2019

Hi Everyone,

It's "Dahly" here. It's been a year since I saw your beautiful faces and they still cross my mind daily. I wonder what all of you have been doing . . . maybe celebrated the year-ender bender we never had? Or all playing pond hockey with Elgar? I just really hope you are doing well and supporting each other!

It hurts me looking through your Instagram pages and old videos/photos of the memories we created, as I know they radiate each of your personalities. It bothers me to see many people lost and grieving your absence . . . including myself. It's the worst knowing there's no way to bring you back or reverse the accident. If there was a way for me to do it, I would.

However, I know that's not in my control. You will forever be family to me. I have continued to be that positive guy that you occasionally got sick of. In turn, it has allowed me to live my life to the fullest in honour of you. I wore number 16 again this year, which has become more meaningful having you there to Enjoy the Grind with me! Even though my injuries prevented me from playing, I have still done my best to succeed in all aspects of life and not take a second for granted.

The support and strength I have received from those close to me, the twenty-nine families, and the world, is unbelievable and something I couldn't be more thankful for.

You guys should be proud of the impact you have on our world, including new bus laws, semi laws, health notions, etc. You have reminded us how valuable life is and, by doing so, have made this world a better place. I am very proud of the mark you have left.

I am extremely grateful we had the opportunity to be

involved in each other's lives. I have learned lots from everyone and will cherish our memories forever. Whether it was how to carry yourself as a man or how bad of a singer some of you are in Rookie Idol, these lessons and memories will never fade.

Today, tomorrow, and forever, I will do everything in my power to honour all 16 of you brothers and sister. I will live my life to the fullest with you by my side.

I love and miss you all sooo much.

Your teammate, friend, brother, son,
Forever #HumboldtStrong

Dahly

That day, I was in Toronto, preparing for my final exams to finish off my first year at York University. Although I wished I could have been in Humboldt, I knew I had to give everything I had to the future that I was lucky to have. The team would have wanted that. But I couldn't forget about them.

I invited several of my York Lions teammates over to my place. We sat in the living room, beneath my gold Broncos sweater, which I'd hung on the wall above the couch. They all wore Humboldt gear. There are many people who deal with tragedies in their lives that don't get nearly enough support—or sometimes no support at all. Once again, I found myself lucky to be surrounded by friends.

Together, we watched the final game the Broncos played a year before. The epic battle against Nipawin on April 4, 2018.

The fans were on their feet, cheering wildly. It just kept going and going. We battled into triple overtime. We played as though it was the last game of our lives.

It felt like it might never end—and in my heart, it never would.

EPILOGUE

—

We left Saskatoon early in the morning on August 24, 2019. Dad drove our SUV, with Mom in the passenger seat. I sat in the back with Paige.

We had avoided making this trip for as long as we could. It had been sixteen months.

It was a cold and dreary day. The sun hid behind a thick blanket of grey clouds. We drove northeast from the city, up Highway 41, and stopped in Aberdeen so that Paige and I could take a photo in a wheat field, among the stalks almost ready for harvest.

It was one of my last few days at home before heading back to Toronto to start my second year at York University.

The first year hadn't gone as the doctors expected. I finished on the dean's list and as a U Sports Academic All-Canadian, with an *A* average. I'd named several new Diabeauties, expanding the program into Ontario. I'd proved the doctors wrong. Not only could I survive away from home in university, but I could thrive. I was determined to return for another year to do the same.

But it hadn't gone entirely as *I'd* planned, either. All of my injuries were healed, except for the most important one. I'd quietly come to accept the fact that the lesions on my brain will remain—and I will never be cleared to play competitive hockey again. My heart was broken, but my life has taught me to accept the things I cannot change. I would remain part of the team, I'd be a Lion, even if I wasn't able to contribute on the ice. I'd find new ways to help us win. With time, I'd realized that there was so much more that goes into a team than actually playing the game. It was a lesson that I started to learn while playing junior, especially in Humboldt, where so many people contributed in essential ways.

That year, I'd be named our team's representative on the varsity athletics sport council and run community events for the Lions. I'd step into a training role with my teammates by setting up the exercises and working with them in the weight room, encouraging them to enjoy the grind. I'd practise with the team every day, mentoring new recruits and players on the bubble of the main roster. I would meet with our coaches regularly, acting as a liaison between them and the players. I'd step into a recruiting role, scouting talent across the country and building relationships to bring the best and the brightest to York's future.

Paige and I climbed back into the back seat and Dad drove on. We rode in silence. Gold wheat and green canola fields stretched out across the prairie, kissing the clouds in a skyline we could never reach.

Nearly two hours went by before we passed through Melfort—heading north, instead of east. We hit Fairy Glen and carried on to Gronlid.

I thought about what I might remember.

The doctors told me that the return could bring it all rushing back, even though any memories of those moments were still hidden in my mind.

What if I could see it all? What if it came back and I could never forget it again?

I worried about that, but I knew I couldn't hide from it. I couldn't avoid it any longer.

Mom could still see it all. She was quiet in the front seat, watching the passing fields. She didn't want to come along, but I'd asked her to. We needed to do this as a family. We each carry our own wounds, every one of us who is connected in some way to the people on that bus. We had to face it together.

We turned east at Gronlid.

Highway 335.

The road was rough and unfinished.

I thought about the final moments on that bus, rushing north towards the end. A semi-trailer barrelled west at the exact same time. The billions of seconds of our collective lives funnelled into one, like specks of sand in an hourglass.

I felt gravel groan beneath us. We rumbled over train tracks. The crossroads lay ahead.

We could see the white crosses, lined in two rows. Hockey sticks leaned against each one.

Dad pulled off the road and parked. We walked up to the memorial as quietly as we had driven, each heading separate ways to take it in. No one said a word.

The memorial had grown and grown since the crash, accumulating fragments of the lives lost and the memories of those left behind.

There were flowers, tiny solar-powered lights, and jerseys around hockey sticks that had been nailed together in the shape of a cross. Pucks with messages of love written across them. There were green and gold hockey gloves and helmets. Small pinwheel fans and ribbons blew and chimes sang in the breeze. All among them were the specific items that had been left behind to honour and remember our lost friends. Photographs of happy moments. A pair of glasses for Parker Tobin. A can of beer for Conner Lukan. Logan Schatz's childhood stick, with his last name written by him on the top of the shaft. A large York Lions banner for Mark Cross.

I brought along red and white bracelets with *Enjoy the Grind* printed on one side and *Dahlgren's Diabeauties* on the other, along with the York University and Humboldt Broncos logos. I had thought long and hard about what I wanted to bring. I thought a bracelet could endure the cold weather and hug each individual's cross. It was a symbolic gesture, so that they would know I'd be with them forever. I stopped at each cross, tightly wrapping a bracelet around the wood.

Across the road, I noticed six more white crosses—three tall, three small—faded and worn but adorned with fresh flowers. They marked the spot where six members of a family had been killed in a crash two decades earlier. I wondered where the people who loved them were now and how they carried them in their hearts.

Mom stood to the right of me. She took our return to the site the hardest and quickly walked back to our vehicle, unable to linger any longer. Dad walked behind me, remembering where everything had been that day—a field scattered with metal, peat moss, and beautiful lives.

Mosquitoes buzzed around us. There had to have been thousands of them, swarming any life that visited that place. I'd never seen so many at one time. I slapped them away as best I could, taking time to remember each life despite the bites and constant buzz.

The day was still dark and cool. No cars passed by. It was just the four of us, silent and alone—just as I'd hoped it would be. I didn't want to see other people there. I didn't want to interact. I needed to return with the people I love—the four of us—as a family.

I looked across at Paige as she walked among the crosses, paying her respects. She looked up at me and smiled softly, as if to make sure that I was all right.

I was.

My memory remained void of the moments that turned this corner of the Prairies into a nightmare. I clung to the joy of everything that came before and my hope for everything yet to come. I remained determined to live for those who couldn't.

Paige rubbed my back as a tear ran down my cheek.

We'd planned to stop in Nipawin to bring coffee and donuts to the doctors and nurses who had fought to save our lives that day—a small token of thanks. We would complete the journey, together.

The three of us walked back to the SUV, joining Mom. Paige and I sat in the back seat, hand in hand. We were quiet, still.

Dad pulled forward slowly, gravel crunching beneath us as the memorial passed in the windows. We came to the crossroads.

Highway 35.

We turned north towards a grey horizon, beyond fields of green and gold.

ACKNOWLEDGEMENTS

—

There is nothing more valuable than saving lives.

I will donate a portion of my proceeds from this book to STARS (Shock Trauma Air Rescue Service), an organization that has saved countless lives in the face of enormous tragedy, especially on April 6, 2018. Thank you for continually making a difference.

To the sixteen angels I think of every day, I will always treasure the memories we made and the bonds created in the time we had together. I will love you forever and I hope this makes you proud.

To the sixteen angel families, thank you for giving me strength and support in all aspects of my life. I have so much love and respect for each family affected by this tragedy, and I will forever work to honour the memory of your loved ones who were lost in the crash.

To my twelve survivor brothers and the Broncos who did not make the trip that day, thank you for inspiring me to be a better person every day and being understanding of my healing process. I love you all. To the twelve survivor families, thank you for your love and support as we continue to move forward as a Broncos family.

I sit here today in complete astonishment! Never in my short twenty-three years did I ever think I'd write a book, but here we are. I am beyond grateful for the opportunity to share my story. Writing this memoir was challenging, emotional, cathartic, and enlightening. I was able to reflect on all the various crossroads in my life, the people who helped me navigate them, and those who have shaped me into the person I am today.

Like the old saying goes, it takes a village to raise a child. In this instance, it took an enormous team to get me to where I am today and to complete this book. I could literally write a 300-page book full of thank yous, and it still wouldn't capture every person I am thankful for. Although I am unable to mention everyone here, please know that I have immense gratitude for every person who has helped me get to the point where I am today.

I would like to thank my mom, Anita, and dad, Mark. Without your unconditional love and support, I would never have put my thoughts to paper. I could not be luckier to have such a wonderful relationship with both of you. I am forever appreciative of your assistance in my life and throughout the writing process. I know it was not easy for either of you to fill in the days that I still do not remember. I appreciate your courage and I love you both so much.

An important thank you goes to my partner in crime, Paige Watson. The moment I met you, I knew you were special. Your daily check-ins and caring attitude were essential when you came into my life and throughout this process. Some parts of this book were not easy to write, but your beautiful heart and calming personality were there to help me through these times. I am beyond grateful to have you in my life, and I'll always love you the most.

I want to thank my immediate family, on the Sentes side and the Dahlgren side, for all of your love, support, guidance, nurturing, and confidence in me. I am lucky to have been raised and supported by such great individuals: Rudy and Stella Sentes; Myron and Doreen Dahlgren (in memoriam); Rick, Shelley, and

Dominique Sentes; Linda and Mike Muntean; Sandra, Shantell, Brandon, and Andy Dahlgren; Jamie, Alex, and Courtney Dahlgren; Wayne, Lori, and Emma Dahlgren.

I would like to thank my "chosen" immediate family for taking me in as if I were one of your own and influencing me to be the person I am today: the Hancox family, the Tyndall family, the Ingram family, the Doepker family, the Grant family, the Korol family, the Ehrmantraut family, the Watson and Wright family, the Kulchycki family, and the Bitove family.

Thank you to my billet families, who took me into their homes as a stranger and let me leave as a part of their families: Anne Cole and Ryan Haughian in North Battleford; the team billets in Wilcox, Bobbi Churchill, Rick Pow, Bryden, and Taytum; and in Humboldt, Carla and Wes Clement and their children, Jaya, Rowan, and Madden.

Thank you to the communities and people of Moose Jaw, Saskatoon, North Battleford, Wilcox, Humboldt, and Toronto for providing me with places I will always call home.

To my brothers from another mother, thanks for being the siblings I never had and for being there by my side throughout the challenges I've faced. To Wyatt Tyndall, Connor Ingram, Brody Doepker, Wyatt Grant, Michael Korol, Adam Ehrmantraut, Lane Pederson, Evan Weninger, Josh Roberts, Jarrett Fontaine, Josh Lilly, Derek Frater, Keegan McBride, Kaelan Holt, and Brayden Richards: I love you guys.

To my roommates whom I became close with and who also had to deal with me being a neat freak, thank you. We will always be tied together and I love you all: Brett Pongracz, Tyler Podgorenko, Riley Mohr, Stephen Wack, Bryce Fiske, Jeremy Lucchini, and Mark Wilson.

Thank you to all my teammates throughout my younger years for the memories forged over mini sticks in the hallway and as we grew together each season. Thank you to my Battlefords AAA

Stars teammates for helping me mature into a young man and gain independence during some of the hardest years of my life. Thank you to my Notre Dame Hounds teammates for developing me into a fully rounded person and player. Thank you to my Humboldt Broncos teammates for creating a culture like no other and for memories I will always cherish. Thank you to my York Lions teammates for accepting me as a Lion and pushing me to improve in all aspects of life, every single day.

Thank you to all my coaches, managers, mentors, strength and conditioning coaches, athletic therapists, trainers, equipment managers, and everyone else within the team family over the years. Each of you have had a hand in shaping the person and player I am today.

Thank you to all of my teachers for instilling knowledge and values in me—you're the unsung heroes of the next generation. Thank you to everyone at Palliser Heights Elementary School, Lakeridge Elementary School, Holy Cross High School, John Paul II Collegiate, Athol Murray College of Notre Dame, the University of Regina, and York University for all of your guidance and encouragement.

To all my diabetic friends and the various diabetic communities that I have been a part of since I was eighteen, thank you for your unconditional support and being at my side as we move forward in life together on our quest for a cure. Thank you to JDRF, Dexcom, and Diabetes Canada for giving me a platform to use my voice and ignite awareness around type 1 diabetes, hopefully making lives a little bit easier. To all of my Dahlgren's Diabeauties and their families, thank you for all the love and support you have given me. I am so lucky to watch each of you continue to grow into an amazing individual. I love you all and am thankful that you are in my life.

Thank you to the Humboldt "taxi crew" for all the fun times and all the support you offered me. I love you guys. And thank you to all of you on the Special Olympics floor hockey team. I always looked forward to Monday night floor hockey, and I will always consider all of you good friends. To the rec hockey community, the Grade 5 class at St. Dominic Elementary School, and the Villa Care Home residents in Humboldt, thank you for brightening my days.

To the 2017–18 Humboldt Broncos organization—the board, the Elgar Petersen Arena staff, the Humboldt Community Centre employees, and everyone else who had an impact on our team— thank you for your love and all that you do to support Broncos hockey.

Thank you to those that stopped on the highway immediately after the impact and brought blankets, offered first aid, and assisted all of us until the first responders arrived.

To all the first responders, EMS personnel, firefighters, responding RCMP officers, and any other incident response teams, thank you. Your training, expertise, and professionalism saved lives on April 6, 2018.

Thank you to all the staff at the Nipawin Hospital for doing your absolute best to care for me under incredible demand and heartache—I know it wasn't easy. And thank you to the nurse and doctor who were with me the entire time I was in the Nipawin Hospital.

Thank you, Saskatchewan Air Ambulance and Saskatchewan STARS Air Ambulance, for all of your support on April 6, 2018. And thank you to Alberta Air Ambulance for transporting me safe and sound.

Thank you to the staff at Royal University Hospital and City Hospital for the kind, compassionate, and professional care I received. My sincere gratitude to those who helped me in the healing process.

Thank you to all the medical professionals that have helped me throughout my life—you all have given me inspiration to follow my passion in the medical health field! Thank you, Dr. Best,

Dr. Leakos, and Dr. MacKenzie, for all the years you have been by my side. I appreciate it.

Thank you to the Saskatoon restaurants that provided the Broncos families with free meals while we were in the hospital. (It sure beat hospital food.)

Thank you to all those who helped me with my recovery, through chiropractor treatments, physiotherapy, acupuncture, massage therapy, personal training, osteopathy, energy healing, and more.

Thank you to those friends and old teammates of mine who lined the hospital hallways to visit me and offer support. I know that many of you did not get the chance to see me, but it meant the world to hear your names.

Thank you to those around the sports world who reached out to me following the tragedy. The visits, phone calls, FaceTime, video messages, jerseys, sticks, signed pictures, dedications, and many other gestures were integral to my recovery. There are so many individuals I could name, and that is something I am beyond grateful for.

Thank you to the survivors of the Swift Current Broncos bus crash for the visit when I was in the hospital and your advice on moving forward after an incident like this.

Thank you to the NHL for bringing the Broncos survivors to the NHL Awards ceremony to honour and represent our coach. Also, thank you for bringing the Stanley Cup to the hospital and for sending my family and me to the Stanley Cup final in Washington, D.C. It was the trip of a lifetime and something I will remember for the rest of my life.

Thank you to everyone who left a porch light on, left a stick out for the Broncos, or wore a jersey on jersey day.

Thank you to everyone who sent me hand-drawn pictures, finger paintings, crafts, banners, handmade jewellery, poems, letters and books of encouragement, and so many other creative articles. I took the time to read, touch, and look at every item sent to me. Thank you to every person who sent a message, showed their support with a social media post, wore a ribbon or bracelet, donated to the GoFundMe campaign, sold clothing, stickers, and bracelets, made blankets and quilts, organized a tribute concert or event, or was responsible for one of the many other initiatives. Your compassion has been a game changer in my healing. I was overwhelmed by all of the support you gave me and I am still speechless to this day. Thank you!

Thank you to RCMP Staff Sergeant Murray Chamberlin and the Major Crimes Investigative Team, and the other specialized RCMP officers from Saskatchewan, Alberta, and British Columbia. Thank you also to the multi-partner agencies who provided investigative support, including the Saskatoon Police Service, Calgary Police Service, Alberta Safer Communities and Neighbourhoods, and Alberta Sheriffs. I appreciate your thorough investigation, and that you were open and honest with my family to make sure no stone was unturned.

To all the media staff I interacted with following the crash, I appreciate your kindness and respectful sharing of my story. Thank you.

Thank you, Russ Herrington, for taking a chance on me and offering me a spot on the York Lions men's varsity hockey team. You didn't have to honour the commitment after the crash, but you not only honoured it, you provided the spot unconditionally. I will never forget that you were the one who made my university dream come true. From the bottom of my heart, thank you.

Thank you to the York University varsity athletics administration—Jennifer Myers, Gillian McCullough, Bart Zemanek, Hailey Jones, Mack Abbott, Kathryn Johnston, and the rest of the team—for supporting me from day one and giving me every opportunity to succeed. Even though I was never cleared to play, you allowed me to be a member of the Lions family, and I am forever grateful.

ACKNOWLEDGEMENTS

Thank you to my York University rehabilitation team—Andrea, Tracy, Brittney, Dr. Shukla, Dr. Howitt, Dr. Tator, and so many others. I cannot imagine having a better group of people to help with my rehabilitation. From the moment I set foot on campus, you were there for me and still are today. I would not be where I am in my recovery without you.

Thank you to Liam Richards for shooting the book cover and Josh Martin's Nipawin RCMP team for closing the highway and patrolling traffic. It took two shoots, but we got it!

Here are a few more supporters and friends I am thankful for: Laura Goebel, Maddy Schenn, Connor Odelein, Brandon Lesko, the Pool family, Tristan Hermanson, James Piller, Chance Longjohn, Conor MacLean, Randy Durovick, Evan Fiala, Hailey Manderscheid, Ted Tilbury, Hayley Wickenheiser, Jess Moskaluke, Carmen Choney, Brynn Sussman, Cord Ivanco, Sherri Pockett, Steven Hoffner, Tara Leithead, Dr. Walter J. Perchal, Chris Pronger, Kate Beirness, George Canyon, the James Barker Band, Victor Micallef and the Tenors, Rod Black, Troy Vollhoffer, and HEROS. The crew at NLT—Chad Martin, Kelly Riou, Chad Stoski, Ben Verrall, Colton Stephenson, Chandler Stephenson, Brayden McNabb, Brayden Schenn, and Scott Richardson. Performance coaches Casey Bartzen, Scott Dutertre, and Jason Weber. My neighbours the Leontowicz family, the Rodych family, the Fitzsimmons family, the Chew family, the Shout family, and many others. Our family friends: the Reiter family, the Mendoza family, the Yee family, the Clarke/White family, the Armstrong family, the LaBarbera family, the Lindros family, and the Domi family. There are so many more I want to list, and I can't thank you enough.

Thank you to those who provided advance quotes and took time out of your busy lives to read the book. It means a lot and I appreciate the selfless support.

I would like to thank the HarperCollins team for believing in my story and giving me the opportunity to share it. It is an honour to have been a part of a renowned publishing company. Thank you to Brad Wilson for making this process smooth and dedicating your time to making this the best book possible. Noelle Zitzer, I appreciate your oversight with this project and guidance—thank you. And to Lloyd Davis, for your precision and attention to detail, thank you. To Alan Jones, for letting my creative ideas flourish and creating a stunning all-around book cover, thank you. Thank you, Lisa Rundle, for your guidance with the audiobook and for bringing this amazing format to readers like myself. To Mike Millar and Neil Wadhwa, thank you for doing everything in your power to shine the best light possible on this book. Thank you, as well, to everyone at HarperCollins not mentioned. I am extremely appreciative of the care and encouragement I received throughout this process.

Thank you, Dan Robson, for helping me tell my story. It has been an unbelievable experience working with an author of your calibre. I enjoyed spending time with you and look forward to our lifelong friendship. And thank you, Jayme Poisson, for your background work of proofreading, editing, and fact checking for the book. I am really excited to remain a part of your family's lives.

To my agent, mentor, and good friend, Jeff Lohnes: I cannot thank you enough for your unwavering support and guidance throughout life. I would not be writing this if it weren't for your belief in me and that my story might help others. I know you have put in lots of work in the background and this did not go unnoticed. Thank you. To the team at Talent Bureau, thank you for doing everything in your power to present me with opportunities to make a positive impact. You all have gone above and beyond any expectations I ever had! Thank you.

It was nearly impossible for me to write this portion of the book because there are not enough pages to mention every person who has made a difference in my life. It just goes to show that it takes an enormous team to support one individual, and one impact, no matter how big or small, might change the course of a lifetime. I'm beyond grateful for all of the support I have had throughout my life.

And if you have read to this point, thank *you*. You truly do not know how appreciative I am that you took time out of your life to read this book. The goal is to help others by sharing my story, and I hope it has done that. I wish you nothing but the best in your life's endeavours and I hope you can find happiness in the grind of life.

If you want to share your thoughts and stay connected with my life story, you are more than welcome to find me online:

social media: @kalebdahlgren
website: www.kalebdahlgren.com

I hope you enjoyed the read, and thanks again from the bottom of my heart!

Lots of love,
Kaleb